Religious Education in the Small Membership Church

CONTRIBUTORS

NANCY T. FOLTZ

RONALD H. CRAM

GARY E. FARLEY

PAMELA MITCHELL

WILLIAM H. WILLIMON

SUSANNE JOHNSON

BOB I. JOHNSON

D. CAMPBELL WYCKOFF

DONALD E. BOSSART

JAMES E. CUSHMAN

Religious Education in the Small Membership Church

edited by

NANCY T. FOLTZ

Religious Education Press
Birmingham, Alabama

Library of Congress Cataloging-in-Publication Data

Religious education in the small membership church / edited by Nancy
    T. Foltz
        Includes bibliographical references and index.
        ISBN 0-89135-077-2
        1. Christian education—United States.   2. Small churches—
United States.   I. Foltz, Nancy T.
        BV1471.2.R45 1990
        268—dc20   90-41449
                                                                          CIP

Religious Education Press, Inc.
5316 Meadow Brook Road
Birmingham, Alabama 35242
10 9 8 7 6 5 4 3 2

Religious Education Press publishes books exclusively in religious education and in areas closely related to religious education. It is committed to enhancing and professionalizing religius education through the publication of serious, significant, and scholarly works.

PUBLISHER TO THE PROFESSION

THIS WORK IS DEDICATED TO
SARAH AND WAYNE PETERSON, MY MOM AND STEPDAD,
WHO ARE MEMBERS OF THE BARNES CHURCH,
AVERAGE WORSHIP ATTENDANCE 55,
PASTOR, RALPH L. ROMINE SR.

Contents

Introduction

Some conversations never go away. They remain as fresh and clear today as they were four or forty years ago. One conversation that will not go away has prompted this book. I was teaching seminary students about religious education in the small membership church. I asked, "How many of you aspire to serve a small membership church?" Almost all fifteen students raised their hands. "What would keep you from serving a small membership church?" I asked. The answers came quickly: "The pay scale won't be enough to support my family,". . . . "There isn't the respect for pastors of a small membership church among the clergy." . . . "The denomination encourages us to begin at a small membership church; but first church is the carrot!"

Well, not only are there not enough "first churches" to go around but, most importantly, there are many persons in seminaries who know they are called to ministry in the small membership church.

Religious Education in the Small Membership Church is a comprehensive resource on religious education in small membership churches. The approach to all chapters is necessarily theoretical, but practical application for specific religious education in the small congregation is suggested.

This book is written to encourage those pastors who are serving and who want to continue to serve in the small membership church. The intent of this book is to encourage pastors in their role as religious educator. This book is for denominational leaders who are removing institutional barriers so that men and women may choose to serve the small membership church, not as a "steppingstone," but as "the place" for ministry.

For the past fifteen years I have worked with hundreds of leaders of

1

small membership churches and have been a member of such churches as well. I hear stories about the Sunday school, the CCD, the struggles of surviving on a less than desirable salary and keeping church finances afloat, the insanity of denominational forms that intimidate small membership church leaders. Mostly I hear about how difficult it is for a pastor to maintain a good self-image.

Clergy as religious leaders tell stories of apple butter festivals and homecoming celebrations, of having their church on the history and landmark city tour, and of the ecumenical food banks. Most of all, however, I hear of clergy who love people and want to be faithful to God's call. This edited work is in response to religious educators, clergy and lay, in small membership churches and to the stories they tell.

Overview

The first three chapters in the book set forth the context in which religious education in the small member church is discussed. They are the foundation of understanding religious education in the small congregation. The context chapters include: the overview, which explores descriptions of the small membership church, recent trends, an explanation of research and programs and sociological forces which suggest specifics that impinge on ministry in a dramatic and powerful way. As part of the existing fabric, these critical context chapters include discussion of areas which are important to understand but difficult to change even when change is needed. Frustration mounts when religious educators fail to realize that many factors which significantly affect ministry are part of local history and geography. Chapters four through nine treat the more visible areas of ministry in the small membership church: education, worship, administration, leadership, curriculum, and conflict. Chapter nine, on conflict, deals with the elusive dimension of how we argue and resolve our differences. The final chapter is a word of hope about the future of religious education in the small membership church. Chapter ten reminds us to dream and to work today in order to bring tomorrow's dreams to reality.

Chapter one, "An Overview of the Small Membership Church," by Nancy T. Foltz, includes a size profile chart, a list of characters who exist in local congregations, and a chart of small membership church characteristics. The intent of the overview is to illustrate the wide variation in size, characteristics, and other critical factors which might assist religious leaders, clergy and lay, to more fully appreciate, understand, and to be in ministry with members of small membership churches.

The complexity, intricacy, and delicateness required to understand religious education in the small membership church is suggested throughout the chapter. Perhaps, suggests Foltz, religious educators are the gender-free "heroes" on a journey of ministry.

Chapter two, "The Small Membership Church: Recent Trends in Research and Program," by Ronald H. Cram begins with an overview of basic problems surrounding current discussion of the small membership church. Cram acquaints the reader with selected research, programs, and persons who represent dominant current trends in understanding religious education in the small membership church. Cram discusses three persistent structural issues which appear across denominational lines: economics, status, and seminary education.

The chapter cites recent institutional models which offer innovative ministerial seminary preparation. Cram offers practical suggestions of how some mainline denominations are preparing for religious education with and in the small membership church. Small congregations may, as Cram suggests, "hold . . . keys for opening the doors of church renewal."

Chapter three, "Understanding the Sociological Perspective," by Gary Farley, asks, "Where in America is St. Paul's Chapel?" The two major foci of the chapter are: 1) concepts, resources, and a strategy to understand the "place" of the small membership church and 2) the internal life, including decision-making patterns and organizational structures, and facts concerning other critical areas.

Farley's basic principle is that effective ministry, evangelism, and outreach are grounded in an understanding of setting. Farley takes the reader from the mine tipple to the factory smokestack, from the grain elevator to the golf course to understand that communities organize around a symbol of their founding dream. The challenge of religious education is illustrated in a case study of Boley, Oklahoma, where a founding dream was re-dreamed when the existing community changed.

Worldviews and cultural attitudes are described and noted for their importance in grasping how essential sociological factors are in understanding religious education in the small membership church for yesterday, today, and tomorrow. Farley knows the gathering places, the corridors through a community, and the rhythms and sequences of ministry in the small member church as well as the steps in discovering the inner life, and suggestions on staffing. The author offers a useful blend of a theoretical and practical perspective on how sociology shapes religious education.

Chapter four, "Educational Ministry, the CCD, and the Sunday School," by Pamela Mitchell, suggests different possibilities for developing religious education using four organizational guidelines. Mitchell begins with constructing the church's story rather than with forms, charts, and questions. Mitchell cautions the reader to avoid over-organizing and falling into the "generic religious education mentality of a large-scale design." Mitchell describes four models which are consistent with the organizational guidelines.

The clarion call for educational ministry, CCD, and the Sunday school, is for simplicity, clarity, and unity of design that maintains the small membership church focus on persons and relationships. The communal character of religious education in the small membership church is central to the teaching and learning ministry.

Chapter five, "Worship—Ministry within the Scared Space," by William H. Willimon, discusses ways in which worship in the small membership church is the center of congregational life. Readers are offered ways to improve worship.

Willimon understands the potential for creative and flexible use of space. The examples suggested in the chapter are for small membership church leaders who are wrestling with problems of space in small or large buildings.

This chapter walks leaders through the basics of worship and the singing of familiar and unfamiliar hymns as well as other issues related to sacred space. Willimon reminds us that "we shape our buildings, but they also shape us."

Chapter six, "Administration: Equipping the Saints for Religious Education Ministry," by Susanne Johnson, states that creative, faithful church administration arises in the dialogue between what actually now is and what a church theologically is called to become. Johnson explores the creative tension between the "sociological is" and the "theological ought" in church administration.

The chapter examines a practical theological approach to administration. Methods of budget construction such as line item, zero, and program budgets are discussed. Johnson challenges religious educators in the small membership church to be proactive in denominational decisions that affect its future.

Chapter seven, "Lay Religious Education Leadership and the Planning Process," by Bob I. Johnson, challenges religious educators, clergy and lay, and offers step-by-step suggestions which include: how to find leaders, then develop, support, and most of all release them for their work as religious educators.

Recruiting leaders to share ministry is a primary task for Johnson and is part of his basic approach to leadership and the planning process. People do resist change, and we do tend to support what we have created. Johnson's chapter calls for intentional ways to develop lay leaders in purposeful planning. The challenge, states Johnson, is for the religious educator to leave a legacy of planning that is consistent with the overall missional objective of the church.

Chapter eight, "Curriculum in the Small Membership Church," by D. Campbell Wyckoff, goes to the grass roots to ask small membership church religious educators questions: "Who does the actual educational planning?" . . . "What educational resources and curriculum materials are used and recommended for them and why?" Wyckoff gathers this information from Roman Catholic, Southern Baptist, Presbyterian, U.S.A., and the Assemblies of God churches.

This chapter addresses the central question of how a small membership church puts together a comprehensive and practical plan that takes into account everything it knows about religious education—the teaching, the mission of the church, the character of the Christian life, the learning process, and the challenges and opportunities in the situation of the learners. The basic premise in Wyckoff's chapter is that the situation of a church conditions its educational plan and differences point to unique curriculum needs.

Chapter nine, "Conflict, Feuds, and Border Wars," by Donald E. Bossart, tells why conflict is harder to manage in a small membership church and describes how the creative resolution of conflict is affected.

Bossart relates eight basic characteristics of the small membership church to three major sources of conflict. He explicates dynamics of conflict and then describes specific steps of consensus building with suggested implications for religious educators.

This chapter gives practical guidelines for religious educators who have been in the middle of conflict in the small membership church and who want help in not repeating past errors.

Chapter ten, "The Future of Religious Education in the Small Membership Church," by James E. Cushman, offers a prophetic sign of hope. Cushman assesses the problems and identifies a roadmap for revitalization. The small membership church may not be "trendy," but it may be the "one place left where the true meaning of human community can still be experienced."

Cushman delivers a clear message for central office leaders as well as for religious educators in the small member church. His clarion call is for a major attitudinal change. The richness, vitality, and energy of ministry are described in three hopes for a dynamic tomorrow.

There are many persons to thank for their help in the creation of this book. Pastors and lay leaders of small membership churches who permitted us to share ministry through consulting and working together: friends and colleagues who were willing to read and give suggestions. I want to thank Sharon Schwab, who gave tremendous suggestions from her pastoral experience and the students at Pittsburgh Theological Seminary, who want to be called affectionately "That Class Ed. 29, 1987." Many other colleagues and friends: Dorothy Hill, Kevin Rippin, Seth Bower, Jim Moss, Paul McCormick, Ed McElroy offered valuable suggestions and support. A special "thank you" to Peggy Sholich who figures out how to type "impossible" charts.

To Warren Hartman, whose impeccable work inspires and encourages me I am grateful. James Michael Lee's honesty and encouragement are greatly appreciated. To my husband, Bob and sons Drayton and Nelson, who know how to support and encourage with just the right kind of humor, I am indebted. My appreciation to each contributing author who made deadlines and most of all who made their wisdom and experience available to you, the religious edcuators of small membership churches. If you the reader finish this book feeling supported, encouraged, and clearer in your understanding of religious education in the small membership church, then we, the contributors, will have done our work.

Chapter One

Overview of Religious Education in the Small Membership Church

NANCY T. FOLTZ

A pastor sat in my office describing his church's location as "two corn-fields away from Ohio." He talked about the struggle and pain of trying to meet the denomination's expectations, those of the congregation, and his own hopes for the small membership church he serves.

"Sometimes when I go to denominational meetings, I feel like I'm speaking a different language than I speak in my church." He described his ministry: "Sometimes the hopes and dreams from various groups wear me down."

Later in our conversation the pastor raved about what the church people do exceptionally well. "They have a Strawberry Festival that serves the county. I suspect that's the one area we do best," he said.

A pastor, a woman, was appointed to a three church charge. Moving in, she arranged her lawn furniture on the front lawn, and a church member came by the parsonage to remind the pastor, "Don't get too comfortable . . . pastors don't stay here too long." This pastor has served those three small membership churches for the past ten years.

This book examines events in the life of the small membership church that demonstrate ways to teach and learn the faith, ways to create faithful community, ways to understand religious education. Collectively, the events, and the leaders as the faithful are the essentials for effective religious education in the small membership church.

This book is written by and for people who love the small membership church. The purpose of writing such a book is to offer a perspective, a vantage point, from which to see the potential for religious education.

This chapter divides into five sections: 1) definitions; 2) size profile; 3) congregational culture and worldview; 4) primary groups and their characters; 5) conclusion.

I. DEFINITIONS

Religious Education

How do you define "religious education" and "small membership church"? What does the world of the small membership church look like? Who are the religious educators? What are the dreams and hopes for the future of the small congregation? What does the journey of religious education look like in a small membership church? What are the obstacles which barricade the doors to change?

The purpose of religious education is to help persons respond to God. Religious educators are environmental shapers and directors. We create environments, shape them to teach and learn, and are shaped by them. At our best we are environmental directors of religious education, creating environments that will teach who God is. We offer individuals opportunities to interact, to passionately express their love for God and for one another. Religious education is not about curriculum resource, building, and position. Religious education is about knowing that we are the curriculum; we are the designers of space; and the ultimate issue is how we position ourselves to God and others.

Religious education is defined in our day-to-day interpersonal interactions. At its best, religious education is the culmination of our expressed life. We live out that life shaping and being shaped by environment. The way we feel, think, act, and most importantly live tells who we are.[1]

---

1. Nancy T. Foltz, "The Context of Wanting," in *Does the Church Really Want Religious Education?"* ed. Marlene Mayr (Birmingham, Ala.: Religious Education Press, 1988), pp. 174-175.

The litmus test of credibility is life lived.

In the small membership church religious education is "exaggerated living." There is an intensity to life together that demands clarity on the "why and how we teach" and "how we learn." Obviously the "why" and "how" are important, but the "where" also brings clarity to the scope of environment. The "why" we teach tells how persons understand and interpret the scriptures and faith experiences in light of their living. The "how" and "where" may tell more about personal history and experience.

Religious educators bring a definition whether stated or unstated to their ministry place. Whether that definition is too small or all-encompassing is rather critical for it informs and transforms the way the religious educator will begin "to be" with others. Intentionality in religious education means shaping the way hours are used or abused; knowing what kind of learning experiences persons want, need, and have.

I do not believe there to be any one all-encompassing definition of religious education that will make every religious educator jump with ecstasy; the point is that definitions set the boundary of the work. If the boundary is too small, it can be redefined; or if too large, it can be narrowed. Whatever the case, it is important to mark our area for concentrated work.

Religious Education in the Small Membership Church
Perhaps the complexity of religious education in the small membership church is best described by reviewing some of the most noted writers on the subject:

Carl S. Dudley: The Effective Small Membership Church
Dudley's love for the people who serve and live in the small membership church is evidenced in his writing and lecturing. When Dudley defines the culture-carrying, history-bearing, single-cell organization, he describes the effective small membership church as "a composite of several churches that have stabilized in their relationship to their particular environment. They seem to have a positive attitude toward themselves, and a constructive relationship with their pastor."[2] Dudley makes clear the notion that affirming the strengths of smallness will not necessarily lead to church membership growth.[3]

---

2. Carl S. Dudley, *Making the Small Church Effective* (Nashville: Abingdon, 1978), p. 17.

3. Ibid., p. 16.

Rachael Swann Adams: Size and Advantages

Adam's definition suggests "a congregation of one hundred or less meeting in a building of one or two rooms."[4] The distinctive advantages of religious education in the small membership church include: homes are natural meeting places, the out-of-doors and total environment are teaching places, creativity is stimulated in working with leaders, resources, and facilities.[5] Not only are small membership churches everywhere from rural to urban, but facilities are as varied from small to large, from two rooms to twenty rooms. Perhaps the constants in Adams' work are the advantages which, regardless of location or size, continue to exist.

Paul O. Madsen: Assets

The three basic assets of the small membership church are defined as: 1) warmth and intimacy of fellowship, 2) possibility of identifying and concentrating on mission, and 3) flexibility in approach—minimizing structure.[6]

These assets sound so basic, and they are; but they are foundational in understanding the critical dynamics of religious education. High relational needs with the ability to focus, and high flexibility on the one end and low structural needs on the other represent a clear definitive description of religious education in the small membership church.

Donald L. Griggs, Judy McKay Walther: Four Essentials

Understanding religious education in the small membership church means grasping the necessary essentials which guide the work. The essentials suggest that religious education is: 1) more than children's programs, 2) offered at times and in places in addition to Sunday, 3) involves the pastor in planning and leading, and 4) applies sound educational principles to all aspects of the church's ministry.[7]

Old images take a long time to change. Donald Griggs and Judy McKay Walther suggest we permit, encourage, and actively work toward an all-encompassing age spectrum of educational ministry when teaching and learning in the small membership church. Keeping religious education synonymous with children's programs or Sunday morning events

---

4. Rachael Swann Adams, *The Small Church and Christian Education* (Philadelphia: Westminster, 1961), p. 9.

5. Ibid., pp. 14-16.

6. Paul O. Madsen, *The Small Church VALID VITAL VICTORIOUS* (Valley Forge, Pa.: Judson, 1975), p. 29.

7. Donald L. Griggs and Judy McKay Walther, *Christian Education in the Small Church* (Valley Forge, Pa.: Judson, 1988), pp. 16-21.

exclusively presents unnecessary limitations on the potential of religious education.

Steve Burt: A Dozen Guidelines

In a chapter entitled, "What can the small church do?" Burt suggests a dozen guidelines for examining ministry, mission, and program: 1) content is relative to context, 2) program addresses real needs, 3) input comes from a wide cross-section of the church and community, 4) people's talents and gifts are used, 5) ideas can translate or adapt from one context to another, 6) realistic, 7) creative, 8) leaders' needs are balanced with leaders' church responsibilities, 9) ministry and programs are consistent with the church's purpose and goals, 10) programs and resources are prioritized, 11) recognition, acknowledgment, and appreciation are built in, and 12) evaluation and review are necessary.[8]

What is particular for the small membership church in this list of guidelines? Perhaps it is the high need for intentionality in making sense out of the guidelines and their usefulness for religious education. The translation of the dozen guide-lines is "common sense" coupled with high skill in planning and implementing
using the ordinary gifts of many people rather than the extraordinary gifts of one leader. The cornerstone is certainly maintaining consistency between religious education and the church's purpose and goals.

Religious education in the small congregation is not something unrelated to ministry; it is woven into the fabric of the entire life of the church.

David R. Ray: Ten Essentials

Small membership churches are different from their larger "ecclesiastical cousins," suggests Ray, particularly in the ten essentials: 1) common expectations, 2) almost everyone knows everyone, 3) a sense of family, 4) almost everyone feels, and is, important and needed, 5) group functioning is simple, 6) identity is in its collective personality and experience, not in its program, 7) common history and future, 8) theology is understood and is alive in personal, relational, and historic ways, 9) mission is implemented in immediate and personal terms, and 10) clergy is seen as a person, pastor, and generalist.[9]

---

8. Steve Burt, *Activating Leadership In the Small Church* (Valley Forge, Pa.:Judson, 1988), pp. 81-90.

9. David R. Ray, *Small Churches are the Right Size* (New York: Pilgrim Press, 1982), pp. 43-50.

Ray's order of essentials carries a message of people "first" and position (clergy) "last"; it also hints at the intangibleness of religious education. Theology and mission are often fused and visible in the unfolding of life experiences. Loyalties to family and the collective history are critical for positioning effective religious education with consistency in content and context. Some of the struggles of religious education in the small membership church center on the unexpressed intangibles which people have as common expectations.

Lyle E. Schaller: Characteristics

Schaller's intention is to differentiate between small and large churches. Schaller describes the subculture which exists in small congregations. It is this "culture within a culture" environment in which religious educators must be knowledgable and adept. The major cues of religious education are found within the comparisons. Knowing the importance of "kinship" as compared to "skill and knowledge" is essential in identifying and developing leaders. This does not suggest that one precludes the other, but rather that kinship is first and skill is second. Often the cues are learned on the job rather than in seminary education.

Summary

Collectively, these eight authors provide a way to view religious education in the small membership church. Perhaps one critical clue in understanding religious education in the small membership churches is to listen for consistency in the language of people as they speak about their relation to God. Who are they and what are the ways God calls, comforts, encourages, and directs? Listening around the edges of a faith community tells who God is to these people. Listening and watching the actions of persons, responses, interactions, and outcomes tells how these persons respond to God. Religious education is about hearing God and responding, it is about knowing God and acting, it is about consistency between who we claim to be and who we are.

Jackson W. Carroll prefaces his work by stating that "new possibilities open to small member churches to celebrate their smallness as a positive attitude and to develop their potential as vital, caring communities of faith."[11] Religious education is first, relational. There are many variables which affect why and how we do what we do; the basics, the essentials,

---

10. Lyle E. Schaller, *The Small Church Is Different* (Nashville: Abingdon, 1982). This chart was developed to visualize what Schaller has written about the distinct differences which exists when comparing size of congregation.

11. Jackson W. Carroll, ed., *Small Churches Are Beautiful* (New York: Harper & Row, 1977), p. xiii.

SMALL MEMBER CHURCH	CHARACTERISTICS	LARGE MEMBER CHURCH
Average worship attendance less than 50		**Average worship attendance 250+**
• Everyone	1. A place for	• Most work on special needs: singles, etc.
• Rewards generalists	2. People and performance	• Rewards specialists
• Very important, lower "dropout rate" helps to select officers	3. Kinship ties	• Does not enter into leader selection or decision making
• "Counts who is absent" "Counts faces"	4. Takes attendance	• "Counts those present" "Counts pews"
• Consider bloodlines/and the right marriage	5. Selective officers	• Officers earn their positions • The office needs able leaders
• Volunteer, other than pastor and an occasional part-time secretary	6. Staff	• Pastor, secretary, choir director, etc.
• Intergenerational	7. Age-grouping	• Same age cohort
• Individuals	8. Who does the work	• Committees
• Clan leader or worker	9. Leaders	• Tribal chief, assistant medicine man
• To the congregation as a whole	10. Loyalty	• Toward the minister, an adult Sunday school, or some other sub group
• Four to six hours a week for a leader to be reasonably well informed	11. Leader's time to be reasonably well informed	• In a middle-sized church – eight to fifteen hours a week
• The pastor loves every one of us, the pastor cares, the pastor gets around and gets acquainted	12. What the minister does best	• Preaching, administration, sermons, teacher, leading worship organizer
• Emphasize the relational dimensions of the person (RELATIONAL DIMENSIONS)	13. Members appraise the strengths of their pastor	• Concentrate on the functional and symbolic dimensions of the office (FUNCTIONAL DIMENSIONS)
• Is not used to classify adults	14. Marital status	• Is used to classify adults
• Each other, that meeting place, kinfolk ties	15. The nature of the commit- ment of the members – in addition to religious com- mitment	• The minister, specific programs, ministries, the denomination
• Considerable time given to fellowship needs of members	16. Meetings	• Agenda is task-oriented, functional needs are primary
• Shorter time frame for program planning	17. Planning	• Longer time frame for program planning
• Participatory democracy • Owned and operated by the laity	18. Decisions	• Central authority in a small number of leaders • Dominated by the clergy
• An asset—is dependable and accurate	19. Grapevine	• Carries more erroneous messages than accurate bits of information
• Tough – usually can survive a succession of disasters	20. As an institution	• Fragile – highly vulnerable to erosion, internal or external
• Internal clock	21. Time	• External clock
• Influenced by seasons, family reunions, language and nationality differences, ethnic customs, congregational traditions	22. Calendar	• Liturgical and/or traditional
• "Attraction model" – new members take the initiative	23. New-member recruitment	• "Proclamation approach" church members take the initiative
• Piano	24. Central musical instrument	• Organ
• Focused on a single theme: it is a community of believers where people come together to worship God and to love and care for one another	25. Resources	• Spread over a wide range of ministries, causes, needs, specialized staff and service programs
• Members respond based on their perceived needs of the congregation	26. Systems for the financial support of the congregation	• Members are not able to perceive the full scope of ministry
• Resembles participatory democracy	27. Form of government	• Resembles a representative system of shared government
• Resembles a CLAN • A clan is a few families • Offers the clan fewer services	28. Anthropological terms	• Resembles a TRIBE • A tribe is individuals, families, clans, other groups • Offers the tribe many services

CHART 1

the characteristics of the small membership church are certainly excellent signposts for the pastor as religious educator.

Another way to examine the small membership church is by size. There are numerous misperceptions about religious education that might be dispelled through the examination of a profile of six sizes and characteristics.

II. PROFILE - SIX SIZES AND CHARACTERISTICS

Membership Size

Denominations tend to define churches by numerical size. The small membership church is defined as under 200-250 members. Unfortunately, most definitions of this kind refer to membership rolls rather than persons in the pew on Sunday morning. The discrepancy between "on the roll" and "present in the pew" is enormous. The basic assumption of this section is that in the small membership church religious education is an all-church enterprise, that each time the people gather there is a potential opportunity to learn and to teach. The unique factor in the small congregation is that the intensity of the setting and interpersonal relationships sometimes overwhelm and immobilizes leaders, and consequently many "teaching and learning moments" are missed. Another assumption is that just the dynamics of size alone . . . is powerful in shaping what can be done.

The sizes shown on Chart 2 range from 1) THE FAMILY CHURCH, 2) THE PASTORAL CHURCH, 3) THE PASTORAL/PROGRAM CHURCH, 4) THE AWKWARD-SIZED CHURCH, 5) THE PROGRAM CHURCH, AND 6) THE CORPORATION CHURCH.

Each size is represented with characteristics such as: the usual context, lay leadership, pastor/priest, church definition, religious education, decision making, planning, communication, and the source of new members. Perhaps this examination can enlighten our perceptions and sense of reality about what is and what can be a realistic expectation of religious educators who serve small membership churches.

Chart 2 (attached separately) indicates some of the critical characteristics which define the small membership church. In examining religious education, understanding the differentiating factors in size may be useful in clarifying what is and is not essential. This examination certainly emphasizes the powerful role of religious educators, clergy and lay, who develop and unfold ministry within an environment which is preset.

In examining the size of a church, it became clear that to fully understand religious education in the small congregation it would be imperative that the full gamut of size be studied. How different is the "very small" from the "very large" church? Viewing the full scope of size gives perspective to the enormous challenge for religious educators.

Lessons Learned

Several points can be made about the lessons learned from the chart. The first thought in developing the chart was to dispel the myth that small membership churches are all the same. Size is not divided into small, medium, and large but rather size contributes to shaping and developing a profile which can assist religious educators in understanding and in designing educational activities that make sense and are consistent with the profile needs of a particular church size. There are four size profiles which are clearly within the general definition of small membership church: 1) very small, 2) small, 3) moderate-middle, and 4) awkward-sized church.

In reviewing the literature the following profiles emerge:

1. THE FAMILY CHURCH (very small)

   0-50 church membership
   Fewer than 35 in morning worship

This matriarchal/patriarchal church may be comprised of one, two, or more families. Everyone knows each person. When attendance is taken, it is informal and faces are counted. Morning worship will bring fewer than thirty-five of the faithful members together, a little over half of the membership.

Key leaders are either a matriarch and/or a patriarch who emerge from congregational life. They may or may not be in attendance at morning worship.

The pastor in his or her role as religious educator is to love the people. This person's task is to listen to the history of the church, appreciate it, and be able to retell the stories. Leadership is more symbolic than operational. Note in the chart that the pastor may be or feel to be outside the church. The pastor's presence does not automatically assure the pastor's participation in ministry. The pastor is something like a visitor waiting to be welcomed. Actually, it is not the pastor as religious educator or a central office leader who determines the pastor's role; it is the church members. This is the "Family Church" that the pastor is to love while often being treated as a denominational "visitor."

The message for religious educators is to "listen, learn, and appreciate." The role of the pastor as religious educator is to cultivate a taste for and the love of local history and tradition. Actually, the pastor is a learner first and then, perhaps, a teacher. In this Family Church some of the real teachers are the persons in the pew as well as the unofficial leaders who chose to lead the church from their homes. Informal and relational teaching is strong in the Family Church.

Each leader's vote is weighted; therefore, a true democracy is a mere figment of the imagination. Leaders exist out of blood ties and position within the family, not necessarily because of their expertise. Leadership is self or family appointed in unofficial more frequently than official ways. Usually the membership is very stable with little turnover. The family church is informal, casual, and relaxed. No one gets too excited about planning let alone long-range planning.

There may be several budgets that emerge as critical needs arise. The pastor is not expected to be overly concerned about finances nor to ask too many questions about the budget. One church of twenty-seven persons told the story of getting a pastor who had grown up in a big church and was fresh out of seminary. He had no idea how twenty-seven people could be a church. Somewhere in his seminary preparation he had been informed to worry about finances so he inquired about the state of the budget. He worried and the people were amused. Finally, a gentle soul, pillar of the church, said: "Pastor, today we need forty more dollars to pay your salary, so next Sunday after church we'll serve pie and dessert and take up an offering." They did, and forty dollars appeared in the basket. The salary was paid. And yet another lesson in religious education was taught. . .postgraduate studies in the small membership church. The Family Church operates on low organizational structure and high relational activity. Make no mistake about it, this church is owned and operated by laity!

Leaders more often than not will inform the pastor about decisions made. The decision-making locations range from the parking lot, the telephone, places where the people gather in the community, to occasionally the church, prior to meetings. Remember, the principle is, the smaller the church the lower the organizational structure and the more informal the decision-making process. Often pastors feel left out of decision making. They not only "feel" left out in the matriarchal/patriarchal church—they *are* left out.

"Events" are critical, programs are not. The smaller the church the more events are valued. There is the strawberry festival, the annual bazaar, revival week, and the community fair. These are the serious places where teaching and learning occur. Leaders are developed, ecumenical ties are strengthened, and persons learn what it means to demonstrate loving your neighbor.

The liturgical year may not be as important to many small membership churches. One Monday morning in the seminary parking lot I overheard two students talking about their churches. "You'll never believe what I was told yesterday. The matriarch forgot to buy candles for the Advent wreath so she told me to reschedule the beginning of Advent to next week instead of yesterday." Pomp and circumstance teaches in the large membership church; flexibility teaches in the small membership church. So how terrible can it be if you light two candles the second Sunday of Advent? Moments such as these are the "teaching/learning moments" of religious education in the small membership church.

The purpose of religious education is to love and to be loved; to know and to be known; to live and to forgive within the context of a single cell, culture carrying, history bearing primary group. The smaller the group, the more intense, dynamic, and potentially volatile the religious education . . . or to say it another way . . . the higher the potential for touching lives!

Where are these churches located? Everywhere from rural to urban to small towns.

2. THE PASTORAL CHURCH (small)

50-150 church membership
40-100 worship attendance

In the Pastoral Church the pastor as religious educator actually moves to a more prominent position of leadership if that person is willing to acknowledge, respect, and defer at times to members of core leading families who dominate leadership positions. The patriarch/matriarch leaders are still critical to decision making.

Other leaders gather often in informal locations to do the work of the church. Persons may change positions but not roles. The same leader may carry the same responsibility for years.[12] Leaders emerge through blood ties and marriages rather than via a formal nominating process. Central offices do not usually determine programs but are important because they provide a tie with tradition.

The pastor is a shepherd to guide the congregation, preach, and care for

---

12. In a study of laity in leadership positions, the research stated that 48 percent of the respondents have been in a leadership position for sixteen or more years. Only 3 percent of the respondents were under age thirty. "A Summary of the Goals Questionnaires in Leadership Development and Mission and Ministry 1984-1987" developed by the Research and Development Committee in the Western Pennsylvania Annual Conference of the United Methodist Church.

the members. Most Pastoral Churches do not want a pushy shepherd. Minding the sheep is one thing; making decisions about the church is quite another. Sometimes the pastor is permitted to guide the flock and other times the organized sheep keep the pastor outside the pasture. Flexibility is the key!

Annual "events" are the primary places to teach and learn. The mission festival, the homecoming celebration are the places where the positive image of the church is enhanced and the leaders feel good about ministry.

The Pastoral Church is like an extended family, a two or three cellular structure. The dynamics are more complicated and still represent intense interpersonal struggles for the pastor and laity. Frequently there are tensions between organizational models for decision making and informal person to person discussions. Often denominational structure is evidenced on paper but in reality is nonfunctional. This dilemma produces not only frustration but a negative self-image in leaders who wonder why they cannot "make it work" or why denominations do not make sense. Warren Hartman tells the story of a brilliant lay woman in a small membership church who told him that their church needed five leaders: a Sunday school administrator to run the Sunday school, a treasurer to handle the money, a trustee to take care of things, a lay leader who would go to conference to get their preacher and hear about the rest of the churches and their apportionment, and a preacher to conduct services, baptize, marry, and bury.

If religious education is, or can be, wherever there is an opportunity to teach and/or learn, then the Pastoral Church is a microcosm for learning about small group dynamics, intergenerational grouping, interpersonal relations, clear communications, and decision making using the most informal of processes. Usually the Sunday school or CCD is very prominent. The pastor as religious educator may or may not regularly be involved.[13]

This microcosm called the Pastoral Church often takes incredible energy and the learning environment produces such stress that religious leaders, clergy and lay, are often weary of the lessons to be learned. Religious education may be viewed by laity as the Sunday school or CCD only;

---

13. Some of the frustration of conversation about new people finding their way into leadership positions is made clear when you realize that in general terms: "If more than one half of today's leaders have been members of this congregation for more than a dozen years, morale tends to be low. If more than one half of today's leaders have been members of this congregation for less than seven years, morale tends to be high." Schaller, *The Small Church Is Different*, p. 61.

however, the pastor's role as religious educator is to observe, point out, and encourage conversation and events that emerge out of the needs of laity. Building on what is, enhancing present events, and affirming through the ministry of encouragement are intentional skills which need to be developed by the religious educator.

One Saturday, working with leaders of the New Brighton Church, the leaders wrote two specific, attainable, measurable goals. The first goal provided a ministry of fellowship. The leaders planned a monthly program emphasizing luncheons and all-church dinners. The second goal of intentional visitation included teams of three persons visiting new residents in the community including inactive church members.

The leadership team worked six hours to develop their mission statement and goals. Facilitating their planning process brought clarity to the notion that to define religious education in the small membership church is to be privileged to work with a pastor and leaders on what they know works best. An amazing revelation came as the leaders worked. They were able to list thirty-one ministries for the spiritual and educational development of leaders and twenty-nine ministries positioned to the community and beyond. These sixty ministries represented what "is." No wonder the small leadership base of sixteen leaders felt overwhelmed.[14]

When the planning session ended, Mid, a key lay leader, brought out a box of albums. She had collected pictures of each person's family dating back to their birth, youth, and adult years. Pictures of their parents and family filled each album. Mid used a t-square to center each picture on the page. The albums were given as a gift to leaders in the church.

Is the small membership church a primary group where there is intimacy? Yes . . . each leader teaches and learns in an environment that unfolds faith page after page, generation after generation. Understanding the historical dimension is central to knowing how religious education can be positioned for the future. To love the history, and to learn the genealogy, of its members is to begin to understand who and why the small membership church is. The religious educator must be a cultural historian and one who loves to hear the stories of local history.

The grapevine is alive and well and nourished in this church. Leaders

---

14. Laity respondents listed four reasons for accepting leadership positions in the church: 1) They could serve God—the church, 2) they realized personal fulfillment, 3) they sensed a need, and 4) no one else would do it. These responses come from the survey of Research and Development, 1984-1987, The United Methodist Church, Western Pennsylvania Conference.

who need to communicate use the grapevine and pastors who care to learn must know how to use and not abuse its use. When a religious educator wants to fax it fast, that person uses the grapevine.

The Pastoral Church is most frequently found in towns and suburbia. It is often an old church and is found in sparsely populated areas such as the plains states of the Mid-West.

3. THE PASTORAL/PROGRAM CHURCH (moderate - middle sized)

150-250 church membership
75-125 worship attendance

One of the dilemmas of the Pastoral/Program Church is the vacillation between a small and a moderate to middle-sized church. This church shifts between having a low, informal organizational structure which is consistent with the small pastoral church and wanting to be a middle-sized church with multiple programs. More attention is given to nominating procedures for electing persons to leadership positions. Lay volunteers are more generalists than specialists.

The pastor is a cross between a shepherd and a program director. Sometimes the pastor is to guide the flock and other times the work means introducing new program ministry ideas.[15] The pastoral leader needs to be "meek as a lamb and wise as a fox." To understand conflict resolution is to survive and enjoy the members of this Pastoral/Program church. Often this church is struggling to support a full-time pastor.

Teaching and learning occurs in fewer intergenerational groupings and appears in more opportunities for broadly grouped classes. There are more distinctive classes and identities. Some groups will organize other than Sunday activities.

As the groups appear, record keeping becomes more formal and more important to the leaders. It is possible to find some records on last year's plans for this year's ice cream social.

The Pastoral/Program Church is usually found in the towns and suburbia.

4. THE AWKWARD-SIZED CHURCH (middle-sized)

200-350 church membership
100-200 morning worship

---

15. In the same Goals Summary Research, 93 percent of the laity named the pastor as primary resource leader. There is no doubt that the role of support for laity is critical and carefully observed by the laity.

The Awkward Church is a middle-sized church. The struggle of "who's in charge—clergy or lay" continues from the Pastoral/Program Church. The Awkward Church is not staff-centered, highly structured, nor family-like. This church does have active formal religious education in a variety of settings.

The pastor as religious educator is the program director. There may be a part- time employed secretary. The perception is that there are just enough programs to produce stress for one pastor but not enough to hire additional staff. The fast pace of the pastor in the role as religious educator may suggest why pastors usually change in the Awkward Church every three or four years. There may be enough ministry activity for additional employed staff but not enough finance. The pastor must have or develop a capacity for working in and understanding ambiguity. The higher a pastor's needs for specificity, concrete, "nail it down" information, the higher the frustration level because the Awkward Church often sees itself as smaller than it is and often lives out ministry in paradoxes. (See Chart #3, page 22.)[16]

The Awkward Church is sometimes a testing ground for pastors to see if they can move beyond the small membership church, can be good administrators, can work with others and delegate responsibility, can manage time, and can really lead and motivate the congregation to action and outreach (often through a building program). This is often (in the United Methodist Church) the first single church charge that the pastor has.

One paradox is the Awkward Church's desire to grow. Generally there is no room in the church that could actually accommodate or seat the entire congregation at one time. Multiple programs move members to participation. Large events assist the several church clans and those new clan members to be assimilated into the membership of the Awkward Church. Two worship services could help to solve the dilemma of too few seats to accommodate all members but the trade-off is the intimacy of the small group. When the seats in the sanctuary are 57 percent occupied, the congregation will experience "resistance pressure." When the occupancy reaches 80 percent of the pew space there will be a "barrier" that prohibits new persons from being assimilated.

Congregations who want to grow numerically will consider a second worship service when the annual average attendance reaches 65 percent of the comfortable capacity of the sanctuary.[17]

---

16. Schaller, *The Middle-Sized Church,* pp. 11-13. This chart was developed out of the writing of Schaller to highlight the paradoxes which exist in the awkward-sized church.

17. James W. Moss, "People Spots" (Churches of God, 1984). Moss's study indicates that a People Spot is a physical space where relationships with others are developed and where felt needs are being met. When the people spots of a church are all filled, new people cannot be assimilated.

MIDDLE-SIZED CHURCH PARADOXES

ONE MINISTER _____ CLERGY _____ TWO MINISTERS

PART-TIME SECRETARY ____ SECRETARY _____ FULL-TIME SECRETARY

ORGANIZED CHOIR _____ CHOIR _____ CHOIR AND PAID CHOIR
                                           DIRECTOR

ONE LARGE GOVERNING __ ORGANIZATION _____ TASK FORCE AND
  BOARD   STANDING COMMITTEES

YOUTH GROUP TOO _____ YOUTH _____ SEPARATE JUNIOR HIGH
  LARGE   AND SENIOR HIGH
                                           YOUTH GROUPS

NEW MEMBER _____ NEW MEMBER _____ A NEW MEMBER
  ENLISTMENT EFFORT   ENLISTMENT
TOO LARGE TO KNOW ____ RELATIONAL NEEDS __ TOO SMALL TO WEAR
  EVERYONE BY NAME   NAME TAGS

TOO LARGE FOR A _____ GRAPEVINE _____ TOO SMALL FOR A
  RELIABLE GRAPEVINE   NEWSLETTER

CHART 3

Religious education occurs in many settings of the Awkward Church. The formal learning classes, the worship experiences, and the music are essentials in the Awkward Church. One of the struggles of religious education is whether to reach out into the community and world or stay in our own church building and membership.[18]

More decisions are made in meetings than in the parking lot. Trial votes may be taken in the choir during rehearsal. Actually, the choir represents a critical group of leaders. Usually the choir is the one group which meets weekly. Their regular meetings often present an opportunity for central leaders to discuss critical issues of religious education. This casual yet interpersonal and more formalized setting gives leaders a chance to test many trial balloons. It is wise for the religious educator to be present before, during, and/or after choir meetings.

The Awkward Church is usually found in larger towns, urban, and growing suburban areas.

---

18. In a study of forty-seven growing churches 81 percent of the pastors indicated that they involve themselves actively in the life of the larger community. "Why Churches Grow," Western Pennsylvania Conference of the United Methodist Church, 1986.

5. THE PROGRAM CHURCH

350-800 church membership
250-400 worship attendance

The Program Church is a moderately large church with a full-time pastor and other employed staff. There is a core of laity who provide specialized leadership in numerous sub groups.

The other employed staff members may be in youth, music, education, or other designated areas of ministry. Each staff person has specific, defined work areas and has responsibility to assist key lay leaders in the implementation of ministry. Assignments are often much broader than in the corporation churches: religious education as youth, singles, children, adult: or evangelism as: minister of visitation, congregational care. By this time clearer lines are seen between programs and services versus administration and policy making. In the smaller churches many (if not most) lay persons make little distinction, but in larger churches and especially the corporation churches the two functions are very clearly separated. It is in the Program Church where these distinctions begin to be seen.

The pastor's role is program director. Knowing how to coordinate the staff, the needs of the church members, and the introduction of new ministries is the work of the pastor.

Religious education becomes more formal with closely grouped ages and interests. More care is given to the curriculum resource used, and the general resources available are expanded. Church members begin to recognize that, contrary to the small membership church, they are not expected to be in church every time the doors are open.

Leaders and resources are often brought in for additional expertise and knowledge. The Program Church leaders, clergy and lay, often provide leadership at denominational and or regional events.

The purpose of religious education is certainly to extend the ministry into the community and beyond. New opportunities for learning may occur in outreach ministry to the homeless and/or abused. Basically, religious education opportunities are offered to help persons cope: e.g., divorce recovery, parenting, dealing with grief, or caring for aging parents.

The Program Church resembles a nation. There is a unified spirit and sometimes a budget that presents a single focus. Each person knows the organizational structure and knows where his or her contribution can be made.

Decision making may include the gathering of research data. There is an openness for receiving new information that originates beyond our collective histories. Demographic studies, census, and age-sex pyramids may be used in examining the feasibility of numerical growth in the five-year plan.

The Program Church is usually found in cities and metropolitan areas.

6. THE CORPORATION CHURCH

   800+ church membership
   350+ worship attendance

The Corporation Church is almost larger than life. This church offers specialized staff and a comprehensive program. There is a full-time pastor and employed staff.

This multistaff church is a complex organization with a wide range of programs and facilities to meet the needs of the church and area. The church may resemble the United Nations. In one such church, there may be numerous nationalities represented, various races, and during morning worship there may be signing for the deaf.

The pastor is viewed as a chief executive officer whose efficiency, knowledge of each member of the congregation, and overall supervisory skills of the staff combine to produce an image of unified corporate life.

The pastor of the Corporation Church is representative of the image the church wishes to project. This person knows how to delegate responsibility and then stand back while the implementation is done. The basic principle of clergy in the Corporation Church is: the larger the church, the longer the pastorate.

Knowing each member of the congregation is almost impossible. It is rare to have a pastor of a church this size who has accurate information on all members. The basic principle of conserving persons in small groups applies. The Corporation Church has a central leadership staff, a lay leadership team, and multiple small groups and leaders.

Decision making is done in a collaborative style among the elected leaders. Power tends to be in the hands of those who hold particular office. The votes are not weighted. Resolution in conflict would probably be done using some form of principled negotiation such as the Harvard management team's *Getting to Yes*. Basically, principled negotiations decide issues on their merits rather than on people and what they will or will not do. The issues are explored based on the potential options available to all parties.

The intent is to resolve the issue with integrity for all parties. A best alternative to a negotiated agreement (BANTA) is suggested to bring resolution to the issue.[19] In the Family or Pastoral Church focusing on particular issues is not the norm. When in conflict, leaders will not focus on particular issues but rather drag out all previous conflicts until the one central beginning issue is submerged, confused, and unable to be identified.

A colleague told of visiting a Corporation Church for Christmas Eve. There were wise men on camels and sheep wandering around the chancel. This is the level at which the Corporate Church operates. The bigger, the more extravagant, the better.

The worship service is the one experience which holds the large Corporation Church together. Worship is the setting in which disparate groups and activities come together to share in one common experience of celebration.

Planning may be done thirty-six months ahead. A formal planning process is used with critical boards who delegate to sub-groups. Lay leaders and employed staff carry out the final stage of implementation.

Usually excellent music and fair to good preaching is prominent in the Corporation Church. In all other-sized churches, small to corporation, the sermon is considered more important than is music; however, in the Corporation Church music is more important than the sermon or liturgy.[20] Obviously the choir is essential, the organist a must, and the choir director full-time. Special music concerts are available and paid vocalists are brought in or are a part of the choir.

Lay persons usually specialize in one or two areas. Leaders are nominated and the process becomes more formal as the size of the church increases.

Religious education includes a full-time staff member with specific responsibilities. The approach includes formal educational activities, closely graded curriculum, numerous special ministries, such as singles, divorce recovery, and persons with handicapping conditions. Curriculum resource,

---

19. Roger Fisher and William Ury, *Getting To Yes: Negotiating Agreement Without Giving In* (New York: Penguin, 1984. This is a practical guide that can assist religious educators to use the process in its most formal or informal settings. It has the potential to be used in conflict with members of the small membership church.

20. In the research of forty-seven growing churches, those churches over 400 in membership indicated that music was most important for the spiritual life of their congregation. Research and Development Study, 1986.

media including video, and satellite capability might also be included. Recruiting, developing, supporting, and releasing a significant number of lay leaders and teachers can be a highly organized effort to support religious education. Special short-term learning opportunities, such as trips to mission areas or notable speakers and workshops are often made available to those involved in the religious education arena.

The Corporation Church is usually found in cities and metropolitan areas.

Summary

Size is important; however size is misleading.[21] Membership attendance is not as important as worship attendance plus attendance at educational events such as the Sunday school, CCD, and any other educational offering. Leadership for clergy and laity varies based on size. The smaller the congregation, the more the people want to know their leaders. The more the religious educators are known, the more vulnerable they become. The smaller the congregation, the more visible the leader needs to be around the community. Often in the small membership church the leaders in the community are the leaders in the church.[22]

Visiting is not an option; it is central to understanding "how" to be present in the small membership church. The smaller the membership church, the more important knocking on doors is. Knowing how to distinguish between what can be retold and what was privileged information becomes a question of critical importance. Visiting is not necessarily for the purpose of increasing the membership.[23]

Pastors need a voracious appetite for history, local history. The ears of

---

21. Warren Hartman, "They Aren't All Alike," *Trends* 3:1 (February 1985).

22. Arthur J. Vidich and Joseph Bensman, *Small Town in Mass Society, Class, Power and Religion in a Rural Community* (Princeton, N.J.: Princeton University Press, 1969), pp. 258-284. Vidich and Bensman discuss "Community Integration Through Leadership" giving particular attention to primary and secondary leadership roles. Of particular interest is their notion that "leadership accumulates leadership even when the individual does not desire the position of leadership."

23. Lyle E. Schaller, *Growing Plans, Strategies to Increase Your Church's Membership* (Nashville: Abingdon, 1983), pp. 15-49. Schaller's observation is that most small membership churches have been in existence for three or more decades. Growing churches are frequently those who have not yet reached their fifteenth birthday. To grow numerically, the small membership church needs a pastor for five to six years to implement a two-part program of serious study of the Bible, of "how to" opportunities for leaders in workshops on church growth.

the pastors will be more important than the voice. Hearing the stories precedes being able to tell the local stories.[24] This is an invariant sequence.

Religious educators come and are present at the births, the weddings of the Joneses and the Petersons. Religious educators come and are present at the rally days, the opening exercises, the vacation Bible school, the short-term and long-term events. Religious educators who excel know when to linger over a cup of coffee, a conversation in the parking lot, waiting out the silences . . . to be present with. Religious educators who excel are cultural historians par excellence! They come to hear about the beginnings, the fires, the tornado that blew the roof two communities away, the flood that took the pews to the next city. These religious educators help to calm the terror within that is too scary to name.

Somehow it is not the programs nor eloquence in the pulpit that makes a difference. It is not the endless recruiting, the filling in at the last minute, the cleaning of the coffee pot and turning off lights that makes a difference. What makes the difference is what religious educators pay attention to. Ministry is about people, their greatest hopes and dreams as well as their fears.[25] Ministry is learning there are people who will help you to live through and beyond your worst nightmares; people who will share your greatest dreams.

Religious educators are environmental shapers and directors who help congregations to "warm up" even to outsiders. These leaders find ways to talk about how to welcome, invite, create space for new people. Religious educators help us to be better at saying "hello" than "good-bye."

In the small membership church, size does not tell it all, it only helps us to see that one size does not fit all.

III. CONGREGATIONAL CULTURE AND WORLDVIEW

Each congregation has a set of internal dynamics, a perspective on living and believing, and a way to talk about the world as they perceive it.

---

24. James Hopewell, *Congregation Stories and Structures* (Philadelphia: Fortress, 1987). This entire work is a careful examination of participant observation of a pastor with two churches. Understanding congregational narrative and the power of narrative gives religious leaders insight into parish ministry.

25. A four-year study of 150 United Methodist churches reports that developing vital congregations requires: "pastors who love people, have known God's grace, and model the gospel they proclaim"; a threefold approach of leadership, nurture, and outreach; in-service training for clergy on practical ministry; long tenures; use of trained laypersons on staff; and emphasis on increasing Christian influence. The United Methodist Newscope, Vol. 17, No. 46, November 17, 1989.

Congregational culture and worldview tell who a congregation is based on their history. . . their story. Religious educators can share in the teaching and learning ministry, which is the living out of a shared history . . . story. A congregation's narrative discourse, their storytelling, has a thread of familiarity which is woven through their collective stories. Their collective stories when stitched together represent their view of the world. This is the parish's worldview.

Religious educators are historical designers of congregational story. Our role is to examine congregational culture—to hear worldview. To identify particular stitches. Ministry is fashioned, designed, out of historical culture and worldview. Listening around the edges of a parish gives opportunity to overhear the stories, laugh at the jokes, and experience the rituals which collectively speak about the uniqueness of this particular people.

Congregational Culture

Lyle Schaller describes congregational culture as the distinctive factor that unlocks the secrets of internal dynamics in congregational life.[26] Members are both the creators of and the products of congregational culture. The uniqueness of a congregational culture tells why particular traditions, customs and habits endure. Eight aspects of a congregational culture include:

values	1. a system of shared values
"the how"	2. a clear understanding of "how we do things around here"
structure	3. the organizational structure a. what is it for planning and decision making b. how is it constituted c. what values and goals are the foundation blocks for that organizational structure
control	4. a control system: "What happens if they don't?"
interaction	5. how shared values, belief systems interact with the organizational structure, the people, reward and punishment system and with the religious leaders to inform and shape what happens.
turf	6. turf is the owning of space for one purpose by one group. For example, the kitchen in the small membership church may belong to the cooks for the fellowship dinner, the adults for a Sunday school or CCD

---

26. Schaller, *The Middle-Sized Church*, pp. 15-29.25.

	class. In the large membership church there may be fewer keys to the kitchen and more ownership of particular space.
legends	7. tribal legends are often "what the stranger sees." Often they are the pictures on the walls. The tribal legends are the furnishings which symbolize the legends, represent ing visual reminders of history and reinforcing the sense of continuity.
people	8. the people represent the heart of the congregational culture.[27]

Congregational culture is the living out of perceptions. Each congregation has a culture which affects how religious education is defined and lived out.

Worldview

A congregation's worldview describes a community's perceptions and suspicions about what is happening in life. Worldviews are fragile and incomplete constructions. James Hopewell suggests congregations tell their worldviews through narration of personal experience. Their parish stories reveal, through local metaphors, not universal propositions, a system within which life occurs. By listening to the parish stories, religious educators hear congregations interpret their view of the world.[28]

The functions of congregational worldviews are 1) persons tend to cluster with those who see the world as they do; 2) most of the members of the local congregation share an idiomatic discourse which projects a mutually recognizable world; 3) through the discourse of its members the congregational story establishes its world setting; 4) different congregations do have distinctive worldviews; and 5) worldviews are not determined by denominations.[29] Hopewell suggests that worldview stories are often told during times of acute crises and that they reflect and give a focus to group experience. The worldview stories provide a way within which words and actions make sense. The elements in a parish culture which may well be the source from which you hear worldview include: jokes-stories-lore, the written material of the parish, conversations that follow administrative meetings, sermons-classroom presentations, use of space, organizations,

---

27. Ibid., pp. 15-29.
28. Hopewell, *Congregation Stories and Structures,* pp. xi-18.
29. Ibid., pp. 95-96.

social groupings, processes of becoming a nuclear member, lines of authority and influence, use of time, ritual, social class, demographic features, history, conscious and unconscious symbols, and conflict.[30] Religious educators can listen for the worldviews that unfold as conversation occurs in the natural environment of the local congregation.

In Hopewell's research about congregations and worldviews, he identified certain correlations between a member's worldview position and other church activities. The correlations are: There is a communicative link between worship and worldview suggesting that persons who attend worship regularly have similar worldviews to those in the congregation; pastors and congregations whose worldviews differ significantly may express their discomfort with each other in conflicts; persons whose scores are on the periphery of the cluster of a congregation's scores are often marginal to the life of the congregation in other respects as well; and lay leaders of the congregation do not necessarily have scores that approximate the mean orientation of the church.[31]

The four worldview categories Hopewell suggests are present in congregational culture include: Canonic, Gnostic, Charismatic, and Empiric. Each category offers a way to hear parish stories and the universe the group constructs.[32] For our purposes, we will explore one worldview. It represents a recurring theme which is often spoken by religious educators in their telling of experiences in congregations they have served or in musing about the possibilities.

Charismatic or "Romantic" Worldview

The Charismatic or "Romantic" worldview, as James Cushman in chapter ten suggests, views life as an adventure and heroic in nature. Evil is present; but through God's Holy Spirit one can be empowered to overcome anything.

More has been written about this view in the last decade through the work of Joseph Campbell, Carol Pearson, Katherine Pope, and others. The beauty of this worldview is the image of the true hero, gender free, who

---

30. Ibid., p. 89.

31. Ibid., p. 98.

32. Hopewell, *Congregation Stories and Structures*. This work brings a new dimension to hearing congregational story and participating as a religious educator in shaping story.

shatters the established order and creates the new community.[33] There are leaders, clergy and laity, within the religious communities who are journeying as heroes of small member churches experiencing familiar routes and quests. Perhaps a recounting of the worldview would be useful to those leaders who may have experienced, or who experience, some commonality with those heroes of old.

In examination of the cultures, and classic writing within various cultures, there is a wealth of material to suggest that such a worldview as the Romantic worldview can help us to understand our experiences of life in a fuller way. Biblical as well as mythical characters can be traced through the seven dimensions of the Romantic worldview.

The Hero

The world of the mythic hero is about men and women who exit known worlds. Heroes are not about courage; heroes are about living life in self-discovery. Heroes remove conventional masks, knowing that to journey is a take a solo venture. "The ultimate aim of the quest must be neither release nor ecstasy for oneself, but the wisdom and the power to serve others."[34] In some respects heroes die to their known world before they can actually begin the journey or quest.

The Known World

The potential hero exists in a world where there is familiarity, and perhaps a comfortableness, but not necessarily a contentedness. Knowledge about "what is" in the known world is compared to "what could be." The restlessness within the potential hero stirs the hero to imagine a different world, a new community. Often the stirring of the hero, the imagination, the external movements, prior to the exit from the known world are unknown to those around the hero.

---

33. For a detailed account of literature on the female hero see Carol Pearson and Katherine Pope, *The Female Hero in American and British Literature* (New York: Bowker, 1981) and Carol Pearson, *The Hero Within: Six Archetypes We Live By* (San Francisco; Harper & Row, 1986). A summary of the hero's adventure is found in Joseph Campbell, *The Hero with a Thousand Faces* (Princeton, N.J.: Princeton University Press, 1968), pp. 245-251.

34. Joseph Campbell, *The Power of Myth* (New York: Doubleday, 1988), p. xv.

The Voice

Because the journey or quest is filled with such terrifying unknowns, there may be one factor that distinguishes the potential hero from a victim in the time of leaving the known world: there is a "voice" which assures the hero that the journey/quest is possible and that the hero has the qualities and resources to pursue to the finish.[35] The voice continues to encourage the hero to take risks, to be fully alive, and to avoid those who would try to stifle the hero's passion and energy. The voice may come in a "blinding flash and other times as the result of a gradual process, that things-as-they-are are not inevitable."[36] Often the voice or call is a common event, a change in circumstances which forces the hero to move beyond the familiar, the known, the safe world.

Campbell suggests that some heroes choose to take the journey and others are heroes who do not choose to take the journey but are thrown into adventures. These individuals are also heroes because they are always ready for the journey.[37]

The Exit

There is an intentional leaving, a separation from what is known and familiar, to what is unknown and perhaps terrifying. To exit means to change, to risk, to journey, to leave people and the present world as the hero knows it and move into the "exit." This is a conscious act, a liberating moment, which may be prompted by a series of events or people which the hero may have welcomed or may have feared. The exit involves a psychological as well as a physical separation, a departure from the conventional. "All heroes depart alone."[38] However, there may be a sense of liberation for those who are left.

The Journey/Quest

For some, there are several paths, but only one at a time. Others tell of no pathways but "thickets, ditches, ponds, labyrinths, morasses, but no paths."[39] The journey or quest may be circuitous, self-doubt may follow

---

35. Pearson and Pope, *The Female Hero in American and British Literature,* p. 84.

36. Ibid., p. 79, 85.

37. Campbell, *The Power of Myth,* p. 129.

38. Pearson and Pope. *The Female Hero in American and British Literature,* pp. 79-80, 132.

39. Margaret Atwood's *Lady Oracle* (New York: Simon and Schuster, 1976) p. 345 in ibid., p. 78.

each positive action, there may be constant searching, a losing of the way, a discovering of unexpected truths about self and the world. The journey may be more adequately described by circular or spiral metaphors than as a linear path. It may be that the hero is unable to understand completely all the ramifications of the single experiences.

The Underworld and Dragons

This is the new, the unknown, the descent into the encounters with life-denying forces, or the "dragons" within. The dragons may be internal or external; they are "the forces of fragmentation, self-loathing, fears, and paralysis."[40] To exist in the underworld is to be willing to experience the new and fearful unknowns with the hope of finding the treasure, the new community . . . to become alive.

The Treasure/The New Community

There is uncertainty when or where the hero may find the treasure, the better way. The departure into the underworld marks a release of the old and a search for the new. Seldom does the hero proceed directly to the treasure.[41] A new way of viewing, a different perspective, a life-changing experience may be a part of the treasure, the new community. The treasure may be "the adventure of the hero—the adventure of being alive.[42]

Summary

Small membership churches have laity and clergy heroes, persons who are viewing "what is" and are asking "what could be?" These leaders are preparing to exit known worlds and to journey into new territory, sometimes terrifying and dragon filled. There are clashes with the larger than life dragons, times in the swamps and marshes. Yet, no one knows for certain what keeps the hero on the journey other than the voice, the call, the sense of something beyond what is. There is an aloneness in religious education that few leaders are prepared for . . . a sense of isolation from the familiar.

Treasures are not something to be held in one's hand; they are environments to be shared, new realities about living together and being alive in the richest dimension. To find the treasure is to experience anew the deepest presence of service to God . . . it is to risk . . . It is to know there is no

---

40. Ibid., p. 63.
41. Ibid., p. 77.
42. Campbell, *The Power of Myth,* p. 163.

guarantee that the treasure will exist . . . It is to enter the unknown for the sake of the community that might be.

The Romantic worldview is one perspective that might be useful to religious educators in examining ministry in the small membership church. It provides a perspective, a vantage point from which to understand the journey, the experience of ministry in the small membership church. Religious education is shaped and formed by our worldview.

Congregational culture unlocks the internal dynamics of congregational life, and worldview suggests that each congregation sees the world in a particular way. The stories we tell, the jokes that make us laugh are ways we share worldview.

So, if each religious educator enters ministry knowing that each congregation has a culture and worldview, how do we talk about and reconcile existing disparities? Acknowledging the distinctiveness of each seems to be a first step. Knowing why some conflicts are likely to emerge, knowing as well that many conflicts are based on diverse perspectives alleviates some apprehension that "this place of ministry is radically different." Perhaps congregational culture and worldview can come clear in the living out of religious education.

IV. PRIMARY GROUPS AND PRIMARY CHARACTERS

The small membership church is about people, people who are a part of a group. These people have uniqueness. This uniqueness is basic to understanding how people become a group. The dynamics include understanding basic characteristics of a primary group.

Primary Groups

Five basic characteristics of a primary group include: 1) intimacy, 2) security of people who can be trusted, even with silence, 3) territorial identity, 4) carrying the culture of a particular ethnic, racial, or national group, and 5) the emerging of primary "characters" held together by blood ties, tradition, and turf. There are two other critical uniquenesses about the primary group. First, the small member church may be a single-cell organization in which every member expects to be known and to know other members. Second, the small member church is a culture-carrying congregation which brings its identity from the past.[43]

---

43. Carl Dudley, "Unique Dynamics of the Small Church" (Washington, D.C.: The Alban Institute, 1984), pp. 5-6. Dudley's source for the characteristics is the

Primary Characters

The specific characteristic of encouraging persons within the group to emerge as "characters" has particular importance in understanding religious education. The small membership church is not only an intense primary group, but pulpits and pews are full of "characters."

The basics of primary group living and the characteristics help to explain why "characters" are so important to religious education in the small membership church. Chart 4 helps to identify who the characters are, clergy and laity, and why they are so critical in religious education.

Characters are larger than life. They are the persons who when you describe them seem almost too exaggerated to believe; but that is the critical element in understanding their role and function within the primary group of the small membership church.

Matriarch/Patriarch

For example, almost all churches have at least one matriarch and/or patriarch. One particular writing called this character "the church boss," suggesting that the pastor needed to give special study to this individual. "It often takes some time for the pastor to actually discover him. But he is usually there somewhere. . . . The preacher must know how and why he works so successfully that the people obey his beck and call." The author suggested that the pastor's own tenure of office depended upon the church boss.[44]

The matriarch or patriarch may literally sit in the center of the sanctuary, or she or he may not attend worship. One student told of a powerful matriarch who moved away. The pastor was elated. A week prior to a critical meeting of the trustees the matriarch wrote a letter advising the trustees how to vote on a critical decision. Physical presence is not absolutely essential to preserving the role and function of a matriarch or patriarch. Other characteristics of the matriarch or patriarch character include: may have passed their prime on age, money, and friends, have lived through

---

work of Charles Horton Cooley, *Social Organization* (New York: Scribner's, 1907), p. 23. The original work of Cooley cites that primary groups include: "those characterized by face-to-face associations and cooperation, they are fundamental in forming the social nature and ideals of the individual, 'we' is the natural expression, and it is not supposed that the unity of the primary group is one of mere harmony and love," p. 23.

44. Charles Otis Bemies, *The Church in the Country Town* (Philadelphia: American Baptist Publication Society, 1912), p. 31.

the history of the church, remember when things were different and "how we got to where we are," are not "irrelevant antiquarian," are informal elders who accept new members and share church history with those whom they want to adopt.[45]

Gatekeeper

The gatekeeper is another central character in most small membership churches. Actually, they, as well as the matriarch and patriarch, are critical in welcoming and adopting new members. The characteristics of the gate-keeper include: linger around the edge of church meetings and congregational worship, are often older men, usually do not have positions of formal leadership, enjoy greeting everyone (especially visitors), like to know everything and everyone, avoid the center of events, "go outside during the sermon, just to talk," and like to interpret the church to new visitors.[46]

Candy Person

One favorite character is the candy man or woman. Sometimes they pass out cookies or gum. Whatever they give, the unmistakable message is warmth, love, and caring for individuals. They represent for a congregation an understanding of hospitality. They are known by the children in the congregation. There is a naturalness in their giving and a delightful playfulness in their presence.

Summary

Religious educators are a part of the pageantry of characters who parade into the small membership church. Dudley suggests that small membership churches have an ingenious way of making the pastors into characters. How? By telling one another the stories of the times the pastor "goofed." When Dudley once said the wrong name at a funeral and buried the person's broth-er, everyone knew by morning.[47] When religious educators, clergy, and laity are at ease with themselves, are able to laugh at their outrageous mistakes, are willing to enjoy the humor in situations, are able to laugh at themselves, there emerges the character, the larger than life, the caricature, the imperfect human willing to risk being known. Living in the small membership church

---

45. Carl S. Dudley, *Making the Small Church Effective,* 1986, pp. 56-57. Lectures by Carl S. Dudley delivered at Pittsburgh Theological Seminary in the fall of 1986.

46. Ibid., p. 11.

47. Carl S. Dudley, "The Art of Pastoring a Small Congregation," in *New Possibilities for Small Churches,* ed. Douglas Alan Walrath (New York: Pilgrim Press, 1983), pp. 46-58.

is about being comfortable, becoming a character among characters.

The intent in providing Chart 4 is that we should see ourselves as religious educators in caricature fashion. These are not necessarily "good" or "bad" . . . they just exist. Many of these characters are the religious leaders in our churches. They may or may not be elected to official office; but they are teaching about acceptance, decision making, and hospitality and humor in learning in general and specifically in small congregations. They are the real leaders, officers, small membership church persons, appointed to live out the future in the shadow of the past."

"There is always an enormous temptation in all of life to diddle around making itsy-bitsy friends and meals and journeys for itsy-bitsy years on end. It is so self-conscious, so apparently moral, simply to step aside from the gaps where the creeks and winds pour down saying, I never merited this grace, quite rightly, and then to sulk along the rest of your days on the edge of rage.

V. CONCLUSION

Religious education in the small membership church begins by defining how eight authors view the challenge of teaching and learning in general and specifically in small congregations. The six size profiles delve into the numerical examination of how size affects religious education and leaders, clergy and lay, in critical areas such as decision making and organizational structure. The congregational culture, worldview section engages the learner in checking perspectives. Understanding the importance of hearing narrative discourse and knowing that persons reveal their worldviews through their discourse give new ways of hearing parish stories. The primary group and characters section reminds religious educators that first we are about people and their learning/teaching exchanges and that there are constraints on our approach based on the dynamics of primary groups. The characters are not foreign personalities, but we are they; at times we are the dragons for others and at times they for us. Religious education in the small membership church is not simple, and the religious educators, clergy and lay, are not facing easy ministries. These are complex arenas which challenge the brightest to stretch and learn, to engage in the journey that will call, sometimes, into the unknown. "We are making hay when we should be making whoopee; we are raising tomatoes when we should be raising Cain, or Lazarus."[48]

SOURCES FOR CHART 4

Charles O. Bemies, *The Small Church in the Country Town* (Philadelphia: American Baptist Publication Society, 1912); John A. Mac-

Dougall, "Small Churches Do Have a Future," Circuit Rider, April 1987, p. 16; Rockwell C. Smith, *Rural Ministry and the Changing Community* (Nashville: Abingdon, 1971); "Ministry Resources for Congregations With Small Membership" (Minneapolis: Augsburg, 1986); Sharon L. Schwab, pastor of Buffalo Charge, United Methodist Church, Western Pennsylvania Conference; "That Class," Pittsburgh Theological Seminary Ed. 29 course of students who experienced the first educational ministry in the small membership church course. Their ideas and suggestions are a part of this chart; Marshall Shelley, *Well-Intentioned Dragons—Ministering to Problem People in the Church* (Texas: Word, Volume 1, The Leadership Library, 1985); Kevin Rippin, Editor of The United Methodist Reporter, Western Pennsylvania Conference; John F. Cowan, *Big Jobs for Little Churches* (New York: Revell, 1917).

CHART 4

Characters in the Small Membership Church

A primary group has five basic characteristics, one of which is its characters holding the group together by blood ties, tradition, and turf. Some of those wonderful characters emerge in the small membership church as clergy/laity.

PRIMARY CHARACTERS

1. { MATRIARCH or
2. PATRIARCH }
("Church Boss")

• sits or is at the center of the church, sanctuary, congregation
• is gruff on the outside, caring person on the inside
• has lived through the history of the church
• the pastor's tenure of office depends on whether this character has been won over

3. GATEKEEPER

• watches the doors
• often older male, usually does not have positions of formal leadership
• enjoys greeting everyone, especially enjoys interpreting the church to visitors
• goes outside during the sermons, "just to talk"
• lingers around the edge of church meetings and congregational worship

DECISION MAKERS

4. INNOVATOR

• can be the pastor or an outsider
• if not the pastor, he/she is helpless unless able to ally support for change
• often the first to recognize a problem and a remedy

5.	LEGITIMIZER	• puts stamp of approval on decisions may give approval by verbal or nonverbal
6.	DIFFUSERS	• carries a discussion wherever they go • senses reaction of others and responds

---

THE MOST IMPORTANT
STONES ARE RELATION-
SHIPS

7.	TOUCHSTONE	• the relationship of the congregation
8.	CORNERSTONE	• often the same leaders are in the church and the community • based on the congregation's perception of a person's personal power
9.	BLARNEY STONE	• communicator of the congregation • tells the pastor what the people cannot tell • sometimes the pastor tells the congregation via this character • rarely fully aware of the message he/she carries
10.	LODESTONE	• points direction • the pastor points beyond the congregation to a vision
11.	PEBBLE	• newcomers • support the stepping stones • the young person, newcomers, or the elderly

---

OTHERS WE KNOW
AND LOVE

12.	SLEEPER	• enjoys worship with eyes closed • is usually able to avoid snoring, dropping a hymnal, or talking out loud during their Sunday church sleep
13.	AGINER	• maybe one of the hardest workers • usually "agin" almost everything • bickers a lot
14.	NEW IDEA	• duty is to bring up new ideas • if the idea isn't accepted, always has another
15.	BORDER GUARD	• familiar with all the families in the congregation • knows who is or is not a part of the congregational community • often the real or honorary "aunt" or "uncle" to everyone in the congregation • carefully watches newcomers • may steer the pastor and newcomers away from family feuds
16.	STORYTELLER	• living historian

17. FIRST SERGEANT • "I'm not in charge, but I represent the one who is."

18. EARLY BIRD • arrives early, straightens up the church, folds the bulletins

19. BELL RINGER • makes sure the bell is rung to start church and gets everyone into and out of class on time

20. PEACEMAKER • works to maintain or to restore harmony between people and/or groups

21. SPARK PLUG • a self-starter
• sees what needs to be done and does it

22. HUGGER • frequently found giving and receiving "hugs"
• the friendliest sort of person; not necessarily outgoing

CHILDREN

23. CHURCH ANGEL • this child is the church's "model child"
• usually able to sit in pews for long periods of time
• the church wants this child to be a minister, rabbi, or priest

24. HOLY TERROR • a child who is everywhere at once and who frequently may be seen running down church halls bumping into patriarchs and matriarchs
• this child often grows up and becomes a minister, rabbi, or priest

THE WELL INTENTIONED

25. BIRD DOG • two legged. . .
points to where the pastor should direct her/his attentions ("so and so is having a problem")

26. THE SUPER SPIRITUAL BIRD DOG • "this purebred strain is more likely to point out things that always leave the pastor feeling defensive and not quite spiritual." "The Lord has laid on my heart that we need to be. . ." "These people like to give the impression they have more spiritual perception than anyone else."

27. WET BLANKET • "it's no use trying. . ."
• has a contagious, negative disposition
• spreads gloom, erases excitement, and bogs down the ministry
• motto: "Nothing ventured, nothing lost."
• they may informally oversee building maintenanc

28. ENTREPRENEUR
- the opposite of the wet blanket
- enthusiastic
- first to greet visitors and first to invite them to his/her home
- equally enthusiastic to sell anything—vitamins, insurance, bee pollen car wax
- people sometimes feel victimized by the entrepreneur

29. CAPTAIN BLUSTER
- graduate from the union steward school of diplomacy
- "speaks with an exclamation point instead of a period"
- everyone else is always wrong
- a steamroller who flattens anyone in his/her way
- does not compromise; does not negotiate
- enjoys fireworks

30. FICKLE FINANCIER
- "uses money to register approval or disapproval of church decisions"
- sometimes withholds offering
- manipulates people and programs with money
- may call the church office or parsonage to see if you are there (wants the pastor to keep regular office hours)

31. BUSYBODY
- "enjoys telling others how to do their jobs"

32. SNIPER
- avoids face-to-face conflict
- "picks off pastors with pot shots in private conversation, such as the cryptic Be sure and pray for our pastor. He has some problems, you know"

33. BOOKKEEPER
- "keeps written record of everything the pastor does that isn't in the spirit of Christ"

34. MERCHANT OF MUCK
- "breeds dissatisfaction by attracting others who know he's more than willing to listen to, and elaborate on, things that are wrong in the church"

35. LEGALIST
- "their list of absolutes stretches from the kind of car a pastor can drive to the number of verses in a hymn that must be sung"

MY FAVORITE

36. CANDY, COOKIE, OR GUM PERSON
- male or female - usually known by the children
- understands the ministry of hospitality
- keeps pockets full of "goodies" for children (of all ages)

37. "WARM SHEPHERD"
- an adult surrounded in the pew, by numerous children, not necessarily his/her own. Children often hug, tease, and in general "attach" themselves to this warm shepherd

38. VIOLET LADY
- gentle flower lovers who gather fresh bouquets and place them on the altar for worship
- "makes a specialty of growing white and purple violets for church decoration, and not a Sunday, rain or shine, but her offering is there"

Chapter Two

The Small Membership Church:
Recent Trends in Research and Program

RONALD H. CRAM

INTRODUCTION

The small membership church is dead.

Not long ago, such a statement would have been taken for granted by
most denominational agencies and theological institutions. The small
membership church represented narrow provincialism, lack of prestige,
and social failure. In the United States, popular conceptions of success and
progress tended to dismiss anything that was small. Big was somehow better than small, and that included the small membership church. The small
membership church was a problem to be solved. The solution normally
consisted of physical plant expansion, numerical "church growth," and
economic success. Often viewed as a sign of professional failure, the small
membership church might be considered by a pastor as the place to wait
until something better came along, but it was rarely conceived of as a place
of first choice for long-term pastoral service.[1]

---

1. For a pleasurable and often lighthearted historical overview of these trends,
listen to the cassette tape by Robert W. Lynn, "The Small Church in the American
Past" (Hartford: Hartford Seminary Foundation, 1976). Available at Union Theological Seminary in Virginia.

There is no doubt that for many today the small membership church is an irrelevant topic for research and program. For these, it *is* dead—or at least should be put out of its misery. But an increasing number of church-related persons and agencies are now pointing to the small membership church as an asset, not a deficit. Recent denominational research does not dismiss the challenges that face the small membership church. Neither does it gloomily predict the complete demise of the small membership church. Rather, current denominational research into the small membership church is generally optimistic regarding its future as a viable context for the embodiment of the people of God.

Beginning with an overview of basic problems surrounding current discussion of the small membership church, this chapter then seeks to acquaint the reader with selected research, program, and persons that represent dominant current trends in this important area of evolving perspectives. This review is intended to be representative, not exhaustive. This chapter concludes that the small membership church, with all of its significant challenges, may be viewed as a viable alternative to larger membership churches. It will be suggested that as culture, a basic and crucial concept for small membership church research, is taken more seriously dominant theological and educational assumptions that guide current and future planning will begin to change in ways that are positive for the entire church.

OVERVIEW OF PROBLEMS

Why do congregations in small communities have difficulty securing and sustaining able leadership? In a recent Episcopalian study by the Standing Commission on the Church in Small Communities, in Cooperation with the Alban Institute and the Order of Ascension, *Clergy Leadership in Small Communities: Options and Issues*, ten frequent answers given to this question by selected church leaders included:

1. Clergy in small communities tend to become demoralized.
2. Small churches and those in small communities are regarded as lower salary jobs.
3. Part-time and minimum salary cures are hard to fill.
4. Part-time and minimum salary cures put financial strain on the clergy family in the present and lead to inadequate pensions in the future.
5. Dioceses often fill these cures with inexperienced or troubled clergy.

6. Most clergy are unprepared for the scale and dynamics of ministry in small communities.
7. Clergy and their families increasingly expect a "professional's" lifestyle.
8. Seminaries tend to reinforce expectations (economic, liturgical, social) which cannot be met in the small community.
9. New ordinands are usually placed in larger, more affluent parishes.
10. Slow movement in the application of certain alternatives.[2]

Viewed as a whole, these ten problems are illustrative of three dominant and persistent structural issues that surface in virtually all denominational studies about the role of leadership in the small membership church: economics, status, and seminary education.

Economics. The interdependence of economic capitalism and small membership churches in the United States is painfully clear. For many Protestant seminary students, the cost of a two-year (normally the M.A. in religious education) or three-year (normally the M.Div. in theological studies) program of academic study *requires* a postgraduation income that is sufficient to meet daily living expenses, plus the repayment of academic debt.[3] Part-time employment positions (that more often than not require full-time attention) or employment positions that offer only a minimum salary typically are not viewed as adequate by the graduate. Within the marketplace of supply and demand, clergy and educator competition for those churches that are able to pay higher wages almost always leads able church professionals to large membership churches. Vocational clarity is often difficult to maintain in light of lower pension benefits that may result from lower wages and basic family expenses, including such things as medical plan deductibles and rising food costs. While the dollar gap between leadership in small membership churches and larger churches may be lamented in many denominations, there is often the sense that the most skilled and competent leaders deserve—and should expect—larger churches, more responsibility, and larger wages. Caught in the sobering reality of economic forces, the small membership congregation often is understood to be a nice place to start professional ministry but in the last analysis only a temporary stepping stone on the road to true ministerial success.

---

2. The Reverend Alice B. Mann OA, *Clergy Leadership in Small Communities: Options and Issues* (Philadelphia: Ascension Press, 1985), pp. 12-17.
3. In the Presbyterian Church (U.S.A.), for example, the accumulated debt for graduate theological education typically amounts from $20,000 to $30,000.

When defined in concert with socio-economic forces, success may lose its focus on faithfulness and vocation. Progress in this context acquires the meaning of "making it to the top." Needless to say, the "bottom" refers to those settings—rural, urban, and suburban—that are socially, economically, and politically marginal. While this rather simplistic economic portrait may not be an entirely accurate sketch for all professional ministers, it is representative often enough to make it rather uncomfortable for those who perpetuate such institutional inequality.

This matter is especially troubling to those laypersons who believe they are called to the ministry of religious education in the local congregation. Almost all graduates from two-year M.A. programs in religious education who desire to serve as lay directors of religious education will almost certainly go directly to a larger congregation. The small membership church rarely is able, unless extremely well-endowed financially, to support both a pastor and a religious educator at the same time.

What, then, is the meaning of Christian ministry? It is very possible that answers to this important question have yielded to economic signs and metaphors that corrupt an understanding of calling and vocation in such a way as to preclude the small membership church from the list of possible areas of service. Even the remote possibility that bigger is better in relation to the church, moreover, calls for a renewed and careful consideration of ecclesiology. A calloused materialistic response alone to basic theological issues that impinge directly on the small membership church will only perpetuate acts of institutional discrimination that will benefit some to the detriment of others.[4]

Status. Warren Hartman has indicated in a popular United Methodist study that seven out of ten small membership churches were *not* involved in leadership responsibilities in their districts; nine out of ten were *not* involved in leadership responsibilities in their annual conferences.[5] Similar parallels have been noted in the Episcopal Church.[6] Power and size appear to be related in these cases.

In addition, racial and ethnic factors often are associated negatively within the context of the small membership church. Both Episcopalian[7]

---

4. This section has been influenced significantly by anthropologist John A. Hostetler's article, "Toward Responsible Growth and Stewardship of Lancaster County's Landscape," *Pennsylvania Mennonite Heritage,* July 1989.

5. Warren J. Hartman, "What Makes Small Churches Grow?" *Circuit Rider,* January 1981.

6. Mann, *Clergy Leadership,* p. 13.

7. Ibid., p. 9.

and Presbyterian Church (U.S.A.)[8] research indicate that almost all their racial and ethnic churches are small membership churches. The lack of pastoral supply in these churches, moreover, is often acute.

Seminary Education. In a random selection of course catalogues from twelve well-known theological seminaries in the United States, this writer found only one course offering directly related to the topic of small membership churches. This cursory overview confirms the contentions of those who have engaged in lengthy research into this matter. At first glance, it might appear that the small membership church was being deliberately ignored in favor of some preconceived bias toward the larger membership church. In fact, the issue is far more complex than that. Barbara Wheeler, President of Auburn Theological Seminary, has suggested that theological schools in general have not paid attention to the congregation in the formation of the curriculum of study required of its students. Wheeler asks a simple and profoundly important question of theological schools, "What might be the effects if the congregation were to be more central the focus of theological education?"[9]

The sad but true fact is that most theological institutions do *not* factor the congregation into curricular considerations in consistently integral ways. In Wheeler's terms, "It is possible to conceive a curriculum that takes the welfare of local communities of believers as its final goal."[10] By neglecting the local congregation as a paradigm for theological education, theological institutions implicitly reject the possibility that the stories of the congregation have curricular importance. This position, planned or unconscious, devalues all congregational life, including the small membership congregation. In this sense, most theological institutions are unable to be more responsive to small membership churches (or churches of *any* size) because of inadequate curricular constructs resulting from a critical interplay between the "academy" and the local congregation.[11]

---

8. Partners in Small Church Strategy, "Report and Recommendations to the 201st General Assembly," February 1989, p. 16.

9. Barbara G. Wheeler, "Talk or Fish: The Congregation's Role in Theological Education," *The Auburn News,* Fall 1988, p. 2.

10. Ibid., p. 7.

11. There are significant exceptions. The University of Dubuque Theological Seminary has a splendid program for those preparing to serve in small membership churches, especially in rural areas; Bangor Theological Seminary has consistently focused on the small membership church through the years; Candler School of Theology's Rollins Center for Church Ministries; and Union Theological Seminary's (Virginia) focus on congregational analysis within the doctoral program in Practical Theology are worthy of mention. They are, however, *exceptions* in theological education as a whole.

OVERVIEW OF CURRENT PROSPECTS

A Cultural Perspective

With these real and significant structural problems surrounding any truthful discussion of the small membership church, why not dismiss it as an irrelevant albatross? The fundamental answer is that small membership churches, as all churches, are living communities with distinct cultures.

What is culture, and why is it important for the conversation about the small membership church? Ann Swidler proposes that culture may be defined "as the publicly available symbolic forms through which people experience and express meaning."[12] She continues by suggesting that some symbolic vehicles of meaning include "beliefs, ritual practices, art forms, and ceremonies, as well as informal cultural practices such as language, gossip, stories, and rituals of daily life."[13]

Community is the cradle of culture. Patterns of culture represent the community's responses to "life together." Because the history of each community is different, so also are the responses to life different. Each community, then, possesses its own culture. Each has its unique patterns of behavior and outlook.

Community is a complex term to define. Anthropologist Ulf Hannerz suggests that a community "has a territory and fairly clearly defined population," "economic and political self-sufficiency," and its own consciousness about who belongs in the community and who does not.[14] Even when external political and economic systems invade the community, which is more often than not the story of community in the United States, there continue to be spheres peopled only by the community (perhaps "partial-community" is a more adequate term here)—"family life, leisure life, and just plain neighborship."[15]

Culture holds on tenaciously even when community is invaded or threatened. Culture is situational because community is context-specific. When there are no longer social processes in place for "the learning and maintenance of modes of behavior within the community,"[16] culture evaporates, community disappears, and the story (what James Hopewell has

---

12. Ann Swidler, "Culture in Action: Symbols and Strategies," *American Sociological Review,* April 1986, p. 273.

13. Ibid.

14. Ulf Hannerz, *Soulside: Inquiries into Ghetto Culture and Community* (New York: Columbia University Press, 1970), p. 12.

15. Ibid.

16. Ibid., p. 185.

called "narrative"[17]) embodied by the community's culture is lost.[18] Culture, then, may be viewed as the necessary starting point of all congregational analysis.

The interplay between theology and culture as it relates to the small membership congregation is worthy of examination at this point. Robert Schreiter in his seminal book *Constructing Local Theologies* writes:

> The experience of those in the small Christian communities who have seen the insight and the power arising from the reflections of the people upon their experience and the scriptures has prompted making the community itself the prime author of theology in local contexts. The Holy Spirit, working in and through the believing community, gives shape and expression to Christian experience. Some of these communities have taught us to read the scriptures in a fresh way and have called the larger church back to a fidelity to the prophetic word of God.[19]

When viewed in this way, the small membership church may not be presumed to be a nuisance to be eradicated. It may, in fact, hold within its life of Christian memory and intimacy keys for opening the doors of church renewal. The small membership church may well be a center of God's prophetic word; indeed, a sacred space of incarnation. Schreiter continues:

> The gospel is always incarnate, incarnate in the reality of those who bring it to us, and incarnate in those who help us nurture the beginnings of faith. Church is a complex of those cultural patterns in which the

---

17. James F. Hopewell, *Congregation: Stories and Structures* (Philadelphia: Fortress Press, 1987), especially pp. 193 ff.

18. This approach to culture is somewhat different than that proposed by Carl Dudley and Douglas Alan Walrath in their very popular book, *Developing Your Small Church's Potential* (Valley Forge, Pa.: Judson Press, 1988), pp. 10, 51. The understanding of culture promoted by Dudley and Walrath would see culture as the whole way of life of a group of people. As used in this chapter, culture points to specific symbolic vehicles of meaning. The distinction is important for further research in this area, since the former understanding of culture was pre-Geertz, while the latter is post-Geertz. See Clifford Geertz, "Religion as a Cultural System," in *Anthropological Approaches to the Study of Religion,* ed. Michael Banton (Edinburgh: Tavistock, 1966), pp. 1-46.

19. Robert S. Shreiter, *Constructing Local Theologies* (Maryknoll, N.Y.: Orbis, 1985), p. 16.

gospel has taken on flesh, at once enmeshed in the local situation, extending through communities in our own time and in the past, and reaching out to the eschatological realization of the fullness of God's reign.[20]

The culture of the small membership church may be a place in which the gospel is incarnated. That incarnation occurs in concrete situations where God's word may be heard afresh.[21] While such theological and cultural perspectives may not be common among all who are concerned with the small membership church, the renewed interest in it almost always has basic concern with analysis (often formal, but just as often intuitive) of the congregation within its social context. The following data reflect this developing interest and concern.

Centers of Education

Long known for its innovative curriculum designed for career changers who desired to focus on the ministry, Bangor Theological Seminary, located in Bangor, Maine, may well become one of the leading centers in the United States for small membership church research and ministerial preparation. Douglas Walrath is Director of the Small Church Leadership Program at Bangor. Closely related to the United Church of Christ, and approved by the United Methodist Church, Bangor's program focuses on pastoral preparation in the small membership church, lay leadership development, and research. A year-long residency requirement for seminary students in a small membership church, and a careful structuring of the pastoral studies and field education programs help prepare students for effective ministry in rural, urban, and suburban settings. In many ways still in its experimentation stage, the program began with a planning grant from Lilly Endowment, Inc. Later, the Pew Charitable Trust awarded Bangor a grant of $211,000 to implement the program. What is especially striking about this emphasis at Bangor Seminary is the institutional affirmation of

---

20. Ibid., p. 21.

21. This writer in no way is attempting to conclude that just because a church has a small membership that it is a sacred place of incarnation. In the words of Jürgen Moltmann, "Christian life is a form of practice which consists in following the crucified Christ, and it changes both man himself and the circumstances in which he lives" (*The Crucified God* [San Francisco: Harper & Row, 1974], p. 25). A presumed discipline and faithfulness is presumed in *any* congregational setting in order for this framework to have any theological validity.

the "marginal," including the small membership church, as the organizing center around which seminarians will be educated.

The Rural Ministry Program of the University of Dubuque Theological Seminary and Wartburg Theological Seminary opened its doors in September 1987. Lutherans, Presbyterians, and United Methodists (who comprise about 30 percent of the whole) may take advantage of this program in order to serve in small membership rural churches upon graduation. A rural semester for seminarians from all over the country is offered yearly. In addition, the Rural Ministry Program has a cooperative relationship with the Rural Outreach program at Mercy Health Center of Dubuque that helps train and place nurses in rural congregations.

Another innovative approach is a continuing education curriculum for rural ministry. Rural Social Science by Extension (R.S.S.E.) curricular options are a joint venture of the Texas Agriculture Extension Service and faculty from the Department of Rural Sociology at the Texas A & M University System, with design input from representatives of the Texas Conference of Churches, the Baptist General Convention of Texas, and Resource Center of Small Churches. At the time of this writing (1989), Presbyterian, United Church of Christ, Lutheran, Roman Catholic, Christian (Disciples of Christ), and United Methodist representatives are part of the design team. Rural Social Science by Extension correctly assumes that many pastors serving in rural and small town ministries are not prepared academically or socially for such contexts in most theological seminaries. This perceived lack of adequate seminary preparation has resulted in a combination of home study and small group learning meetings (no less than six and no more than ten members) that result in a predetermined number of continuing education units, awarded upon completion of the work by Texas A & M University.

The curriculum is worth reviewing as a whole, since the required topic areas represent one of the most thoughtful educational approaches to date. Other theological institutions would do well to review this curriculum in light of their current offerings. The seven units in the core curriculum include:
1. Orientation
2. Basics of Rural Sciences
3. The Rural Scene
4. Culture and Values
5. Economic Base
6. Dynamics of Leadership and Power
7. Effecting Change

Once a group of learners has finished the core curriculum, the group may choose one or more of the following electives:

1. Conflict Management/Understanding Criticism
2. Dynamics of Church Growth—Social Science Perspective
3. Rural Family Structures
4. Characteristics of the Rural Church
5. Pastoral Role in a Rural Church
6. Delivery System for Community Services in a Rural Setting.
7. The Pastor as Change Agent
8. The Future for Rural America—Trends, Predictions
9. The Church and Community Planning
10. Community Analysis
11. Life of Clergy Families in Rural Parishes
12. Population Analysis
13. Special Groups—Poor, Ethnic, Aged, Immigrants, Service Persons, etc.
14. Allies in Rural Communities—Support Systems
15. Rural Justice
16. Leadership
17. Dynamics of Small Churches
18. Technology and Rural Ministry
19. Rural Schools/Education
20. Health Care Delivery
21. Communication Systems
22. Mapping Needs of Evangelism/Congregationalizing
23. Responding to the Rural Crisis
24. Churches in Dying Communities
25. Pastoral Care and Nonresident Pastors

By reviewing the curriculum, one is able to discern not only the many areas of expertise that are required by the rural pastor but also the state of the rural community and rural church in the United States as well. Each of the curricular areas may be thought of as desired outcomes that are meeting perceived needs of those who lead in the rural context.

One of the most attractive aspects of this program is that continuing education is viewed as an integral part of the pastor's ongoing professional education. The concept of "lifelong learning," rarely acted out in theological settings for the professional, is given form and coherence in this comprehensive and innovative program. Still in its infancy, the program's evolution will be well worth watching. The curriculum was tested with fifteen pilot groups in 1988, with ongoing refinements anticipated. This unique approach to theological education by extension is worthy of emulation in traditional theological settings.

These three recent institutional models all have one thing in common. The focus of ministerial preparation on cultural context shapes curricular options in order to help leaders develop more effective skills. The institutionalization of such a viewpoint strengthens the socially perceived importance of the small membership church.

Denominational Responses

Rather than dwelling on what denominational central office agencies are *not* doing in regard to the small membership church (an extremely tempting option in light of limited programs and literature available), let it simply be noted that it is extremely difficult to discern any consistent patterns of response that are readily visible across denominational lines. Systematic, eclectic, formal, and informal approaches appear to coexist even within denominational centers themselves. This is a time of experimentation and innovation; therefore, such diversity is often a sign of institutional health.

An example of an informal approach to the study of the small membership church may be found in the Diocese of Richmond (Virginia). In this diocese, some 60 percent of its one hundred thirty-five parishes have one hundred households or less.[22] Walter F. Sullivan, Bishop of Richmond, has taken time to visit and to learn about each of the one hundred thirty-five parishes in the diocese. This direct observation by an important church leader of small membership churches is a simple yet innovative and needed model for all denominations.

A more complex model has arisen within the Presbyterian Church (U.S.A.). In what may become a historically significant attempt to gain financial and programatic support on the denominational level for the small membership church (at this hour, there are few Protestant bodies that are willing to overtly and publicly affirm the importance of the small membership church as a central "plank" of its stated mission), the 199th General Assembly (1987) approved the response to a referral from the 198th General Assembly (1986) that focused on the need to engage in research and

22. Within the Diocese of Richmond a small membership parish is considered to be one hundred *households* or less. In many Protestant churches in the same area a small membership church is considered to be two hundred *members* or less. The distinction between households and members is an important one as Protestants and Catholics talk together about the "small membership church" in the area.

program regarding the small membership churches in rural, suburban, and urban areas. At the 198th General Assembly, Carl Dudley of McCormick Seminary in Chicago made the following comments that will probably be referred to as foundational for all future small membership church research:

> Some two-thirds of Presbyterian churches are small. They tend to be churches that are overlooked. I think the church is ready for some kind of genuine response to the small church concerns reflected here. . . . I want to suggest specifically that if this committee is to be helpful, from my experience, it would urge the Assembly to create a network of existing networks of small congregations throughout the country . . . and urge the networks of people who are already concerned on a national and ecumenical basis, so that those people that are already concerned about small churches can themselves be interrelated to develop a program.[23]

In brief, the Presbyterian Church (U.S.A.) response to small membership church issues may be said to be network-centered, national, and ecumenical. This approach has two basic goals: 1) small membership church network developments, and 2) small membership church advocacy and coordination among the ministry units of the church. A "Partners in Small Church Strategy" meeting was held in 1987 of those Presbyterian Church (U.S.A) groups that could work together on issues of mutual concern. The groups included: New Covenant Presbytery, Small Church Conference; Synod of the Covenant, Association of Town and Rural Congregations; Synod of the South Atlantic, Small Church Network; Philadelphia Presbytery, Small Church Development Project; Pittsburgh Presbytery, Small Church Network; Northwest Area Ministry of Kiskiminetas Presbytery; Appalachian Ministries Educational Resource Center; Racial Ethnic Ministries, Austin Presbyterian Theological Seminary; Rural Ministries Program, Theology and Land Institute, University of Dubuque Theological Seminary; Johnson C. Smith Theological Seminary, Presbyterian Tentmakers.

The Partners in Small Church Strategy has accomplished a great deal in a very short time. They are raising the visibility of small membership church concerns in a systematic way within the church; they are identi-

---

23. Partners in Small Church Strategy, "Report and Recommendations to the 201st General Assembly," February 1989, p. 3.

fying existing denominational and ecumenical networks; they are establishing an inter-unit staff team (which includes representatives from existing Evangelism and Church Development, Education and Congregational Nurture, Racial Ethnic, Vocations, and Theology and Worship units); they are compiling existing presbytery small membership church strategies; they are sponsoring a General Assembly booth; they are establishing good relations with Presbyterian theological institutions; they are developing programatic and bibliographic resources, and they are broadening the vision of the Partners themselves.

The Partners in Small Church Strategy reported to the 201st (1989) General Assembly the following types of "strategies" worth consideration by a presbytery regarding small membership churches. These approaches have useful implications across denominational lines.

1. *Congregational Redevelopment:* Redevelopment involves an intentional reorientation of the ministry of a congregation to reach a new population of persons which is presently not being reached by that congregation. Congregational Redevelopment can be a program of the presbytery or it can be planned in partnership with the Synod and General Assembly as a Mission Program.

2. *Congregational Revitalization:* Revitalization is a planned effort to raise the vitality of ministry of a given congregation. Revitalization can result from several different types of congregational development strategies.

3. *Facilities Development:* The presbytery assists a church in the repair, expansion, or improvement of its facilities as a planned part of a redevelopment or revitalization project.

4. *Yoking:* Two or more congregations covenant to share the same pastoral leadership as a means of increasing resources and of expanding their ability to do ministry.

5. *Cooperative Parish Development:* Several churches covenant to plan and resource certain areas of ministry jointly. A cooperative parish may or may not involve the sharing of clergy leadership. Cooperative parishes can be planned ecumenically.

6. *Area Ministry:* Presbytery, in consultation with participating churches, hires an Area Minister as a presbytery staff person. The Area Minister is appointed as Stated Supply for several congregations in the Area Ministry project to provide pastoral care, supervise the work of lay preachers, and work with sessions in developing the program life of congregations.

7. *Clustering:* Several churches in a natural geographic area plan ecu-

menically or denominationally in order to consolidate and diversify
local programs of ministry and to draw outside resources.

8. *Merged Congregation:* Two or more congregations covenant to merge
   into a single congregation in order to increase resources and the ability
   to minister effectively.

9. *Community Ministry:* Specialized ministry: A congregation or group
   of congregations plans a special community ministry. Such a project
   may qualify under specialized ministries as a Mission Program Grants
   Project.

10. *Ministry of Presence:* A congregation develops a specific plan with
    the presbytery to enable it to maintain a Ministry of Presence in the
    area.

11. *Dissolution of a Congregation:* Having determined that it no longer
    has the resources, will, or capacity to carry out its ministry a congre-
    gation covenants with the presbytery to plan an orderly dissolution of
    the congregation celebrating and committing to God the witness it has
    shared.[24]

These eleven "options" described by the Partners provides the small membership church with an invaluable listing and explanation of possible courses
of action. For the religious educator, pastor, and the lay committee, such a
resource may be used to begin discussion for the future work of the church.

Literature: Religious Education

In the second half of the twentieth century, three popular books in religious education immediately come to mind when considering the importance of the local congregation: Lewis Joseph Sherrill's *The Gift of Power*
(1959), C. Ellis Nelson's *Where Faith Begins* (1967), and Craig Dykstra's
Vision and Character (1981). Interestingly, at one time or another, all three
of these persons had teaching and administrative responsibilities at
Louisville Presbyterian Theological Seminary in Kentucky.

Sherrill's understanding of religious education was theologically
grounded in his understanding of the church. He did not deny the local
church's location within social structures, yet he pointed beyond the social
order alone to "koinonia."[25] Nelson's book focused on the communication
of faith within a "community of believers."[26] He noted the importance of

24. Ibid., pp. 14, 15.
25. *The Gift of Power* (New York: Macmillan, 1959), p. 10.
26. *Where Faith Begins* (Richmond, Va.: Knox 1967), p. 50.

taking culture seriously in the communication process, and sought to
define the relation of the individual to the group, and vice versa. Dykstra,
in the process of giving criticism to Kohlberg's understanding of human
moral development, suggested that Christian education for the moral life
"is the introduction of persons to and the incorporation of persons within
the experience of the repenting, praying, and serving community."[27] While
none of the three persons specifically analyzes the small membership congregation, all three focused on the concrete reality of the church in such
a way that the interplay between theological understandings of the church
and "real life" understandings of the church became expected aspects of
any theory of religious education that sought to focus on the local congregation thereafter. Donald Miller's *Story and Context* (1987) and Maria Harris's *Fashion Me a People* (1989) stand in this heritage.[28]

Yet it is not inappropriate to conclude that while such literature alerted
the field of religious education to the need to take the local congregation
seriously in its theory, the on-site research methods of anthropology and
sociology were not defined in any concrete ways. Said another way, while
the social sciences entered into discussions about the local congregation,
practical guidelines for on-cite congregational analysis that reflected socio-
anthropological practice was not provided. It is not enough to presume that
general discussions of culture and the congregation will help persons carefully study the congregation. The methods of cultural analysis must be provided as well as definitions of culture.

John Westerhoff[29] and Ronald Cram[30] are two examples of those in the
field of religious education who have attempted to sustain methodological
dialogue between sociology, anthropology, education, and theology. In
general, however, it may be concluded that religious educators as a whole
do not possess levels of sophistication in the methods of anthropology and
sociology necessary to engage in congregational analysis of the Barbara
Wheeler or James Hopewell sort. The church, whether small membership

27. Craig Dykstra, *Vision and Character: A Christian Educator's Alternative
to Kohlberg* (New York: Paulist, 1981), p. 121.

28. Donald E. Miller, *Story and Context: An Introduction to Christian Education* (Nashville: Abingdon, 1987); Maria Harris, *Fashion Me a People: Curriculum in the Church* (Louisville, Westminster/Knox, 1989).

29. See John H. Westerhoff III and Gwen K. Neville, *Generation to Generation* (Philadelphia: United Church Press, 1974).

30. Ronald H. Cram, *Cultural Pluralism and Christian Education: Laura
Thompson's Design for Anthropology and Its Use in Christian Education*. Dis-
sertation, Princeton Theological Seminary, 1985.

or not, is all the poorer for this lack. Theological and educational reflection on the congregation is inadequate without sound skills in the methods of research available in anthropology and sociology. Without such skills, critical praxis suffers on the altar of commonsense notions about the local congregation.

The only current resource in religious education available that seeks to look at the congregation with sound skills and methods in the areas of cultural analysis, education, and theology is one written and edited by D. Campbell Wyckoff and Henrietta Wilkinson, *Beautiful Upon the Mountains: A Handbook for Church Education in Appalachia,* published for Joint Educational Development and The Commission on Religion in Appalachia by the Board of Christian Education of the Cumberland Presbyterian Church.[31] The book should be read by *any* person interested in the small membership church.

Before concrete models of teaching and learning are introduced in the book, the reader is invited to take seriously the culture of Appalachia and the culture of the local Appalachian congregation. In the introductory pages, Wyckoff explores the land and the people, the role of religion in Appalachian life, and contextual values. An example from one section of the book will help illustrate this fascinating approach:

Appalachian *culture* is what a people does, says, lives, dies, celebrates. It includes:

• a particular routine;
• the primary functions of sustaining and enhancing life;
• an emphasis on personal relationships while developing individuality;
• a personal life-and-death kind of religion;
• institutions reflecting an individualistic and local focus.

Appalachian *values* are the accepted guidelines within cultures, the attitudes of relative importance that lead to the development of culture.[32]

Imagine engaging in the process of teaching and learning in such a cultural context without taking seriously these contextual elements! Cultural

---

31. (Memphis: Board of Christian Education of the Cumberland Presbyterian Church, 1984).
32. Ibid., p. 29.

analysis has concrete practicality for the religious educator. Wyckoff concludes, based on his analysis of culture in the region, that religious education leaders in the Appalachian context need to:

1. Include reflection on experience.
2. Start with Appalachian values.
3. Respect Appalachian [institutional] structures.
4. Use media in teaching.
5. Center Christian education in the family and in the community.[33]

Such an approach has significant implications for the creation and use of religious education curriculum materials, especially for the small membership church. Because of pragmatic economic considerations, most denominational agencies involved in curriculum production have chosen to produce *national* curriculum resources. They are typically produced by nationally centralized publishing houses. With such an approach to curriculum production and centralized distribution, economic efficiency is often attained at the expense of congregational and/or cultural specificity. The "one size fits all" approach may hope for (and encourage) local tailoring, but this rarely takes place at the congregational level in any systematic or informed manner. Even those curricula that seek to tailor their lessons for small membership situations consistently omit any helps for the teacher in understanding the relation of education and culture *in their own setting*.

Chances are the small membership church, including those small membership churches composed of racial and ethnic persons, would fare far better with an educational resource person who could help in the selection, design, and creation of educational resources appropriate to the specific culture of the congregation. At the moment, however, this approach is not the norm of most denominations. This is a matter that deserves sustained attention by all denominational education units.

Literature: Small Membership Church

In one of the most refreshing and interesting books that centers on understanding the culture of the small membership church, Anthony Pappas concludes that:

1. The small church is a stable, not a dynamic, organization. Its nature is to replicate not rethink its previous patterns of behavior.

---

33. Ibid., pp. 36-37.

2. The typical small church is in a "little world to itself." This world is satisfying and meaningful to those within.

3. The typical small church sees the past not the future. It registers what has been, not what can be.

4. The typical small church functions out of reflex and habit not from goals and strategies, rationally defined.

5. The typical small church lives on the level of relationships and not tasks.

6. The typical small church lives on the experiential not the theoretical level.[34]

Pappas developed his ideas as the result of serving as pastor of the First Baptist Church on Block Island, Rhode Island. His insights, however, appear to transcend Block Island. Seminary graduates and/or denominational decision makers who do not seek first to understand the culture of the small membership church will probably end up hurting the church and themselves even as they attempt to "help." It takes time, time, time, to understand the cultural integrity of the small membership church. In a world of immediate satisfaction and rapid demand, approaching the small membership church *on its time* is a counter-cultural act in itself.

Charles Wilson and Lynne Davenport provide an invaluable case study text that instinctively communicates the relation of the small membership church and cultural context.[35] Their study was sponsored by the Standing Commission on the Church in Small Communities of the General Convention, Episcopal Church, U.S.A. The authors repeatedly illustrate that before an attempt is made to change the small membership church, it is necessary to understand it in terms of its own cultural integrity—an integrity that may very well hold a story that could transform the church.

CONCLUSION

The small membership church must be taken seriously. Despite its significant challenges, it is a viable alternative to larger member churches. To view the small membership church from the perspectives of education, sociology, anthropology, and theology is not merely a passing fad. Rather, it is a way to begin hearing the word of God afresh in all of our churches. The Christian cultural experience of the small membership church is a gift to be treasured.

---

34. Anthony G. Pappas, *Entering the Work of the Small Church: A Guide for Leaders* (Washington, D.C.: The Alban Institute, 1988), pp. 73-74.

35. Charles R. Wilson and Lynne Davenport, *Against All Odds: Ten Stories of Vitality in Small Churches,* (Frenchtown, N.J.: Jethro, 1982).

Chapter Three

Understanding the Sociological Perspective

GARY E. FARLEY

INTRODUCTION

Where in America is St. Paul's Chapel?
- Next to the commissary in a Piedmont mill town.
- Surrounded by skyscrapers in a major metropolis.
- Down Church Street, across from the Baptist and the Disciples churches, a block off the square in a Delta countyseat town.
- On a gravel section-line road surrounded by Iowa cornfields.
- Up Guadalupe Avenue in a barrio in Southern California.
- On Main Street in a dying West Texas ranch and oilfield service town.
- On the corner of the intersection of two busy streets in a city neighborhood experiencing racial and economic transition.
- On the poorer side of the tracks in a Great Lakes industrial town.
- In an isolated black community in farmed-over rural Alabama.
- In a rapidly urbanizing, formerly rural, community on the growing edge of a major city.

Small membership churches all. Varied reasons for this smallness. Different contexts. Varied prospects for the future. Diverse needs. Unequal resources. Contrasting opportunities for ministry. Where in America is your St. Paul's Chapel?[1] It can be in almost any sociocultural, physical, or community setting.

Place

This chapter has two major foci. First to introduce you to some concepts, some resources, and a strategy that will aid in understanding the "place" of your small membership church. By identifying three sets of questions and by discovering answers you learn about the setting for your church. The questions will guide you in learning about the historical development, cultural heritage, and social processes of your community. This chapter is different from others in this volume. It falls into the genre of "applied sociology." It asks you to "do" sociology, to use your sociological imagination, and it gives directions in this process. Consequently, it is not a theoretical or scholarly presentation, but if it is successful it should enhance your practical use of the concepts developed in the other chapters.

Setting or place is a most important category for understanding religious education in the life and work of a congregation. Place impacts what a church is and what it may become. Place provides challenges for ministry, outreach, and evangelism. If a parish makes a mark on the lives of its members, it will likely make a mark on its community also.

The sociologist who studies the small congregation may have a second focus—the internal life of a church. Topics of interest include decision-making patterns, leadership style, organizational structure, relations and social bonds, institutional image, and attitudes. In the latter portion of this chapter, concepts, resources, and processes will be introduced which you might employ to better understand the internal life of your congregation.

---

1. I struggled to identify a generic location, neutral name for a church. Bethel is the most common among Southern Baptists (after First), but it has a rural bias. Saint (whoever) is not used by evangelical denominations very often. Many urban congregations take their name from their location, e.g., Garfield Avenue. Many rural churches choose a hoped-for condition, e.g., Harmony or Unity. So, writing from an evangelical stance, I decided to go with a mainline name, St. Paul. I hope that it will be acceptable to everyone. And I am using chapel rather than church because it is more frequently associated with a small congregation.

The Outside/Place

Where in America is your St. Paul's Chapel? A number of excellent books are available to assist you in the study of your place—either the community or the church.

You will want to access resources that treat specifically the history, culture, or the condition of the place where you serve. A helpful librarian, the community historical society, a city planning and zoning office, or the county manager's office can assist. The basic principle is that effective ministry, evangelism, and outreach are grounded in an understanding of setting. So, if you do not have deep experiential knowledge and understanding of your context, then some homework is called for. Some questions which will guide your study of your place sociologically are in order.

While the questions are applicable to most settings—city neighborhood, new suburb, old town, and rural community—the focus of this chapter will be on old town communities, as will be the illustrations.

If your St. Paul's Chapel is in a city or in an open country congregation, some adaptation may be required. However, if your place has a "sense of place," then most of the questions will be of use to you.[2]

---

2. "Types of American Small Towns and How to Read Them," in *Order and Image in the American Small Town,* ed. Michael Fazio and Robert Crenshaw (Jackson, Miss: University of Mississippi Press, 1981), pp. 105-135. This section of the chapter draws heavily from this essay. The social sciences have a rich tradition in the study of place or community. The discipline of sociology arose out of the concern to address the loss of the closeness and order of small town community in the face of growing individualization and bureaucratization through urbanization. Emil Durkheim, Max Weber, and Karl Marx all focused on this issue. Sociology was conceived as a science that society's leaders could use to design a modern social order in which the good elements of social solidarity found in the village could be transferred to metropolis with its capacity to enhance material life and promote cultural developments because of its greater scale.

The resultant study of communities by sociologists and anthropologists has yielded a rich fruit of insights, concepts, and theories. Robert Warren and Larry Lyon, in *New Perspective on the American Community* (Homewood, Ill.: Dorsey, 1983), pull together a collection of the most influential writings on the community.

To my mind, the clearest treatment of this issue is by Robert Nisbet in *Quest for Community* (New York: Oxford University Press, 1953) and in *Social Change and History* (New York: Oxford University Press, 1969). I am particularly impressed by the fact that he draws upon and affirms the writings of Reinhold Niebuhr. They agree that humankind has a deep-set need for the order that community can provide. (Certainly, a major theme in the writings of both Reinhold and H. Richard Niebuhr, as well as their social gospel precursors such as Walter

Your Place as Place and its People

Let's begin with a series of questions about the history and culture of your community.

1) How did it come to be? What was the founding dream? What was the convenant on which the community was built? Utopia, commerce,

---

Rauschenbush and their successors such as Harvey Cox and Gibson Winter, has been community. And currently, liberation theology is addressing this theme as well.)

You will probably be sympathetic to Nisbet when he argues that basic to humankind is a "quest for community." He sees community as representing four specifics which people need:

Place: Rooted in surroundings which are familiar and hospitable. This is "my" place.

Turf: A feeling that I am in control in this place. I can manage. I can cope.

Security: I can depend on the support of others. This is home base, time-out, a resting place.

Truth: All is not relative. In community, there are eternal values upon which one can count.

This listing reminds me of the affirmations of Psalm 23. Perhaps this is one reason why it has been so popular. It strikes a responsive chord in the hearts of men and women because, deep down, we do indeed desire community.

You will find that this definition includes both the idea that community is *place* and is *spirit.* In my discussion of place, I am including both. Those of you who work in a church where the community has a sense of place, as you work through the process and gather the data culled from this chapter you will become more aware of the social order, values, expectations, and patterns of everyday life that wrap around the place and those who dwell therein.

Consider how, in your role as religious educator, you can help people understand the community, create community, or even change community.

Other scholars also address the subject of community or place. Among them is social historian, Fredrick Schroeder. These articles by him have greatly influenced my understanding of community: "Local History and Newcomers," *History News* (July 1985), pp. 18-21; "The Little Red Schoolhouse," *History News* (April 1981), pp. 15-16; "Exploring the Fourth Dimension," *Small Town* (March-April 1982), pp. 8-13.

And from literature, Garrison Keillor and Wendell Berry have profoundly impacted me. Keillor, in *Lake Wobegon Days,* seems to capture the dynamics of small-town life. But it was Berry who first introduced me to the term "place." Berry, more than Keillor, takes on the role of contemporary prophet. He sees the loss of a sense of place as too great a price to pay for the trinkets of modern life. A recurring refrain is "Does Community Have Value," *Home Economics* (San Francisco: Northpoint Press: 1987), pp. 179-192.

resource exploitation, freedom, safety, and the good life are examples of the dynamic which drove the founding of many American communities. In some the dream was broadly shared by the pioneers. In others only the leadership owned the dream. And in "company" towns, mill and mining, the town was but a means to the realization of the dream of investors far distant from the town.

In time, with change, often the founding dream becomes obsolete. The seam of coal plays out; a producer in another country makes the product for less money and forces the plant to close; children grow up; pioneers move away; and the racial and economic base of the community changes. Perhaps new dreams are needed. What is the situation in your place?

2) What is its symbol? The courthouse tower, the mine tipple, the grain elevator, the smokestack of the factory, the railroad yard, the lake, the golf course, or the college administration building? Many communities are organized around the symbol of its founding dream.

3) What is/are its chief economic function(s)? Often this is integrated with the dream and the symbol. Several have already been named—farm service, industrial, institutional (college, prison, military), county government, and mining. Others would include bedroom suburb, retirement, recreational, transportation break, or art colony.[3]

The primary challenge facing many small towns today is finding new economic functions as changes in agriculture and manufacturing threaten their continued viability. Is this true in your place?[4]

Boley, Oklahoma, was founded in 1891 as a haven for blacks. Freedmen from Alabama were enlisted by "boomers" to homestead on recently opened land. These new landowners raised crops of cotton which were brought to Boley to be ginned. An active business district with stores and services run by black entrepreneurs emerged. But by the 1920s the land began to fail, and the boll weevil found this corner of the cotton belt. Families began to drift away. New life was pumped into Boley in the 1930s when a tuberculosis hospital was opened by the state on the edge of town. In time the incidence of this dread disease lessened, and Boley again faced an uncertain future. However, in the 1970s the hospital was transformed

---

3. Gary Farley, "Community Typology," in *Change in Big Town/Small City,* ed. Robert Wiley (Atlanta, Ga: HMB-SBC, 1982), pp. 93-100.

4. David Brown et al., *Rural Economic Development in the 1990s: Prospects for the Future* (Washington, D.C.: USDA/ERS Report 69). This important collection of articles by leading social scientists provides a useful introduction into the field of rural community development.

to a prison. And one of Boley's sons invented a machine for processing barbeque. With a Small Business Administration loan he built a factory which now employs 125 residents of the Boley community.

Do you see the founding dream? Freedom, independence, a new start. Do you find the community symbols? The cotton gin, a prosperous main street, the hospital/prison, the new factory. Do you see how Boley has been impacted by changing conditions? Do you see how the dream was re-dreamed and re-dreamed? Perhaps it will be again.

Boley's nearest neighbor is Prague, a town settled about the same time by Czechs. The dream was similar. But its agriculture was built on general farming with a mixture of small grain and livestock. It has maintained a strong agriculture base, so strong that the grain elevator rivals the huge Catholic church as the symbol of the town. In recent years the annual Kalachi Festival has become a time for celebrating both cultural heritage and the realization of the founding dream. Since World War II Prague has emerged as the dominant trade town for fifteen to twenty miles in each direction. For example, it has captured the retail trade of Boley. It remains to be seen what the impact will be of the opening of a regional mall about twenty-five miles away in Shawnee.

Now, build upon this little case study to consider the founding dreams, the symbols, and the economic functions of your community. What changes have been experienced across the years?

4) Who are the honored and the despised of the community? Most communities have their heroes and heels, past and present. What are the criteria for labeling a person a hero or a heel? Finding this out will provide a yardstick for the next task.

5) What worldview, what values inform the everyday lives of the residents?
• *Time*. Do they dwell on the past, live in the present, or focus on the future.
• *People*. Essentially good, evil, or a mix and capable of either.
• *Activity*. Getting by, goal oriented, just busy for the sake of being busy.
• *Interpersonal relations*. Kin oriented, peer oriented, or personal choice.
• *Nature and the Supernatural*. Fatalistic submission, cooperation, domination.[5]

Anthropologists teach that the cultural attitudes of a community toward these five concerns—time, people, activity, interpersonal relations, and nature/supernatural—shape the character of persons, their relationships,

---

5. Florence Kluckhohn and Fred Strodtbeck, *Variations in Values* (Evansville, Ind.: Row, Peterson, 1961), pp. 10-20.

and their social institutions. Social values and norms find their authority
in these basic attitudes. Sherwood Lingenfelter and Marvin Mayers have
prepared a very useful questionnaire for getting at these and other elements of worldview. While they are addressing the needs of foreign mis-
sionaries, their material also should be useful for those of us who were
raised in one subculture of America but find ourselves ministering in
another.[6]

For example, if your St. Paul's Chapel is in an isolated Appalachian village you may find that the dominant worldview of the congregation is
rather fatalistic, present oriented, and kinship based. You may also note
that people may be perceived as being essentially bad and that getting by,
rather than setting and seeking goals, is normative. And you will find evi-
dence of this in how people do business, how they respond to education,
and even how they worship.

Visit around the country and listen to the anecdotes that residents share,
analyze the attitudes and values that they illustrate. Make note of the common "prayer lines," e.g., "I want to thank you, God, for letting me live
one more week so I could come out here to your house to worship you
among my friends and relatives." What values/worldview does such a line
reflect?

Certainly, some cultural attitudes and values will be in opposition to
Christian values. What does this say about your agenda of preaching and
of religious education? Does it say anything to you about communication
strategy; e.g., repetition of prayer lines, hymn selection, the use of oral stories to illustrate biblical values, inclusion of folk expressions in litany? The
values the pastor as religious educator shares and lives out in time become
a part of the stock of values of persons and of the community.

But more frequently, as Lingenfelter and Mayers contend, the cultural
values are not so much un-Christian as they are one-sided and incomplete.
They note, for example, that one can find in the teaching of Jesus statements that can be interpreted to mean that we should not plan for the future
but rather live for the moment—see the Sermon on the Mount (Matthew
5-7) for several instances of this. Conversely, in other settings, Jesus
emphasized the importance of planning and strategizing (Luke 14:24-35).
How does one explain the differences? Demands of the context. Christians
ought to be sensitive to what God is doing in this moment, in their lives,
in their settings. For some persons, for some times, for some contexts focus

6. Sherwood Lingerfelter and Marvin Mayers, *Ministry Cross Culturally*
(Grand Rapids, Mich.: Baker, 1986), pp. 28-36.

on the needs of the moment is appropriate. For others a goal-setting orientation is right.[7]

A pastor as religious educator should not come into a setting where the activity orientation is "getting by" and chide the people for not being "goal-oriented." If the pastor does, then the pastor may be guilty of preaching the gospel of modern corporate America, not the biblical message. All three "activity" orientations have their place. Each has a role to play. Rather, she should help the people discern the will of God for that time and place. Similar points can be made about the other four basic worldview orientations.

6) What cultural/ethnic/racial groups are present in the community? How do these impact the life of community? Some communities are characterized by a richness of diversity; others, by conflict and by caste-like separation. A few may be monolithic.

7) What are the barriers that separate persons? Are they visible or invisible? Race, religion, education, status? Consider how you can deal with this. Certainly, one function of the gospel is reconciliation. What strategies seem possible? What does God want done? Can tension for change be applied without destroying what is currently good about the community?

8) What are the sins/hurts of the community? As you listen to the stories by which members and friends share the history of community, church, and family you will pick up on these. Is healing needed? Can you retell the story to illustrate Christian values?

9) What has become of its sons and daughters? The story of most older towns in America includes accounts of the out-migration of many of its brightest and best offsprings to the cities. Many have made their mark. In many a humble village home is a fireplace mantel crowded with pictures of children and grandchildren. Ask about them. Listen with interest. One Sunday you will meet them. You may have opportunity to minister to them. And certainly you will bless the parent as he/she gains a sense of self-respect because of the successes of the children.

10) What is the people's perception of the place; awareness of other's perception? Most people have a deep appreciation of their place. They magnify its qualities and successes. They ignore its defects. To an outsider it may appear much like a thousand communities of similar size and function across the nation. But not to the resident. Listen. Learn. Identify. The pastor as reli-

---

7. Robert Bellah et al., *Habits of the Heart* (New York: Harper & Row, 1985). This very important study builds off the dialectic between values of personal freedom and community responsibility.

gious educator must earn the right to speak before he/she suggests change.

11) Does the community have distinct "subcommunities"? For example, by the time a small town grows to about 2,500 persons it has enough diversity that specific subcommunities evolve based on class or race. And, consequently, it becomes increasingly difficult for a single parish to draw significant numbers from the various subcommunities. Normally, the church will draw primarily from only one. This is when a subcommunity will be interested in establishing a small membership church which incorporates their needs and interests.

12) What seems to be the future of the community—its dreams? Who is responsible for dreaming? Communities are born; some grow and flourish; some plateau early; some grow for a while and then fall into decline; some change and either grow or decline. And there are other variations.

A useful tool employed by sociologists in understanding communities is POET—people, organizations, environment, and technology.[8] We use POET to get a snapshot of the current life of a community. How many people live in the community? How many in each age cohort? (Many traditional small-town communities have very high levels of older persons, while new suburban communities will have high levels of younger persons.) What about their income, education, ethnic/racial/cultural heritage? This kind of information is available concerning your community. Check with city hall or the county court clerk to discover who is responsible for planning in your place. They will gladly share with you data about the people in your area.

Similarly, they can provide data about the organizations—business, industrial, professional, medical, educational, governmental, fraternal, religious, and so forth, which serve your community. The diversity of organizations in your place may be surprising.

Historically, natural environment has played a key role in the location and development of communities. For example, milling towns were established where rivers furnished power to drive turbines; forts were raised at strategic transportation junctions; and grain elevator towns appeared every seven to ten miles along railroad lines across the Midwest and out on the Great Plains.

The last example also illustrates the impact of technology on communities. Hundreds of American towns were founded because of the use of

8. Samuel Wallace, *The Urban Environment,* (Homewood, Ill.: Dorsey, 1980). Wallace builds off the POET anagram to present a very useful analysis of urban life, but it can be applied elsewhere.

railroads to move products. From farm, forest, fields, and mines came products to the town to be shipped to the cities. From the factories of the cities came products to be sold to the folk of the hitherland by the merchants of these towns. But in the past two to three decades trucks moving along interstate highways have become the major movers of goods. Consequently, rail lines have been abandoned and some small towns have "dried-up."[9]

The emerging technology in the world is "information transfer" driven by the microcomputer and the fiber optics telecommunication systems. Some futurists suggest that the networking of fiber optics will be to the twenty-first century what railroad building was to the nineteenth and the system of interstate highways has been to the twentieth.[10]

Consider the data available about your community's people, organizations, environment, and technology. Some persons in government, at the chamber of commerce, and in banking and real estate are thinking about the future of your community. Talk with them. Find out what their reading of the future is. Is it one of stagnation or decline? Is it one of growth based on existing resources of people, technology, organizations, and natural resources or strategic location? Or are community leaders looking to new developments that will provide opportunities for growth in the community?

What happens to the community in responding to the changes brought by the coming of the Information Age will impact religious education and the people to whom you minister and the church which you lead. So you need to know. This knowledge can prepare a congregation in adjusting to changes. For others the knowledge can guide as you provide leadership in helping the community respond to opportunities that change will offer. And still others may be impressed of God to speak a prophetic word when it seems that community leadership may be jeopardizing community well-being by greedy or shortsighted responses to change. In any context it would seem that a pastor as religious educator should announce and apply biblical values and criteria to the evaluation of change and religious edu-

---

9. Richard Lingerman, *Small Town America: A Narrative History 1620 - The Present* (Boston: Houghton Mifflin, 1980).

10. Don Dillman, "Social Issues Impacting Agricultural and Rural Areas as We Approach the 21st Century," in Joint Economic Committee, *New Dimensions in Rural Policy: Building Upon Our Heritage* (Washington, D.C.: U.S. Congress, 1986), pp. 19-31. This is a very important collection of the best scholarship in rural social science.

cators should help persons learn about and evaluate change. Religious educators also train others in how to effect change.[11]

Let me be more specific. Many of you may be pastoring or leading in a St. Paul's whose community's livelihood is based on agricultural production or on traditional industries. Current changes may threaten the continued viability of that function of your community. Many such communities are now looking for alternate functions—services, prisons or other governmental institutions, hazardous waste dumps, retirement community development, or recreational usage. For many, it is a matter of change or die. But some changes are not good. Consider what role God wants you to play in this process.[12]

Others may be in communities which cannot help but prosper as a result of changing technology. What of the old should be carried over into the new?

13) What is the story of your community? How/why has it evolved as it has? The previous twelve areas lead to this one. You need to know the story, to identify with the story, to appreciate it. Any response of the community to its future will be grounded in its past.

A pastor went to an isolated East Kentucky town soon after World War II. It had no paved streets, no public water, no fire protection, and no industry. Most of the men worked as steamfitters several hundred miles away in Ohio. When he retired thirty years later, the community was much improved. And the men, as they retired back into the community, found their way into the life of the church which he pastored.

Your Place as Process

What seems to be happening? Why? How? What are the routines of everyday life in your place?

1) What are its magnets? What places, activities, and events draw people? What is the rhythm of everyday life? For many years the decisions concerning the governance of Jefferson County, Tennessee, were made at the lunch counter in Doc Bible's pharmacy and then ratified over across Gay Street in the courtroom of the courthouse. The pastor did his most

11. Gary Farley, "The Walmartization of Rural America," *Ozark Watch* (Fall 1989), pp. 7-8; and "Revitalizing Rural America and Her Churches," *The Baptist Program* (August 1989), pp. 6-8.

12. Robert Chambers, *Rural Development: Putting the Last First* (London: Long Scientific and Technical, 1983). This excellent work comes at development from a biblical perspective in the best sense.

effective ministry while drinking coffee at Bell's Sweet Shop in Mossey Creek. He learned the rhythm of the community and quickly fit into it. In Camden Point one learned that Vacation Bible School, revival, and stewardship emphasis needed to be calendared around the cycle of planting and harvesting. If the pastor did not learn the pastor did not last.

Rural and small-town places have their magnets and their rhythms. The pastor as religious educator of people in such places should bend to these processes. They want to see their pastor in the junctions of everyday life. They do not call for appointments and come to the church office.

2) What are the patterns of movement? Post Office. Bell's office. Lunch at Bell's or Bible's, except on Thursday when the Lions Club meets. Work, except for Wednesday when it's golf. Bank. Home. In many small towns the business, professional, and retired persons have a pretty well-set routine. They move along certain corridors through the community in certain sequences. To see persons, to gather information, to become involved in the discussion of issues, and to participate in the decision-making processes, learn the patterns, and intervene. Of course, to really impact religious education in the decision-making process you will have to pay your dues. But this will come more quickly if you have made yourself accessible in the places and patterns of everyday small-town life.

3) How are decisions made? Who are the powerbrokers? Who are the major "get things done" persons in the place? What is the route to leadership? As you move along the corridors and in the gathering places, listen. Hear how decisions are made, who has influence, veto power. Watch and participate as community events are planned and carried out. Bankers, lawyers, physicians, owners, and managers of major businesses and industries—typically, these are the powerbrokers. But there may be others.

Remember, these people will have some biases about the practicality of pastors. And of course they know that you do not know the whole story of the place and why things are as they are. So they will not automatically listen to you. In the early years your role will likely be more that of a "staff" person, raising questions about proposals for action. Only later will you be allowed to have a say in the really important decisions.

There are some "Boss Hoggs" and some "Black Barts" in small towns. But most leaders are wanting to do good, while protecting and perhaps promoting their own interests. Like all of us leaders have their "blind spots." So, the pastoral role as religious educator is to gently remind leaders that "they see in part" and consequently only "know in part." There are other positions and opinions that need to be considered.[13] Your role as religious educator includes the presentation of other ideas for consideration.

4) What are the routines of everyday conversations? What are the taboos? I have lived in several regions of our nation. In each I have been fascinated by the routines people do in everyday conversation concerning greeting, leave-taking, teasing, transacting business, courting, and making requests. Similarly, various ethnic groups have their routines for these and other common interactional events. For example, in Appalachia the phrase, "Won't you come and go home with us," is a common leave-taking expression. It says that the persons are having such a good time together that they wish that it might be continued. This phrase is often met with a counter offer of hospitality or by an arrangement to get together soon at some appointed time and place. Know what these routines are. Understand them for what they are.

Likewise, each community has its rules of etiquette and taboos. Consider the set of expectations related to the event of someone dying. How is the pastor to relate to the family of the deceased? Who is to be involved in the key roles? How is the body to be disposed of?[14]

Further, there are places and activities that are sacred and those that are profane. There are roles, relationships, and routines that are appropriate for pastors as religious educator and those that are not. One must learn these rules and be sensitive to them.

5) How do people make a living? The communities served by many St. Paul's Chapels are dominated by a single vocation—farmer, factory hand, or railroader, but this is less common than a generation ago. The activities, rhythm of work, values, attitudes, concerns, and organizational structures and processes of the workplace often carry over into the life of the church. For example, historically a mill village congregation may have difficulty

---

13. Gary Farley, "Unit 6: Community Power and Decision-making," in *Core Study Text-Reader: Rural Social Science by Extension,* ed. Gary Farley, (Cooperative Extension Department, Texas A&M University, 1988). The classic sociological study of power in small towns remains Arthur Vidich and Joseph Beresman's *Small Town in Mass Society,* rev. ed. (Princeton, N.J.: University of Princeton Press, 1989).

14. Gary Farley, "Role Theory in Christian Perspective,": in *A Reader in Sociology,* ed. Charles De Santo (Scottdale, Pa: Herald Press, 1980), pp. 303-316. You may wish to study role theory more deeply. Begin with Ervin Goffman's *The Presentation of Self in Every Day Life* (Garden City, N.Y.: Doubleday, 1989).

in finding strong lay leadership because this trait has not been encouraged in the workplace.

Consequently, get to know the work of the persons to whom you minister. Discover how this impacts their worldview, their decision-making processes and personal conduct. Draw upon this in your sermon illustrations and your pastoral care. Let it impact your leadership style. Move to complement the style of the lay leadership. What implications may vocation have for your approach to religious education?

6) How does your community relate to other communities? Is it the dominant community in the area; one among several competing rivals; dependent upon a larger community; or a despised and feared place? How are these relationships expressed in your church, the other churches, interfaith and denominational events? For example, longtime rivalry between two towns over which got the county seat, the railroad line, the U.S. highway, the consolidated high school, and the like, will be carried over into church life.

7) Where and how do people play? Fall Friday nights at the high-school football field are almost sacred times of community affirmation. Note the urbanizing of rural recreation—golf courses, video rentals, and trips to amusement parks in "regional city." Note the shift in the past half-century from intellectual-cultural pursuits for recreation to physical activity. What does this say about our culture? What does it say to our churches and our church programs? Is church to be seen as a recreational alternative or is it central to life? How can religious education be reflected in and through the recreational activities of the community? What does this say about approaches in religious education programing?

8) How does the community assimilate persons? The fate of many clergy is to always be "marginal" persons. They move or are moved with regularity and can never really put their roots down deeply in a community. In some sense this is useful for the pastoral role. You can see problems and opportunities that might be overlooked by the locals. People will share deep concerns, hurts, and sins because they know that they will not have to see you everyday for the rest of their lives. And when faced by serious difficulty you will know that you can move on to a new and different context.

But while there one of your concerns is helping those new and marginal to the life of the community to become assimilated. If you are pastor of a long-established church, you may be a "bridge" person. By this I mean that you have acceptance by the leadership of the church and of the community, so your acceptance of a new person can help him/her gain broader acceptance. Their involvement in the life of the church, which you sponsor, can be an aid also. Further, positions in the religious education program of the church are an important resource for the assimilation of new people.

In summarizing this section let me suggest that by understanding the processes of the community, accepting them inasmuch as is possible, working within their frame, and seeking to improve them as opportunity comes, will enable you to be assimilated within the life of the community. Granted that you will likely always be seen by many as a marginal community resident, you can be assimilated as "their" marginal person.

The Place of your Church in the Place

Though small in membership, your St. Paul's Chapel may be the leading church in your community. Or it may be a "special purpose" church serving only one segment, such as the poor in that town. Or it may be the "chapel" of an extended family group. Another small membership church in the place may be in but not of the community. This is often the case with evangelistic sects and charismatic groups.[15] These congregations are gathered along doctrinal lines from across community bounds. They have little "parish" or community focus in their life. There are some questions to ask as you look at congregations that have a sense of belonging in their place:

1) What role does your congregation play in the place? Leader, cooperator, secondary?

2) What kind of reputation does it have? Friendly, aloof; rich, middle-class, poor; formal, ordered, informal; loving, conflictive, combative; community serving, self-serving?

3) What is the relationship between your church and other congregations in the community?

4) What community resources are available to assist your church in the work of religious education?

5) What ministries, programs, events, and activities in the community receive the support of your church?

6) What community leadership roles are filled by active members of your congregation?

---

15. Douglas Walrath has given special attention to typologies of small churches by location. See pp. 33-61 in Jackson Carroll, ed, *Small Churches are Beautiful* (New York: Harper & Row, 1977) and Carl Dudley and Douglas Walrath, *Developing Your Small Church's Potential* (Valley Forge, Pa.: Judson 1988), pp. 32-38. Also, Gary Farley, "Typology of Churches" in *Change in Big Town/Small City*, ed. Robert Wiley (Atlanta: HMB-SBC, 1982), pp. 105-135.

7) How does the community relate to your congregation? Embraces, holds at a distance, rejects?

8) Does your church seek to serve or to dominate the life of the community?

As you work through the answers to those questions, a picture of the place of your church in the life of the community will emerge. Next, ask if this is the picture that is needed, appropriate, and wanted. If not, consider steps that might be taken to change it.

In the preceding three sections of this chapter, I have shared the topics from sociology that can assist in comprehending the setting and the culture in which you serve. And I have suggested some topics to investigate in order to get an understanding where your church fits into the life of the community. Again, I have written for St. Paul's Chapels in small town settings. If your parish is in a rural or a metropolitan setting, some adjustments are needed, but most of the topics are applicable.

Characteristics

In the past decade or so several very useful books have been published that can guide you in understanding the interior life of your church, again from the sociological perspective. These characteristics are useful in examining religious education.

The findings of these studies can be summarized in these twelve basic characteristics of smaller membership churches:[16]

1) More like a family than a corporation
2) Resistant to change
3) Limited resources available
4) Lacking in intentionality
5) Locally owned and operated
6) Focused on worship
7) Focus on caring ministry to members and to community
8) Membership by adoption
9) Works best through projects
10) The event is the thing
11) Pastor as caring shepherd
12) Critical mass/rule of forty

---

16. Gary Farley, "Of Smaller Churches; A Dozen Characteristics," *The Baptist Program* (April 1988), pp. 4-5.

Think about small membership churches you have known and loved (or perhaps hated). Does this list fit your experiences? Intensely relational. Maintenance of fellowship is central. Decisions made by consensus. Events are intergenerational. It cannot do all of the religious education programs suggested by the central offices because it lacks the resources. If it grows much beyond forty active members, it becomes something different. If it falls much below thirty-five, it may experience difficulty in doing its work. It does not want its pastor to be a "professional" with office hours and appointments. Rather, it seeks someone who cares, who listens, who walks alongside, who is known and respected in the community. Religious education is about experiencing God in an event, or renewing the fellowship; this is what is remembered and retold.

Leading

A common criticism is that future pastors and religious educators in seminary are being trained to manage a church following the modes of corporate America. Consequently, they are ill-prepared to lead a small parish. The new pastor comes to the first pastorate with one set of expectations and understandings and finds a church with a very different set. The stage is set for conflict and hurt.[17] Let me suggest some steps to take in discovering the inner-life of the small membership church.

First, as a very relational group, the people want to know about you—your upbringing, your pilgrimage of faith, your beliefs. Be transparent and autobiographical in messages and conversations. Of course, be sensitive to their taboos and expectations as you do this.

Second, demonstrate real interest in the "story" of the congregation. This might be done by preaching a message on the basic tasks of the parish in morning worship. This provides parameters for a "talk-back" session in the evening where members share their founding dream and the work of the church. Seek to integrate discussion of how the community came to be. Focus on "change" which the worshipers have observed in the life both of the church and of its community. Weeks later people will be sharing anecdotes about events and changes.[18]

---

17. Anthony Pappas, *Entering the World of the Small Church* (Washington, D.C.: The Alban Institute, 1988).

18. Carl Dudley, *Making the Small Church Effective* (New York: Abingdon, 1979). James Hopewell, *Congregations: Stories and Structure* (Philadelphia: Fortress, 1987). Rockwell Smith, *Rural Ministry and the Changing Community* (New York: Abingdon, 1971).

Third, identify the "bell cow" (leader). Most smaller congregations have experienced times of poor and/or of no pastoral leadership. In this vacuum strong lay leadership has emerged. Typically, it is good to encourage this lay person to become your mentor. Learn from that individual how the church functions, how decisions are made, where the "land mines" are. Realize that his/her endorsement of a project may be crucial. Although the time may come when disagreement and even estrangement may occur over changes you want to initiate; do not seek conflict when cooperation is possible.[19]

Fourth, use the letters to the seven churches in the Book of Revelation to identify strengths and weaknesses common to churches. Devote a message to each, followed by a forum where the congregation can discuss the presence of these in their church. Discuss how they might draw upon their strengths to be a more effective church. Discuss how they might address their weaknesses.[20]

Fifth, involve the church in active, aggressive prayer that God will help the church use its strengths and overcome its weaknesses in effective religious education ministry.

Sixth, identify an event/project that the church might do successfully. Many small membership churches suffer from an inferiority complex. A successful project is needed to build a sense of confidence.[21]

Seventh, integrate what you learn about the church, its religious education, and your community. Give special attention to identifying ministry needs, persons who are unchurched, and those who are without faith.

Eighth, share your observations. See if the congregation concurs. Ask that these be incorporated in the list of prayer concerns.

Ninth, identify the annual events—revival, homecoming, Vacation Bible School, cemetery decoration, Christmas program, community Holy Week observance—and use them as the core of the annual calendar planning. Help the leaders of each to do well.[22]

Tenth, seek to identify other events and projects that the church might

19. Gary Farley, "Where Are You Headed," *The Baptist Program* (September 1988), pp. 6-7.

20. Gary Farley, "And Now Presenting the Small Church," *Tennessee Baptist and Reflector* (February 17, 1988).

21. Gary Farley, "The Single-Staff Church and Its Annual Events," *Church Administration* (July 1988), p. 128.

22. Gary Farley, "Annual Planning in the Small Church," *Church Administration*. Forthcoming.

do, sponsor, or cooperate in. Ask the church to consider and adopt these ideas and incorporate them into the planning process. Address what seems to be the basic flaw in many small congregations, the lack of intentionality. Further, ask for additional time and money from the people as well as real-location of existing resources. There is risk involved in this. Hear objections, take them seriously, and seek consensus if at all possible. When introducing change, take incremental steps. Get people to do well and then adopt the idea. If opposition arises, ask for a "trial" period for the new project, event, or program.

Eleventh, this expanded and intensified level of activity calls for skill training. This should become the motivation for and determiner of the religious education curriculum.

Twelfth, it is probable that the renewed activity and ministry of the church will attract some estranged back to it as well as some nonbelieving and unchurched persons. Certainly, if the members feel good about their church and its success, they will be talking about it and inviting others to become a part of it. Here is another problem in many small congregations, they are not very intentional about including new people. And they may be slow to forgive old wrongs. Being forewarned, take steps to prepare. Identify the gifts the new persons bring, involve them in ministry, arrange for their needs to be met, forge linkages with the old members, and provide religious education activities and events that will bind the old with the new.

Thirteenth, be missionary. So many small membership churches seem to have slipped into a "survival" mentality. This seems to hasten their demise. Encourage leaders to look beyond themselves and help other churches and people. This may help in restoring vision and getting small membership churches moving again.[23]

Fourteenth, lead the parish to consider and cooperatively seek consensus on what the will of God is for this church. What religious education ministries will it major on? Who will it seek to evangelize? How will it assist believers in spiritual growth?

Fifteenth, assist the congregation in organizing itself and in allocating its resources to do the ministry of religious education.

Staffing

Most small membership churches cannot afford a pastor full-time, fully supported. The work load may not really merit a full-time placement. So what are the options:

---

23. David Ray, *Small Churches are the Right Size* (New York: Pilgrim Press, 1982).

1) Bivocational. About 30 percent of the churches affiliated with the Southern Baptist Convention are served by bivocational pastors. They hold a variety of secular employments. Some lack adequate training in theology, homiletics, and church administration. Some see their role as preachers, more than as pastors in the role of religious educator. But the level of quality seems to be improving. Many are very effective. Some see this as their way of giving expression to their ministry calling. Others see it as temporary. They hope to grow their church to the point that they can become fully supported. Or they hope to move to such a congregation.[24]

2) Circuit or field of churches. This approach has been used widely by the United Methodists and the Roman Catholics. The acute priest shortage among Roman Catholics is leaning more and more to several churches sharing one pastor and one religious educator. Two, three, four, or more congregations share a pastor who works with and leads them all. A common problem with this approach is that very different congregations are linked. This makes it difficult for the pastor to get his/her work done. Another problem is that most circuit riders seem to be overworked. The demands of the congregations tax their resources of time and energy.[25]

3) Yoked parish. Often this arrangement is a blending of the first two. Several churches, even those of differing denominational affiliation share a common staff of specialists. For example, each of four congregations may have a worship leader, but share religious education, youth, and/or counseling specialists.

4) Subsidies. Aid from mission boards and central offices makes possible pastoral leadership in many small membership congregations, particularly those that are relatively new, or are in impoverished regions. Unfortunately, the process of being weaned from this aid is often painful.

Conclusion

Where in America is your St. Paul's Chapel? Know the history, social structure, processes, dynamics, and culture of the place. Take steps to discover the inner social and cultural dynamic of the chapel itself. And, finally, make good use of this knowledge to lead the church to be more effective in its ministry of religious education; to be all that God wants it to be.

---

24. Luther Dorr, *The Bivocational Pastor* (Nashville: Broadman, 1988).
25. Tom Sykes, ed., *The Field of Churches* (Atlanta: HMB-SBC, 1989), (mimographed)

Chapter Four

Educational Ministry, the CCD, and the Sunday School

PAMELA MITCHELL

INTRODUCTION

In the past, I used Robert Bower's *Administering Christian Education* as the basic textbook in my "Developing a Church's Educational Program" class . . . until I took a position teaching in a midwestern seminary. Here, most of my students serve "small membership" churches, for whom Bower's highly efficient schemas of organization and management would be overkill. In fact, many of the students serve multiple-point charges consisting of two, three, or more very small membership churches; adding all of them together would barely produce a "flow chart." In this context, I quickly became aware that religious education for small congregations is not simply scaled-down large church programing, but is a particular *approach* to religious education. What characterizes that approach and how can small membership churches make the most of their religious education programs? To answer this questions, I turned first to a bit of history.

HISTORY: THE SMALL COMMUNITY AS BASIS

It seems almost too obvious to state this, but at one time in the western expansion of the United States most Protestant churches were of small

80

membership. Newly established towns were small, close-knit, relational communities, and the church was one center of town life. As Lynn and Wright put it, "The Sunday school was there so early and fared so well west of the Appalachians that most editors of American history texts and popularizers of frontier manners treat it as normal early American scenery."[1] In a young, developing country, the Sunday school in each town was obviously numerically small, yet it was of great import to the community as a key element in an "ecology . . . of institutions . . . consciously engaged in religious education."[2] As Americans pushed westward, small towns grew up with their own integral system of religious education: the community, the extended family, the public schools, the neighborhood church, popular religious publications, and the Sunday school all worked together.[3] In this milieu, the Sunday school was a small community institution functioning as one lay-directed piece of the total educational matrix. Even with the rise of common schools in the nineteenth century, a partnership that served the needs of school and church still flourished.[4]

With the industrialization and urbanization of the United States came a shift in the character of communities *and* in the Sunday school. The manufacturing success of highly organized, well-managed plants suggested general trends and techniques to those in education, which was viewed as a kind of human production field. This industrial pattern combined with the burgeoning post-Darwinian view of education as a science, complete with theories of learning, instruction, discipline, and development, created a vision of large-scale proficient religious education.[5] This vision of a care-

---

1. Robert W. Lynn and Elliott Wright, *The Big Little School,* 2nd. ed. (Birmingham, Ala.: Religious Education Press and Nashville: Abingdon, 1980), pp. 40-41.

2. John Westerhoff III, *Will Our Children Have Faith?* (New York: Seabury, 1976), p. 13.

3. See John Westerhoff's discussion of the pattern of religious education prior to World War II, in ibid., pp. 13-15.

4. See the discussion of this period in Anne M. Boylan, *Sunday School: The Formation of an American Institution 1790-1880* (New Haven, Conn.: Yale University Press, 1988), pp. 22-59.

5. Elliot Eisner makes this point succinctly and strongly in *The Educational Imagination: the Design and Evaluation of School Programs,* 2nd. ed. (New York: Macmillan, 1985). There, he cites the influence of Edward Thorndike in envisioning education as a science of "tested principles and procedures for managing the student's learning" (p. 8). This line of thought was picked up in curriculum design and became the norm; thus, by the 1920s W.W. Charters analyzed the tasks adults

fully crafted science of education moved into the church as well and shift-
ed the role and expectations placed on the Sunday school. It became
"important that the school of the church be recognized by the public as
equally effective,"[6] and thus the "major concern of Christian education was
with gaining educational validity through curriculum development and the
perfecting of the educational plant."[7] To become a technological competi-
tor, the Sunday school had to undergo a change from a lay-directed, intergenerational community hub, to an efficient complete system of professional education. The profession of religious education was born.[8] Large
Sunday schools modeled after industries and businesses, managed by professional religious educators with an eye toward efficiency and production
became the ideal. In this era of professionalism, the small membership
church was unable to compete.[9] Large Sunday schools in large churches
in large towns and cities had educational plants, while the small membership churches and small communities had neither the budget nor the personnel to follow the trend. To an extent, small membership church education lost its identity and became a lesser sibling trailing around behind
professional religious education.

In United States Roman Catholicism, the CCD had similarly begun as
a lay-directed, local community-based movement. The first CCD in this
country, gathered in the New York parish of Our Lady of Good Counsel
in 1902, was a volunteer group of lay persons concerned with the low level
of doctrinal knowledge in the parish.[10] Like Protestant Sunday schools,
which filled a central role in the community, the CCD was a neighborhood
entity.

This small, community character of the CCD continued into the 1930s,

---

must perform in our culture, delineated educational objectives to prepare for those
tasks, and recommended the design of programs to neatly achieve the objectives.
(See W.W. Charters, *Curriculum Construction* [New York: Macmillan, 1923], pp.
34-66). By the time of Henry Harap's *The Technique of Curriculum Making* (New
York: Macmillan, 1928), education could be referred to as a systematic technology.

6. Dorothy Jean Furnish, *DRE/DCE—The History of a Profession* (Nashville:
Christian Educators Fellowship, 1976), p. 18.

7. D. Campbell Wyckoff, *The Gospel and Christian Education* (Philadelphia:
Westminster, 1959), p. 66.

8. Furnish, *DRE/DCE*, p. 19.

9. Lynn and Wright, *Big Little School*, pp. 124-129.

10. Mary Charles Bryce, "The Confraternity of Christian Doctrine," in *Renewing the Sunday School and the CCD*, ed. D. Campbell Wyckoff (Birmingham,
Ala.: Religious Education Press, 1986), p. 30.

with Edwin O'Hara's establishment of a multiparish cooperative summer religious education program in Oregon.[11] O'Hara's CCD was integrally colored by the character of his small farming community context; the CCD was localized and small, not a generic, nationally imposed program. In Robert Lucey's Spanish-speaking CCD in the Southwest, a similar cultural community specificity was also embodied.[12]

The CCD has always been an *alternative* for children not attending a Catholic elementary or secondary school. At one time, full parochial schooling was the norm, but as the number of, and enrollment at, Roman Catholic schools has declined, the CCD has become a more important educational mode. As Roman Catholic communities and neighborhoods have broken up, the need for the CCD has increased.[13] Thus, while Sunday school in small membership Protestant churches has been eclipsed to some degree by large-church professional religious education, the Roman Catholic Church has been gradually seeing more need for the CCD.

The question is: How can the particular character of *small* membership churches be honored in religious education? How can the community-based nature of the Sunday school and the CCD be celebrated, as O'Hara and Lucey celebrated the particularities of their own small communities in the earlier parts of this century? As Rachel Adams once wrote, "A basic principle to keep in mind is that a program of Christian nurture must be worked out in each particular church, taking into account the character and needs of its members, the place of the church in the community, its relationship to other institutions in the community, its tradition and heritage, and its resources and opportunities. If this principle is followed, it will mean that the small church will not try to imitate the large church."[14] The important point is to recognize, recover, and honor the character of the small membership church.

UNIQUE CHARACTERISTICS OF THE
SMALL MEMBERSHIP CHURCH

As Steve Burt points out, "Small churches are not smaller versions of large churches. They are qualitatively, as well as quantitatively, dif-

---

11. Ibid., pp. 32-33.

12. Ibid., p. 37.

13. See Michael Wrenn, "Religious Education at the Crossroads," in *Religious Education and the Future*, ed. Dermot A. Lane (New York: Paulist, 1986), pp. 34-35.

14. Rachel Swann Adams, *The Small Church and Christian Education* (Philadelphia: Westminster, 1961), p. 12.

ferent."[15] There *is* a special character to small membership churches and
to their Sunday school or CCD, when the overwhelming trend toward
large-scale professionalism is peeled away. It is my contention that this
special character is what was honored in the earlier efforts sketched in
the preceding history.

This character has been succinctly described by Carl Dudley, for whom
small membership churches are primarily characterized by the strong
attachment and sense of ownership felt by the members; the small membership church is identified as a single-cell "primary group."[16] This means
that "small" does not have an essentially quantitative measure; you cannot
designate "all churches under 100 members," or all churches under *any*
enrollment figure as necessarily "small" churches. A 100-member church
may be a dying old large church or a newly formed, potentially large
church. "Small" does *not* refer to number! "Small" refers to the qualities
of the church, to the character of relationships, the mode of acting, and the
ethos of the church, as a primary group.

As a primary group, the two dominant features of a small membership
church are 1) the closeness of relationships and proximity among the members, and 2) the church's function as preserver, bearer, and locus of culture.
Closeness entails a certain intimacy that pervades relationships in the
church; like a family that has grown up in one house, the members know
one another "warts and all." Church gatherings are not meetings of mere
acquaintances but are gatherings of a clan. This closeness lends a feeling
of trust and security to the congregation; "church" is the name of the
extended family that is always there and can be counted on when the chips
are down. This does not mean that everyone gets along harmoniously;
there are disagreements, fights, divisions, and offenses, as in any family,
but that primary relational bond is always there.

The cultural role of the small membership church is manifest in the traditions that are shared and carried into the present and future. The church
is not an impersonal imposer of liturgy and denominational activities, but
the locus of very personal custom, belief, and practice. The small membership church often has a very territorial identity: Providence Church is
not just located in the farming country of Louisa County, but its name, its
worship style, and its Christmas traditions are tied to its territory. Thus,

---

15. Steve Burt, *Activating Leadership in the Small Church* (Valley Forge, Pa.:
Judson, 1988), p. 5.

16. Carl S. Dudley, *Unique Dynamics of the Small Church* (Washington, D.C.:
The Alban Institute, 1977), p. 5.

as in earlier Sunday school history, the local community identity is bound up and expressed in the church's life. In this life, time is not calculated by the calendar, the fiscal year, or the denomination's schedule of emphases, but is closely tied to the community's life; time is marked by *events*. The year of the flood, the time of year when one church family was wiped out by fire, harvest time . . . whatever the significant events in the life of the church have been and are, become the units of time. Thus, the small membership church functions primarily as a *conserving* community, keeping alive the memories, stories, practices, events, and relationships that provide community identity.[17]

These two characteristics strike closer to the heart of "small church" than any numerical measure of demographics. The small membership church is a quality, a primary group characterized by closeness and cultural conservation. This qualitative description applied to small membership churches in earlier eras of American life, and as Dudley argues, it holds true today.

PROBLEMS FACING RELIGIOUS EDUCATION IN THE SMALL MEMBERSHIP CHURCH

As the brief historical sketch suggested, the twentieth century has not consistently honored the qualities of the small membership church in designing religious education programs. Instead of educational programs designed, organized, and operated for the particularity of a small membership church as a community culture, religious education has been envisioned for "the church"—a generic, generally large institution that is *not* a primary group. This generic religious education mentality has created a variety of problems for the small membership church.

First are the problems of organization and administration. As envisioned in most Sunday school and CCD administration planbooks, religious education begins with an assessment of the program, evaluating the physical plant, resources, and educational opportunities currently offered. The standard procedure is to ask questions like:

Are our facilities comfortable and attractive?
Is the equipment appropriate for the age level?
Is the equipment in good repair?
Is the space adequate for the class using it?
Do we have vacant rooms that might be used for additional classes?

---

17. Dudley, *Unique*, p. 10.

Are the facilities accessible to all persons?
Do we have a library or media center?[18]
In what settings does religious education now take place?
What is the purpose of each educational program?
What ages are included?
What day of the week is the event held?
How many total hours is it offered?
How many times a year is it held?
How does it relate to other parts of the congregation's life?[19]

These are all important questions that raise a church's awareness of what is, and suggest important programatic features; my point is not to dismiss such analysis. However, such objective, evaluative measurement of features may not tell the story of the small membership church. These are questions addressing features of a large institutional program—the industrial/business/science of education—not the questions one asks of a primary group. An educator would not try to understand a family through an inventory of its kitchen facilities or a chart of its weekly schedule; similarly, an educator does not understand a small membership church through itemization and diagrams. As a relational, close, culture-bearing community, the small membership church is not adequately described or served by technical evaluation. The small membership church may not have the space, the equipment, the budget, or the personnel that are readily described by these evaluative tools. Planning that proceeds on the basis of such evaluation ignores the character of the small congregation and sets up expectations that cannot be met.

Second are the content problems "generic" large-scale religious education design raises for the small membership church. In most denominations, and in many independent publishing houses, curricular resources are designed and written to be as general as possible, thus fitting the broadest market and receiving the widest use. If one central characteristic of the small membership church as primary group is it cultural specificity, then such generic teaching resources may be a mistake. This is not to say that we should foster a myriad of different Christianities, developed by each congregation, but simply that the lack of relationship to the cultural

18. Roy H. Ryan, ed., *Christian Education Planning Handbook* (Nashville: Discipleship Resources, 1988), p. 5.

19. Paraphrased from Carol Wehrheim, *Planning Your Educational Ministry: A Guide for Congregations* (Atlanta: Presbyterian Publishing House, 1988), p. 28.

specificity of the small congregation diminishes the effectiveness resources and creates problems for the users. Denominational mission resources that focus on the year's United States/Soviet relationship theme may be far removed from the life of Maysville Church, in rural Buckingham County, where farm crises and housing shortages are the crucial facts of life.

In addition, most curricula are designed for religious education programs in a large church: The materials are age-specific, often assuming the presence of a CCD or Sunday school class for every school grade; the format is geared for groups who do not know each other very well; and the style is technically correct "lesson plans." Again, these features are not to be belittled, but such resources do not match the communal character of the small membership church.

The problem, organizational and content-oriented, is that Sunday schools or CCDs in small congregations, looking for help with their educational program, seize the planning guides and curriculum resources designed for the generic large program and then attempt to operate as a scaled-down generic program. This mode of operation ignores the vital character of the small membership church as a primary group and does not develop an educational program that honors, uses, or serves the small congregation.

DIRECTIONS FOR THE SMALL MEMBERSHIP CHURCH

If the "generic" religious educational tools do not serve the small membership church well, where can these churches turn for help with Sunday school or CCD? I believe it is essential for the small congregation to work from the strength of its basic character to:

1. Develop a form of program organization and administration that uses the closeness of the congregation and fits the cultural specificity and conservative function of each small membership church.
2. Develop content and resources geared for the small membership church, resources that fit the communal nature of the church and relate to the real life of the congregation.

This means a move away from strict reliance on generic planning manuals; religious education program organized around the specifics of each church's own particular life becomes the focus. It means a move away from standardized generic curricula; content and form related to the specificity of each church becomes the need. It does *not* mean each small membership church must be left totally alone to forge its own isolated educational trail. It is possible to offer some guidance and suggestions for both organization and resources appropriate to the character of the small congregation.

Organizing For Religious Education In The Small Membership Church

In his recent guide to religious education in the small membership church, Donald Griggs writes, "The setting of a church greatly influences the specific goals, programs, and approaches to ministry appropriate to the church and the community that it serves."[20] Indeed, Griggs has suggested the appropriate starting point for organizing small membership church religious education. The first organizational step is: Begin with the characteristics of the particular church itself. This does not mean enumerating the rooms, equipment, classes, and teachers, constructing a flow chart of all jobs, or passing around questionnaires. Remember that the small membership church is a primary group, and begin with a holistic description of the church as, and in, a community. The stories of the church, the events that identify it, the lives that embody it, the history and the memories, the engagements and opportunities—all of these are the starting point. This means that rather than beginning with forms, charts, and questions, the religious educator begins with narratives and pictures which combine to describe the small membership church as a whole.[21]

There are innumerable ways to describe the church through constructing its story. Conducting interviews with members, old and new, asking for their stories as Eliot Wigginton and his students did for *Foxfire,* and then putting together a tape or book that tells the identity story is one possibility. Scouring old scrapbooks, archives, and bulletins for stories and photos to create a montage is another possibility. Many published confirmation curricula include several sessions on learning and knowing the congregation's story;[22] so a church might choose to participate as a whole group in a several-session event using such a resource. Donald Griggs offers a four-step

20. Donald L. Griggs and Judy McKay Walther, *Christian Education in the Small Church* (Valley Forge, Pa.: Judson, 1988), pp. 12-13.

21. Burt, *Activating Leadership,* p. 15.

22. For example, see the "Building a Church Family" session in *Growing Together,* from *Living the Good News* curriculum; activities include developing a mural of your church's life, and engaging older members in storytelling. Or, see Mac N. Turnage and Anne Shaw Turnage, *Explorations Into Faith,* Leader's Guide, and Judith Sutherland, *Explorations Into Faith, A Journal,* (Philadelphia: Geneva, 1977).

process, including description of the community, listing the programs and activities now offered, exploring beliefs, and identifying challenges.[23] The list could go on . . . the point is simply to begin with constructing a holistic picture of the small membership church as a life, using whatever tools are helpful. Religious education program needs are then framed directly out of this vision of the church as a living, closely knit whole.

Describing the small congregation in this way sets the stage for an educational program that is intrinsically rooted in the particular characteristics of the primary group. Without this step, the church is setting itself up to take ownership of a program that may not be an integral part of its identity and life. *With* full description as the basis, the stage is set to develop a program in which the group feels strong attachment and ownership. Recall that one of the central characteristics of the small congregation is the sense of belonging, ownership, and personal responsibility felt by the members; this characteristic must be carried into the religious education program.

The second organizational step, then, is: Develop lay member ownership and leadership of the educational program. As religious educator in the small church, there is a responsibility to foster and nurture the group's ownership and leadership of the religious education program. Steve Burt writes, "Small churches need good small church pastors . . . who can provide leadership rather than management, who can build up the laity and inspire them so they trust themselves to make decisions and follow through on them."[24] The same might be said of "good small church educators."[25] However, the need for congregational ownership and leadership of the program is not just a pragmatic matter, it is essential to the character of the small membership church as a primary group. The religious educator is not managing a large manufacturing plant but working in a *relationally* oriented setting in which all parties must feel a crucial stake.

---

23. Griggs and Walther, *Small Church*, pp. 28-37.

24. Burt, *Activating Leadership*, p. 25.

25. In reality, very few small membership churches have professional religious educators, since that job is primarily limited to larger churches that are able to participate in the technological system of education. Generally, small membership churches have religious education programs run by volunteers or supervised by the pastor. Practically speaking, the pastor of a multiple-point charge cannot physically be "the leader" of religious education programing in all three churches—in-house responsibility is a must. Those small membership churches that do have a religious educator generally share that educator in a cluster of churches. In either case, the professional manager model is not applicable to the small membership church. The pastor serves as resident religious educator.

Once again, there are a host of methods and tools for helping with this step; the appropriate tool will vary with the particular church. Steve Burt advises a system of using interest inventories, *listening* to people, encouraging lay input into the church's program, developing leadership apprenticeships, cultivating personal relationships with the laity, encouraging small *sui generis* groups, and visibly appreciating members' work.[26]

The third organizational point then emerges as a caution to both the religious educator and the church members taking primary responsibility for the parish's religious education program: Maintain the simplicity of the single-cell primary group in plans and designs. At times the educational technology machine looms large, and the systems of generic large-scale religious education invite the small congregation to over-organize, yet the character of the small membership program should be "inviting, where people feel at home and part of the whole, not overwhelmed or depersonalized."[27] Formality, rigidity, and heavy structure grate against the grain of the small membership church; the religious education program needs a simplicity, clarity, and unity of design that maintains the focus on persons and relationships.

Again, there is no one way to structure such a program. For some churches, single-cell simplicity may mean intergenerational Sunday school or CCD led by a different family unit each week. For others, it may mean a weeknight CCD that meets in someone's home. Still others may develop education centered on congregational worship in which children are taught the meaning and practice of worship, while adults participate with the pastor in sermon discussion. The exact form is wide open, within the parameters of simplicity and relational focus.

A fourth organizational point also arises directly from the relational, communal nature of the small membership church: The religious education program should not be compartmentalized but should be part of the overall life of the congregation. Since the small membership church functions in such a holistic, all-involving way, the careful separation of religious education from other elements of church life works against the nature of the group. Instead of designating separate times, places, and activities as "the education department," the religious educational life of the church can infiltrate and mesh with the whole fabric of community life.

---

26. Burt, *Activating Leadership,* pp. 48-52.

27. *Ministry Resources for Congregations with Small Membership* (Minneapolis: Augsburg, 1986), p. 57.

POSSIBILITIES FOR ORGANIZATION

There are several different possibilities for developing small member-ship church education that follow these four organizational guidelines, fit the flow of the congregation's life together, develop lay/member ownership and leadership, honors the character of the primary group, and break the bond of generic large- scale education design:

1. Cooperative Ministry with Other Churches

In some communities, a number of churches may join together to offer particular forms of programing. For example, five churches of different denominations may share a program of seasonally based education. Rather than Sunday school and CCD meeting weekly in each church, the five reg-ularly join forces for Advent, Lenten, and Pentecost series. The planning for the programs is done by a committee drawn from all five churches, the pastors of all five churches work with the program, and the events rotate through the different church buildings.

Or, Lakeside Presbyterian and Epiphany Episcopal may run their own Sunday schools, but work together each year to conduct Vacation Church School. The director attends one church, the assistant director attends the other, each class has teachers from both churches, and the entire commu-nity is invited to attend.

If the small membership church is indeed intrinsically tied to and central in its community, then such cooperative religious education ministries make sense. Cooperative ventures honor the specificity of the cultural community and increase the opportunity for the church to maintain a focal role in community life.

2. Intergenerational Religious Education

An option that builds on the communal nature of the small membership church might be Intergenerational Religious Education, in which:
- Two or more generations learn together
- Intentional, planned interaction between the generations occurs
- Generations share in planning and leading, as well as learning[28]

The intergenerational model is based on social analysis which shows "segregation, isolation, and insulation of persons [as the] prevailing con-

---

28. Ruth McDowell, ed., *Intergenerational Learning Experiences* (Nashville: Graded Press, 1980), p. 3.

ditions"[29] of our society. Amid this alienation, the faith community is essentially intergenerational in nature and seeks to teach a "faith lifestyle that creates wholeness in persons and the world."[30] In its very nature, the congregation is intergenerational in form and content. Intergenerational religious education draws on this nature of the church to develop a congregational model of religious education. Specific forms may range from weekly intergenerational CCD and Sunday school classes to special events, intergenerational camps, or a worship/education program for the entire congregation.[31]

Intergenerational religious education avoids the very practical small congregation problem of too few students for each class. Rather than dividing the congregation into separate age and interest groups, with perhaps only two persons in some classes, the intergenerational program brings everyone together for the time of learning and sharing. The members participate in planning their studies and share in leadership, as the whole congregation gathers each week.

An intergenerational model builds on the relational nature of the small membership church, treating the congregation directly as the family unit rather than breaking the membership into subgroups. The involvement of the entire church in planning, leading, and learning similarly strengthens the program's ties to the real lives, interests, concerns, practices, and traditions of the community.

3. Family Cluster Programs

An organizational alternative to Sunday school or CCD is based on the work of Virginia Satir, Herbert Otto, and Margaret Sawin: education in "family clusters."[32] While it too is intergenerational, the family cluster model goes beyond the intergenerational model; while it "encompasses an intergenerational approach because of the age variance in families . . . it also is based on the strength and emotional cohesion of the family as

---

29. James W. White, *Intergenerational Religious Education* (Birmingham, Ala.: Religious Education Press, 1988), p. 1.

30. Ibid., p. 15.

31. Ibid., pp. 40-58.

32. See Herbert A. Otto, *Marriage and Family Enrichment: New Perspectives and Programs* (Nashville: Abingdon, 1976); Virginia Satir, *Peoplemaking* (Palo Alto, Calif.: Science and Behavior Books, 1972); Margaret Sawin, *Family Enrichment with Family Clusters* (Valley Forge, Pa.: Judson Press, 1979).

a system."[33] The family cluster model is built on an understanding of the family as both the basic social unit of our lives and a microcosm for all other relational groups.[34] Twentieth-century changes in the patterns and lives of families have called forth a need to care for the family unit, support the entire family, and offer learning within the family.[35] In response, the family cluster model proposes a system of family groupings. Each cluster is a contract group composed of four to six different family units (singles, nuclear families, etc.) that meet regularly, over an extended time period, to share learning experiences that provide "mutual support, training in skills which facilitate the family living in relationship, and celebration of their life and beliefs together."[36] Rather than attending traditional age-specific CCD and Sunday school classes, persons belong to and learn in these family clusters, which may meet at different times of the week. Goals generally include:

> building an extended family group
> exploring each family's religious history
> biblical learning
> celebrating religious seasons and events as a family[37]

Family cluster education seems natural for the small congregation. Since one of the primary characteristics of the small membership church is its relational closeness, a model intended as "a way to build a genuine sense of closeness within a church community"[38] serves to reinforce the natural character of the church, rather than bearing no relationship or working against the nature of the primary group. Rather than isolating members in separate classes, family clusters build on the sense of belonging and intimacy. The cluster model also lends itself naturally to the cultural specificity of the small membership church. Issues, topics, means of celebrating, and schedules arise from the life and interests of the family cluster itself.

---

33. Sawin, *Family Enrichment*, p. 41.

34. As Virginia Satir says, "Families and societies are small and large versions of one another" (*Peoplemaking*, p. 290).

35. See Sawin, *Family Enrichment*, pp. 13-19.

36. Ibid., p. 27.

37. Mel Williams and Mary Ann Brittain, *Christian Education in Family Clusters* (Valley Forge, Pa.: Judson, 1982), p. 11.

38. Ibid.

4. Learning Center Classes

For those churches that value the age-specific teaching possible in "traditional" closely graded Sunday school and CCD classes, yet find that they do not have the number of students or teachers to operate a large-scale graded program, a learning center Sunday school or CCD may be possible. Popularized in the early 1970s as "open education," this model allows each person to "learn and work at their own individual initiative in activity areas. . . . They freely talk and move about."[39] Content is broken into manageable blocks, and different activities at each learning area or center involve the students in this content. The students move at their own pace, following instructions and using materials in each learning center.[40] These learning centers allow each individual to work at his or her own pace and give the teacher freedom to interact with individual learners, while accommodating fluctuating numbers of participants and making the most of the small church's space.

While a permanent learning center Sunday school or CCD may not seem as communally engaging as intergenerational or family cluster models, it can build on the personal interactions characteristic of the small congregation. Instead of highly organized and structured class time in which an entire group is focused on the teacher, learning centers allow individuals to move and engage at will, talking with one another, working together, pursuing their interests, and relating to the teacher individually. The relational nature is not as "whole group" as with some other models, but the freedom of movement and engagement builds on the familial nature of the small membership church while allowing different levels of learning to develop.

The cultural specificity of the small membership church is also well served by a learning center model, since flexibility is the hallmark of the approach. The particular content, style, number, and arrangement of the learning centers can be developed for the specifics of the church. For example, a series of learning centers on stewardship might be personalized for Maysville Church by developing a center on land use, a center on community responsibility, and a center on the biblical concept of shalom; on the other hand, Lakeside Church might pursue stewardship through a center on neighborhood self-reliance, a center on parenting, and a center on shalom. The unique characteristics and traditions of each congregation can

39. Ewald B. Nyquist and Gene R. Hawes, eds., *Open Education: A Sourcebook for Parents and Teachers* (New York: Bantam, 1972), p. 1.
40. See descriptions of the learning center approach for churches in Mary Duckert, *Open Education Goes to Church* (Philadelphia: Westminster, 1976).

be incorporated and emphasized in the specificity of learning centers.

There are obviously numerous other possibilities for organizing small membership church religious education programs, but these four models suggest the importance of building the religious education program around the character of the small congregation: relationship and culture conservation. Whether cooperative ministry, family clusters, intergenerational Sunday school, learning centers, weekday evening CCD, or some other model is enacted, the key is to design a religious education program that makes use of and strengthens the qualities of the small membership church as a primary group.

CONTENT AND RESOURCES FOR THE
SMALL MEMBERSHIP CHURCH

Even if a small membership church has found a model or style of organization that feels comfortable and strengthens its existence as a church, the issue of finding appropriate content and usable resources for that program still looms large. As mentioned earlier, most curriculum resources are designed as generically as possible, for use in as many settings as possible, but this generic nature opposes the closeness and specificity of the small congregation. The important thing is to develop a curriculum and find resource material that relates to and works with the small membership church. This means that wholesale purchase of the United Methodist Church's Invitation series or David C. Cook's curricula may not be the best course of action.

How does the small membership church begin to focus on content for its religious education program and find resources to use? Again, the church needs to begin with its story and image of itself, with its description of who and what this primary group is. The description of the church itself suggests content directions. Then, it seems that Carolyn Brown is correct, and one of three options (or some combination) can be pursued:[41]

Find appropriate curricula designed for small membership churches

There are some encouraging trends in the curriculum market. Resources for the four models discussed in the section on organizing the Sunday school or CCD are available. Some publishers and churches have developed curriculum resources specifically for small membership churches, which are available for purchase. For example, Seedlings Incorporated has developed

41. Carolyn Brown, *Developing Christian Education in the Smaller Church* (Nashville: Abingdon, 1982), pp. 45-46.

a four-year cycle of lesson materials especially for small church schools. The lesson plans are biblically based, self-contained, and provide for flexibility in teaching; they are designed for groups with as few as two students, *and* the materials are inexpensive. For some small congregations, selection of prepared small church resources like Seedlings may be the answer.

Piece together your own curriculum using resources from various sources

Brown calls this the cafeteria approach, in which the small membership church develops its own plan of study, describes the content and type of resources needed, and then selects individual resources from a variety of publishers and materials to piece together the whole program. For example, a church that has decided to conduct an intergenerational Sunday school or CCD, may decide to use *Celebrating Together* from Living the Good News as the starter piece each year, follow *Common Moments for Celebrating* for continuity, but intersperse Bible study sessions from *Generations Learning Together* throughout the year. In this case, the small membership church develops its own vision and plan, then selects individual resources to add up to the whole program.

Develop your own curriculum and resources

For some congregations, the most valuable process is simply to design and create their own resources, rather than using prepared materials. Developing your own resources allows the program to be tailored to the uniqueness of the particular small membership church. The task is not easy, but it can involve the whole congregation in ways purchased materials can never duplicate.[42]

Whichever option a small membership church chooses, the crucial point once again is: Build the content of Sunday school or CCD on the church's identity. The knowledge, traditions, and relationships that give the church its identity need to be the starting point for resource development and selection. Again, this is not to suggest that churches should only be about the business of reinforcing their own idiosyncratic beliefs and practices; the small membership church can be reformed, transformed, or transforming, but only as it honors its character as a primary group and builds on that character.

42. A good guide to developing your church's own curriculum resources is Stephen J. Brown and Carolyn Brown, *Do It Yourself Church School Curriculum* (Nashville: River House, 1980).

HELP FOR SMALL MEMBERSHIP CHURCHES

Although the key to small membership church religious education lies in the particularity of each small congregation, this does not mean each church is alone in its quest to develop solid religious education programs.

This chapter has focused on the starting points and principles for developing small membership church programs, but there are more specific sources and resources to help with enacting each step.

In the area of *human* resources, two growing trends deserve mention. First, I believe the development and use of Regional Resource Centers is an important, promising movement for small membership churches. Resource Centers may be run by the regional central office of a denomination to serve the churches of that denomination, or they may be run by seminaries to serve an area, or they may be ecumenical centers that are sponsored by all the area denominations. The specifics of organization and operation vary with the locale and focus, but the important point is that these centers offer access and help in understanding, organizing, and finding resources for religious education programs. Small membership churches, which do not have large libraries, budgets, and facilities, benefit the most from access to a resource center that helps them chart their course and find the right materials. It is worth the effort for each small membership church to investigate any resource center available.

Second, the development of regional or cluster religious educators bodes well for small membership church programs. Although this development may seem like a perpetuation of the generic professionalism of religious education, the guidance and help an educator can offer to the small membership church may be invaluable. The small membership church program is not *run* by the professional, who only works with the church to organize and resource the program the *church* will operate.

Chapter Five

Worship—Ministry within the Sacred Space

WILLIAM H. WILLIMON

INTRODUCTION

Robert Wilson, with whom I have studied the dynamics of small membership churches, enjoys telling the story of the day he was riding with a denominational central office administrator through a rural area in the Southeastern United States. They passed a little church, "Shady Grove Church," nestled in a clump of pine trees.

"It's sad," said the central office administrator, "but I had the job of closing that little church about two years ago."

"That is sad," commented Wilson. "It is such a beautiful little building in such a lovely setting."

"Yes," continued the administrator, "but it was no longer financially viable, a drain upon the denomination. They only had about fifteen or twenty members left. I led them through a process of closing the place down. Would you like to see the building?"

Wilson said that he would and they pulled off the road and into the front yard of the church. The central office administrator led Wilson up the steps of the church.

"Oh, no!" exclaimed the administrator. "Vandals have apparently broken into the building. They have knocked off the padlock which we put on the front door. Let's see if they have done any damage."

They entered the little church. The sanctuary, with rows of about eight pews, was immaculate. There were fresh flowers on the altar and the hymnboard indicated, not only that three hymns had been posted for the previous Sunday, but also that the offering amounted to $42.25. The administrator was stupefied.

With a bit of smile, Wilson commented, "I'd say that you did a poor job of closing this church."

It was obvious that the people of that small membership church had merely reoccupied their church and that Sunday worship had resumed. It takes more than a church bureaucrat to kill a small membership church. For nearly a century, worship had taken place within the sacred space called, "Shady Grove Church," and there was a good chance that it would take place there for another century—despite the best efforts of church officials to kill it.

One limitation of many church officials, like that central office church administrator in our story, is that they underestimate the amazing resilience of the small membership church — perhaps because many of these officials inadequately appreciate the way in which these small congregations are, for their loyal members, sacred space.

In this chapter we shall explore some of the ways in which the worship of the small membership church is at the center of the life of these congregations. We shall then suggest some of the ways in which these churches can claim their Sunday worship as a unique aspect of their life together and can improve their worship. The underlying assumption throughout this chapter is that for the small membership church, worship may be (as it always should have been for the church) the primary educational event. Pastors as religious educators must take care when they lead worship that they teach the things they really mean to teach.[1]

Like many in the church, when that administrator looked at a church like Shady Grove, he saw a congregation which had failed to meet his standards for a fully functioning, "viable" congregation. Translated, what this means is, Shady Grove could no longer raise the funds to support professional clergy or denominational liturgical programs. In our utilitarian, pragmatic environment, in a culture which places so much emphasis upon size

1. William H. Willimon and Robert L. Wilson, *Preaching and Worship in the Small Church* (Nashville: Abingdon, 1980).

and numbers, the small membership church is bound to appear to be an inadequate expression of the church.

My friend's experience at Shady Grove not only illustrates that small membership churches are incredibly resilient, but that part of the reason for their resilience is that their buildings, and the life which occurs there, make them sacred. A church is not a branch office for the denominational bureaucracy. A church is a sacred space. The prayers and praise of generations of worshipers hallow these buildings and imbue them with holiness.

In our book, *Preaching and Worship in the Small Church,* Robert Wilson and I noted how small membership churches stick with the basics — fellowship, worship, and service.[2] In a larger "full program church," a paid staff plans and directs activities on nearly every day of the week. But in the small membership church, Sunday is the main event. Everything important that happens in the small membership church, happens on Sunday. Sunday worship is for the small membership church, not one religious education activity among many, but the very core of the congregation's life together. Therefore, in turning our attention to Sunday worship in this chapter, we are examining one of the most important aspects of religious education life in the small membership church.

Small membership churches may not be able to fit some of our current images of ecclesiastical success; they may not be able to meet whatever organizational requirements may be placed upon them by their various denominations. They fail in their attempts to provide even the vaguest semblance of a full-program church. But there are no small churches that do not do a reasonably good job of celebrating Sunday morning. Small churches will recover their own unique sense of mission and will restore their positive self-image when they recover and boldly claim the fundamental significance of Sunday for their congregational life and for the life of the universal church. Many larger churches, with their "full programs," sometimes appear distracted, sidetracked from the essential purpose of the church with their preoccupation with so many activities and their neglect of the "one thing needful." The fulfillment of the basic theological purpose of the church never requires a crowd.

PROBLEMS AND POSSIBILITIES

This is not to imply that Sunday morning in a small membership church is without its problems and challenges. In fact, in conversations with pas-

___
2. Ibid.

tors of these churches, pastors frequently cite their dissatisfaction with Sunday morning worship as one of the least fulfilling aspects or their ministry in the small membership church. Inability to produce quality music is the most frequently cited liturgical issue in the small membership church. Many of our people are fond of watching the services of larger congregations of the slick productions of the electronic church on television. When compared to these slick, professionally led musical productions, the music of the small volunteer choir, accompanied by dear Mrs. Smith on the piano, seem amateurish and dull.

In fact, not only in music, but also in many other areas of the liturgy, when the rather vague criterion of "quality" is applied to the worship of the small membership church, the small membership church comes up short. A generation ago the only live music which most people heard, the only sermons which they heard or clergy whom they observed, were the music, the sermons, and the clergy of their own little church. Today, television had had an impact on all areas of our lives. Many people are accustomed to driving great distances in order to obtain "quality" medical care, ballet lessons for their children, and entertainment. These same people are now likely to drive great distances to worship, bypassing the small membership church in their quest for "quality."

Worship leaders within the small membership church should begin by recognizing that quality is an issue. This means that people today may have less tolerance for poorly prepared sermons, poorly performed music, and poorly led liturgy than they may have had in an earlier day. They may be less apt to excuse amateurish leadership. Therefore, those of us who plan and lead worship, and who are developing religious education leadership among the laity, must attempt to perfect our liturgical abilities and creatively to plan and lead Sunday morning worship within our churches.

The small membership church may also want to help its members redefine "quality" Christian worship. If Christian worship is primarily an impressive pageant, led by professional clergy and professional choirs, then the small membership church will always appear second-rate. Fortunately for the small membership church, the liturgical style of the large downtown church with its massive organ, large professionally styled choirs, and sermons by some famous "pulpit prince" are no longer the models for "quality" Christian worship. Recent liturgical trends stress the image of a family gathered around its common table rather than impressive pageantry. Liturgical innovation in the past decade has focused upon the worship of the early church, finding the liturgical practices, theology, and ritual of this period to be especially helpful in contemporary worship inno-

vation. In other words, the new services of Roman Catholics and most
Protestant mainline denominations take their cues from the period before
the church became big, successful, and impressive—before the church's
worship had a chance to become pompous, dramatic, and extravagant—before the Sunday service degenerated into a preacher/choir performance for a gathering of isolated, passive individuals. Directives for
contemporary worship renewal are coming from a church that was still a
family, gathered around a family table, eating a family meal.

This means that the small membership church, when it comes to worship renewal, is not backward and second-rate, rather, it can be at the forefront. With this in mind, let us examine some of the specific challenges
for worship planners as religious education leaders within the sacred space
of the small membership church.

Outmoded Space. The majority of us worship in churches which were
built a number of years ago. The sanctuary or worship space of these
churches was formed by the liturgical ideas of past generations. This
means that every time the church gathers to worship the space in which
it worships may be working against contemporary expectations for the
church. The pastor and congregation hope to achieve a high degree of
warmth and friendliness in their services. But the building forces worshipers to sit in rows or pews, staring at one another's backs, fixed, immobile, and detached. The pastor as religious educator hopes to lead the congregation into the practice of more frequent celebrations of the eucharist.
But the front of the sanctuary is arranged in a way that makes movement
very difficult.

Renewed understanding of baptism calls for a strong, visually unavoid-
able statement of the centrality of baptism. The baptistry is only a small,
insignificant piece of furniture set over to the side of the sanctuary. There
is widespread agreement that Word and Table belong together. The pulpit
dominates everything and the Table has been reduced to an insignificant
sideboard. New liturgics accent the full range of notes within scripture,
and celebrate the rich array of feelings within our faith. The predominant
colors of the sanctuary are dark, dull, and muted, somber and sad.

It is a comparatively simple matter to build a church from the ground
up. We can let current understandings of worship inform the construction
of the sacred space. But it takes a great deal more creativity to adapt inher-
ited space into a form which is more functional with renewed understanding of worship. For most of us, this is the challenge. Whatever is done,
must usually be done under the leadership of the pastor as religious educator. The pastor must exercise great patience and care, being careful to

bring the congregation along as any modifications in the present structure are discussed. As we said earlier, space within the small membership church tends to be sacred. There is usually great investment on the part of the people in the architectural status quo. They will insist that things be left as they are, unless they are convinced that architectural modification is in the best interest of the congregation. If the pastor wishes to change the space, the pastor must be sure not to ridicule the past arrangements which have served the church for many years. Careful, long-term religious education can be helpful. Once the congregation understands that current liturgical understandings may actually suit their liturgical life better than the outmoded spatial arrangements, they may be willing to consider modifications.

Perhaps the congregation can be encouraged to visit some new churches, study their use of interior space, and then evaluate their space. If there are craftsmen within the congregation or the local community, perhaps they could be drawn into plans for new furniture or altarware. A committee could put together a slide show of recent small church renovation projects.

Most of us do what we currently do because we cannot envision any other alternatives. In discussing alternatives, the pastor's approach need not be one of, "Here is the latest thing out of our denominational office and we need to get on board with the latest trend." Rather, the approach should be, "What do we love about this congregation when it gathers for worship?" Then, "How does our pres-ent building help or hinder the expression of our church at its best?"

In all these matters, the congregation must sense that the pastor does not wish to change them into some other congregation than the one they currently are. The pastor's desire as religious educator is to give them the space they need to worship as they desire. In many of our churches we must make do with older buildings where the architectural image conveyed is one of rigidity, stiffness, and colorless, dark inaccessibility. In what ways can the congregation's worship space reflect the friendliness, warmth, and familial atmosphere of the small congregation?

When small membership churches take their architectural cues from larger churches, they miss a single opportunity to embody their unique witness of the Christian faith. For instance, most small churches value the intimacy and simplicity of their life together. There is no need for elaborate organizational structure because everyone knows everyone else. Everyone knows who to call to get the job done. What a pity, if the small membership church builds itself a building in which everything is larger than human scale, the furniture is elaborate and "religious" looking, heavy, uncomfortable, and immobile. A church is a church not because it has a steeple on its roof or because its furniture is neo-Gothic. A church is a church because here God's people gather to pray and to work. The building ought to accent the human activity which occurs in the church rather than overwhelm it. In the small congregation, each person feels special and needed. Why should we continue to construct monumental buildings for our congregations which make individuals feel like lonely spectators lost in the audience rather than actors on stage with an important part to play in the Sunday service?[3]

Lack of Flexibility. Increasingly, congregations, large and small, are finding scarce resources to heat, renovate, or construct church buildings. Therefore, it is important that we get the maximum amount of use out of our buildings. Space which has multiple usage will be more valuable in accomplishing the mission of the church than space which is severely limited in its flexibility.

However, many small membership churches put great value in maintaining things as they are. This attitude carries over even to the way interior furnishing is used in the church. It is interesting how many churches go to great lengths to bolt down their pews, altar rails, communion tables, baptistries, etc. By so doing, they seem to be making a statement that things should never be moved and everything should stay in its place. In many rural small membership churches, people may have lived in the same community for generations. Their lack of mobility carries over into the way they construct their churches.

While it is important for our church buildings to provide us a sense of place and a feeling of stability, why do we furnish our churches in such an inflexible way? Generally, there is no good reason for bolting down pews, pulpits, and communion tables. At the most, usually all that is required to keep an altar rail in place are simple, easily removable bolts or dowels. The church's interior space ought to be adaptable for liturgical drama, dance, movies, as well as for religious education purposes other than traditional Sunday morning worship.

I remember visiting a small Roman Catholic church and school in the MidWest. During the week, their worship space served as the school's gymnasium. But on Sunday, the gymnasium could be quickly and easily converted into a contemporary, but nevertheless worshipful sanctuary. The

---

3. See James F. White, *Introduction to Christian Worship* (Nashville: Abingdon, 1980), chapter 3, for an excellent introduction to the theological and practical interplay of liturgy and architecture.

room had been designed so that a couple of lay-persons could arrive thirty minutes before the service and pull out all the necessary furniture and altar-ware from a closet and set it up. Everything was on rollers or hinged. Within thirty minutes, the church had colorful, contemporary, well-designed, but worshipful space.

With creativity and thought, small membership churches could be made more flexible and the church's meager financial resources could be put to better use. Nothing should be bolted down and fixed in place that does not absolutely need to be fixed in place. New materials and furnishings open up new possibilities for multiple usage of space.

A Small Congregation in a Large, Old Space. The small, rural church which has begun and stayed small throughout its life is one thing. The congregation which once was a large, prosperous church, but which has now declined into a small membership congregation in a big building is quite another matter. Morale is often a terrible problem within such parishes. Every time they gather, the empty Sunday school rooms, vacant pews, and mostly empty buildings conspire to depress and defeat them. The congregation's major resources go into heating and air conditioning the building and in keeping a roof over their heads. For many small membership churches, a small congregation in a large building is their major problem.

Creativity and bold thinking are required to overcome the problem. The pastor as religious educator ought to lead the congregation in a realistic assessment of their situation. Can the building be put to other uses during the week or on Sunday morning? In our inner cities, a number of older, mainline churches are sharing their buildings with other denominations or with new, rapidly growing ethnic churches.

Modifications in the worship space may also be necessary. One congregation of my acquaintance realized that the sanctuary was far too big for their needs. So they eliminated the back twenty pews in the congregation, using the space for a new baptistry which was put in the area where the pews had been removed. They also set up a display of the work of neighborhood artists within this space. The congregation thus ended up with seating which was adequate for their present congregation, a new baptismal and art area, without the depressing sight of empty pews.

Another inner-city congregation hired a lighting consultant to help them with their massive, but very dark, neo-Gothic building. The consultant advised eliminating most of the lighting throughout their sanctuary except for intense, bright lights over the front pews and the altar area. Through the creative use of lighting, worshipers who entered the building were encouraged to move down front toward the light. The lighting, in effect, carved out a warmer, more intimate worship area from the surrounding dark, inhospitable space.

The Problem of Music. In a recent survey among pastors of small membership churches, when asked to list some of the most frustrating and disappointing aspects of their work, a great majority listed problems with music. While music is not exactly a spatial issue, it is definitely at the center of Christian worship and should be considered in the design or renovation of the small membership church.

Music is a problem for the small membership church, in great part because of the advent of radio and television. A couple of generations ago people presumably never had the opportunity to hear music except when it was produced within their local church. Today, everyone has the opportunity to hear the greatest music in the world, produced by the world's finest musicians. So they listen to the Chicago Symphony on Saturday night and then come to their local small membership church on Sunday morning and are confronted by a well-meaning but often poorly trained and meagerly talented pianist who accompanies a half dozen rather poor, albeit well-meaning singers. Although people may appreciate the fellowship, the warmth, and the familial quality of the small membership church, the music of these churches can be quite a burden, particularly for the clergy who may have had more exposure to great religious music than the laity.

This is not a simply solved problem. For one thing, music is an extension of our deepest feelings. What is "good" church music to one person may not be so to another. There may be a great gap between the pastor's and the parish's definition of good church music.[4] Granted all of that, in what ways can music in a small membership church be improved?

Most musicians agree that small churches often attempt music which is outside of the range of their musicians. Most experts in church music advise the small, volunteer church choir to select music which they can sing well. For instance, most advise avoiding difficult anthems, including many of those which claim to be designed for the small church. Often the music and the theology of these pieces is not worth the effort. A better idea is for the small church choir to expose itself and the congregation to some

---

4. David B. Pass, *Music and the Church: A Theology of Church Music* (Nashville: Broadman, 1989) provides a good discussion of some of the basic criteria for "good" church music. See also Robert E. Webber, *Worship Old and New* (Grand Rapids, Mich.: Zondervan; 1982), chapter 14, for a discussion of church music which has relevance to the small church.

of the great hymns of the church. The church choir exists, not to take music away from the rest of us, but to lead the rest of us, to assist the rest of us to sing praise to God, not to perform a mini-concert for the congregation. The beauty of the small membership church is its high percentage of participation. Congregational participation should continue when we gather to worship and to sing. Within any denominational hymnal there are usually dozens of hymns which, though beautiful and meaningful, are unfamiliar to the congregation. The choir could assume more responsibility in leading the congregation in familiarizing itself with this material.

Also, many musicians advise that small membership churches would do better to utilize a good piano for accompaniment rather than a cheap electronic organ. There have been great technological advances in electronic organs, but many musicians still prefer the simple straightforward, quality sound of a good piano to that made by electronic instruments. However, matters of congregational taste should also be considered. For a number of years, military chaplains have utilized taped recordings of hymns sung by church choirs to be used to accompany their worship services in the field. Such tapes are also a possibility for the small membership church which is not fortunate enough to have musicians within the congregation. However, in my opinion much of the taped church music, such as the instrumental tapes which are available for purchase in Christian bookstores, is of poor musical and theological quality, more suitable for Sunday morning television entertainment than for the worship of the people of God.

Part of the problem with our assessment of music within the small church is our tendency to make larger churches and their music into the norm for all other churches. The history of Christian worship reveals that the choir has often been detrimental to liturgical music. The bombastic, hundred-voice choir has a way of robbing the congregation of its rightful place within church music. The music of worship becomes an artistic performance rather than a song of all God's people. The pastor as religious educator of the small membership church should remember that there is something worse than not having a choir on Sunday morning. That is to have a choir that forgets it is supposed to *aid* the congregation in singing and instead sings *for* the congregation. One of the most difficult concerns facing contemporary worship renewal is to give the music back to the people. In the small congregation the people may already bear the burden of music because they have had to do so. Each voice is needed. So the task of religious education is not to build a more impressive choir; it is to enable whatever music leaders the congregation may have to see themselves as leaders and enablers of the congregation, rather than as performers.

The pastor's own commitment to worship through music is important. If a pastor enters into congregational singing with enthusiasm, the congregation will often follow that lead. If the pastor enjoys learning and teaching new hymns, most congregations will respond. While some of the "good old hymns" may be questionable musically and theologically, care must be taken in removing them from a congregation's repertoire. Even some of the worst of the good old hymns may be better than no hymn at all, since in congregational singing participation and fervor often compensate for questionable theology. Unfortunately, contemporary hymnody has not given us many singable, theologically adequate hymns to take the place of the old favorites. Whenever new hymns are presented, it must never be in the spirit of, "Here is a hymn I like, and you ought to like it too!" Rather we should say, "Here is a hymn I think you will enjoy and one that will enrich your own experience of worship."

As in many other small membership church dilemmas, the key may be the pastor's own creativity in meeting and solving the problem, not on the basis of what some larger church may be doing, but on the basis of the unique expression of faith in that particular small membership church.

Poor Acoustics. The problem of music within the sacred space raises the general issue of acoustics. The congregation must be able to see and to hear its worship leaders and one another in order fully to participate in the liturgy. The congregation ought to have a clear line of sight to worship leaders. Lighting must be sufficient for people to read directions in the bulletins and to sing the hymns. These visual concerns are mentioned here because hearing is a visual as well as an acoustical issue. In any congregation, there are people who suffer from various degrees of auditory or visual impairment. Sadly, the architecture of many of our churches aggravates and accents their impairments. A person who has difficulty walking arrives at the church and is greeted by steps, great staircases, steps everywhere. Our desire to make our worship "high and lifted up" results in steps. What religious education message does this give to the person who has difficulty climbing steps?

Likewise, our dim and dark interiors accentuate even average visual disability. We bring people into a poorly illuminated space and then hand them a hymnal and a printed bulletin to read! Such practices are bad in any congregation, but particularly bad in the small membership church. Persons often choose small congregations over large congregations because they are attracted to the openness, intimacy, and small-scale warmth and familiarity of the small membership church. In these churches, everyone has a place. All ages mix and people are more likely to adjust themselves to the limitations and idiosyncrasies of individuals than in a larger congregation. Should not the way we form our sacred space do the same?

Some people have the erroneous notion that our places for worship should be carpeted and padded with the acoustical quality of a bedroom used for sleeping rather than a stage used for speaking and singing to God. Congregational singing and responsive reading are greatly hindered when the church's acoustics swallow up so much sound that everything is muted and dull. Particularly when the choir is small, it needs all the help it can get to project sound. There is nothing wrong with sounds and rustlings coming from the congregation. Such sound is a sign that the congregation is alive and moving rather than quiet and asleep! Carpeting in the sacred space should be kept to a minimum and pews need not have pads in them to be comfortable.

I once heard an acoustical consultant declare that "any architect who designs a room with seating anywhere under six hundred which required a public address system is incompetent." Perhaps he overstated the case, yet it does seem odd that in many smaller churches the room which is designed for a great deal of speaking and listening is so poorly designed that the preacher must resort to a public address system, and one which is often a poor system (i.e., inexpensive) at that. The pure, unaided, human voice is a beautiful thing. Our sacred space ought to be so designed that the voice can be heard, unaided, by all who worship in the small membership church.

SACRED SPACE

Lately is has become fashionable on the part of some Christian commentators to lament the preoccupation of the church with its buildings. Many times the church can be justly accused of having an "edifice complex" in its exaggerated concern and rather obscene expenditures for our buildings and places of worship. Some of these commentators call for the church to divest itself of its expensive buildings and become again a people who are pilgrims and exiles, not limiting ourselves to a place or building but rather giving ourselves over entirely to the ongoing mission of the church, unencumbered by buildings.

Talk of this sort usually fails to understand the peculiar nature of the Christian faith as well as our nature as human beings. While God may be ubiquitous, we human beings find it helpful to have a place, a space which is holy and points us, in a specific visible and tangible way, toward the gen-

eral presence of God among us. A religion of incarnation must have its feet
planted firmly on the ground. God always meets us, not just anywhere, but
somewhere. We do not just think about God or talk about God, we touch,
taste, see, and feel God among us through utterly human activities like
washing (baptism) and eating (the Lord's Supper). Ours is a sacramental
faith. It is no accident that the word "church" has come in our minds, not
only to refer to the active, believing congregation, but also to the place
where believers congregate.

We shape our buildings, but they also shape us. As we have noted here,
sometimes our buildings misshape us and hider religious education, the
church in its mission. Our church buildings also make a statement to the
larger world about our faith. When a person looks at our buildings, what
does that person think? Many might get the impression that the church is
a nostalgic place to walk down memory lane. Why is it that when we build
new churches we so often take our architectural cues from a bygone age
of church building? So, in evaluating the sacred space of the small membership church the congregation must not only ask itself, *What do we want
to do in this building?* but also, *What do we want to say through this building?* Is our building inviting, accessible, and part of the surrounding community? Will visitors feel welcomed? Will they know where to park and
which door to enter? Are times for our services publicly posted or does
one need to be an insider, one of us, before one knows the secret of when
we gather and how to get inside of our building?

One of the unattractive aspects of some small churches is their tendency
to close themselves off from new life, to become an isolated, tightly knit
enclave of people "just like us." The intimate, familial nature of the small
church is thus perverted into a hindrance rather than a help to its mission
as a Christian church.[5]

Today there is much needed emphasis on church growth. I once led a
small congregation through a process of evaluating its potential to evangelize and attract new members. In one exercise, the Evangelism Committee parked their cars in the parking lot of the church and entered the
building, imagining themselves to be first-time visitors. We quickly discovered that our building appeared to convey the impression that visitors
were unwelcomed. Parking was a problem. (Why not reserve spaces for
visitors?) Some of the doors were locked. ("Everyone here knows that the

---

5. The essays in Jackson W. Carroll, ed., *Small Churches Are Beautiful* (San
Francisco: Harper & Row, 1977) underscore this observation from a number of
perspectives.

left front door stays locked," said one of the members.) Where were the restrooms? Where is the infant nursery? We found that we had, quite unconsciously and without malice, formed our sacred space on the basis of the perspective of us insiders rather than on the basis of the needs of outsiders. What does our building "say" about who we are as a church, our religious education, and in what mission we are engaged?

Earlier, we challenged the notion of "quality" and admitted that the small membership church, in order to make an accurate assessment of itself and its worship, may need to redefine just what quality worship, music, and architecture are. However, this does not mean that quality is an unimportant issue. While the small membership church may have different expressions of beauty than the large church (i.e., a song offered by a quartet rather than a hundred-member choir), the small church still knows that beauty is important. From the first days of our faith believers ought to praise God through the beautiful products of human creativity. Sometimes small membership churches and the sacred space they inhabit may look second-rate and shabby because they are. Sincerity of desire or easy utility are substituted for skill and beauty. While God may be worshiped as faithfully in an ugly room as in a beautiful room, believers have a natural desire to (in the words of the old hymn), "Give of your best to the Master."

Beautiful is not necessarily synonymous with expensive. Sometimes, the best money a congregation can spend is in securing the outside, expert help of an interior designer or consultant. An outsider can often see things that we insiders cannot see because of our familiarity with the present arrangements. Sometimes congregations make poor decisions about interior arrangement or decoration because they are poorly informed. They decorate the church using the same criteria they use to decorate their living room at home. A good interior design consultant, a person who makes his or her living choosing colors, selecting fabric, judging visible effect, can often save a congregation needless expense.

For example, one small congregation of my acquaintance was greatly displeased with their old, outmoded, dark Akron-style sanctuary. It did not seem to fit their new, more joyful style of worship. They considered completely gutting their sanctuary and starting over. However, an interior design consultant showed them how, by stripping their pews and woodwork of the old, dark finish; through the judicious use of color and new fabric; they could unlock the beauty of their sanctuary and achieve the visual statement they wanted for a much less expense than starting over from scratch.

I remember a small membership church which wrestled with securing appropriate furnishings for its sanctuary. The furnishings committee looked through church catalogs. All the furniture looked the same—the boring, often unattractive, fake Gothic church furniture offered in church catalogs. They were determined to have something different, something special which reflected their special love for their new church.

A local cabinetmaker was hired, a man whose family was on the roll of the church, but who had not been active in many years. They told him the type of table they wanted for communion, the sort of baptistry they had in mind, for the embodiment of their new understandings of baptism. He drew up plans which were enthusiastically approved and, using local materials, fashioned simple, yet elegant furniture for the chancel area which made this congregation unique.

For no more money than they would have had to spend for the hackneyed and the trite, they had enlisted the God-given talents of someone to make something special for their sacred space.

In a way I take this episode as a sort of parable of the small membership church as it struggles with issues related to religious education and its sacred space. In uncovering and utilizing the unique talents of individuals, no church does it better than the small membership church. In celebrating the simple, straightforward beauty of the human voice, the human body, the human personality in praising and serving God, no church does it better than the small membership church. In what ways can we embody and display these small church gifts in the way we build and renovate our sacred space? This is the challenge before those who love the small membership church, who gather in this sacred space every Sunday to praise and serve God in, as the Bible says, "the beauty of God's holiness."

Chapter Six

Administration:
Equipping the Saints for
Religious Education Ministry

SUSANNE JOHNSON

Grace was given to each of us . . . to equip the saints for the work of ministry (Eph 4:7a).

INTRODUCTION

The pastor as religious educator of a small membership congregation is a preacher, teacher, pastor, liturgist, evangelist, counselor, visitor, servant. He or she is also an administrator. None of these functions of religious education ministry can be effectively done without attention to administration. Each includes an administrative dimension. To be a minister means one must administer.[1]

Unfortunately, many pastors resist administrative work. They are tempted to think of it as a series of distractions from the real stuff of ministry. To them, it is nothing but meetings, mailings, charts, reports, budgets,

---

1. Thomas C. Oden, *Pastoral Theology: Essentials of Ministry* (San Francisco: Harper & Row, 1983), p. 153.

busywork. Or administration is associated with crass business practices unrelated to the mission of the church. Yet, administration is a rich concept, needing to be explored in light of religious leadership and religious education as well as modern-day management theory.

In biblical terms, administration *is* ministry. The key Greek word for ministry, *diakonia,* can also be translated as administration (1 Cor 12:5; 2 Cor 9:12 KJV). Paul regarded *kubernesis* as one of the gifts of the Spirit (1 Cor 12:28). As Thomas Oden points out, *kubernesis* is variously translated as administrators, governors, organizers, managers, or those who have the power to guide.[2] As we shall later emphasize, to be an administrator is also to be a steward of all that God gives to the faith community to fulfill its calling in the world.

At the heart of the New Testament notion of ministry or *diakonia* is service: "Let the greatest among you become as the youngest, and the leader as one who serves. . . . I am among you as one who serves" (Lk 22:26-27). To be a minister, therefore, in terms of biblical images, is to be a servant. Ordained (representative) ministry is to be in the service of empowering lay (general) ministry. All religious education ministry is rooted in service and witness to God's work in the world to mend creation and to create a community of justice and peace. Administration is ministry that ultimately has to do with helping the faith community discern that work and decide how best to participate in it.

Administration thus has to do with leadership exercised in such a way as to equip every member of the faith community for the work of ministry. The scriptures affirm the work of the whole people of God. Especially in the New Testament was there no sharp distinction made between ordained persons and lay persons. Moreover, administrative leadership rests upon the unique nature of the faith community as distinct from any other sociological or organizational entity, though we must also understand its organizational side.

A Practical Theological Approach

An underlying assumption of this chapter is that administration, especially as it is associated with religious education, should be presented as a dimension of practical as distinguished from pastoral theology. This point holds important implications for the practice of ministry in the congregation. In order to make the point, it is necessary to supply a brief historical backdrop.

---

2. Ibid., p. 154.

By the nineteenth century, the fourfold differentiation of theology into biblical studies, church history, dogmatic theology, and practical theology, i.e., the theological encyclopedia, had become standardized. The focus of practical theology was gradually reduced to the study of clergy functions only, in contrast to the study of the work of the whole faith community and its leadership, both lay and ordained. This meant that practical theology become virtually synonymous with pastoral theology. Pastoral theology is the branch of theology that deals with the office and functions of the ordained clergy only![3] The practice of the priesthood of all believers became more obscured as the church's ministry became more clericalized and more professionalized.

Moreover, the theological grounding of clergy functions was dimmed, as both pastoral and practical theology were reduced to a potpourri of practical hints and helps on pastoral functions. These functions were meanwhile being developed into separate specialized academic disciplines. It became all the more difficult for seminary students to grasp a holistic, unified vision of ministry. Moreover, the disciplines tended to be more grounded in secular cognate disciplines than in specifically biblical-theological resources. For instance, after the turn of the century religious education gave most of its attention to developmental psychology and to the short-lived field of psychology of religion.

There is a contemporary effort to push beyond this negative legacy. Practical theology is emerging as a way to recover a cohesive center of ministry. To locate administration and religious education as dimensions of practical theology, therefore, leads us to several important statements.

1. Practical theology is moving away from its image as merely an umbrella term that covers disparate functions of ministry.[4] It is being approached in ways that can provide a holistic view of ministry, helping to overcome the negative fallout of hyperspecialization. The need is to find ways to develop functions to their fullest while also maintaining

---

3. Ibid., p. x.

4. Urban Holmes identifies eight ministerial functions which, with varying degrees of emphasis, have been present at all times in the life of the church in one form or another: preaching, teaching, prophesying, caring, evangelizing, ritualizing, administering, and discipline. The six functions of ministry listed by Seward Hiltner more closely represent present-day practice: worship and preaching, Christian education, pastoral care, evangelism and mission, social outreach, and church administration. Seward Hiltner, *Preface to Pastoral Theology* (Abingdon: Nashville, 1958), p. 28.

their unity in the practice of ministry.

There is valid reason why it is sometimes difficult to draw clear parameters around this or that function of ministry as actually practiced in the
local congregation. Acts of ministry arise out of and lead back to the same
faith vision (however it is articulated by various traditions). Their distinction may be overdrawn because of hyperspecialized treatment in theological education.

2. To recover practical theology is to recover theology as constitutive
to all the various functions of ministry.[5] In a very general sense, practical
theology contributes to and arises out of critical dialogue between multiple
conversation partners, including biblical, systematic, and historical theology, and the various human and social sciences, within explicit socio-
historical experiences and contexts of the church. Any one of these partners has potential to alter the other, so that no one of them is merely the
"errand boy" for the other. Practical theology at its heart is an interdisci-
plinary enterprise. Within this perspective, there is a great deal of freedom
to be informed by the best insights of secular cognate disciplines while not
losing grounding in one's own theological tradition.

3. As it is being reclaimed, practical theology emphasizes the work of
the whole people of God in specific, concrete communities of faith. Its
proper focus is the *ministry of the church*. Practical theology is a form of
inquiry that helps the church think about what it *has done, is doing,* and
ought to do.[6] It is a discipline concerned with helping ordinary believers
in ordinary communities deepen their practical everyday pursuit of the life
of faith. This involves the wisdom of practical knowing, that is, as an individual believer and as a community together, knowing what to do, how,
and why.

4. With the emphasis of practical theology on enabling the religious
education ministry of the laity, we can view administrative leadership as
a fluid function rather than a role that only the pastor fills. That is, admin-

---

5. In following Schubert Ogden's lead (Christian) theology can be defined as
critical inquiry into and critical reflection upon the Christian witness of faith. In
regard to the Christian witness, historical theology asks, "What has it been?" Systematic theology asks, "What is that witness as decisive for human existence
now?" Practical theology asks, "What should it become as decisive for human
existence?" See Schubert M. Ogden, "What Is Theology?" *The Perkins Journal*
26:2 (Winter 1973), pp. 5-8.

6. Howard Grimes, "What Is Practical Theology?" *Perkins Journal* 30 (Spring
1977), p. 36.

istrative leadership does not belong to the ordained clergy alone. Power and leadership and authority can be fluid and shared, depending upon the particular situation. Effective pastoral leadership can be measured by how well it enables the leadership of the laity to emerge. The style of leadership will vary from situation to situation and from context to context. depending upon discernment of need. Administrative leadership, therefore, is service-oriented; it is situational; it is shared.

Administrative Leadership Defined

Administration exists in the creative tension between the church as an organization, on the one hand, and as a faith community (a simple gathering or association of believers) on the other. To talk about administration is to talk about the church as an organization. It is to talk about the structural, institutional, or bureaucratic side of the faith community. According to Arthur Adams, an organization is a social system that overcomes individual limitations, that mobilizes energy for group goals, and that is characterized by specialized structures, processes, and traditions.[7] A faith community must be an "organized body" in order to carry out specific goals related to its sense of mission and ministry. James Anderson and Ezra Jones suggest that the phrase "ministry of the church" always includes four elements: organization, leadership, reason for being, and community.[8]

Administration is one important form of leadership, though in the church there are other important forms of leadership. Leadership can be defined as the process of influencing the activities of individuals and groups in order to help them accomplish their goals in a given situation.[9] Administration is leadership that directs its attention to the organizational side of the church. Administrative leadership has to do with all of the formal and informal, visible and invisible, organized, enduring elements, processes, and programs of the church.[10]

Anderson and Jones distinguish three types of leadership in the church: organizational, associational, and spiritual. They discuss the church as a

---

7. Arthur Merrihew Adams, *Effective Leadership for Today's Church* (Philadelphia: Westminster, 1978), p. 78.

8. James D. Anderson and Ezra Earl Jones, *The Management of Ministry* (San Francisco: Harper & Row, 1978), pp. 18 ff. It is important to note that in this context "community" refers to the total social context or the setting of organizations or institutions from which they draw their membership.

9. See Charles J. Keating, *The Leadership Book* (New York: Paulist 1978), p. 13.

10. Anderson and Jones, *Management of Ministry*, p. 47.

comingled association and bureaucracy (organization).[11] An association is a freely gathered group of persons who voluntarily associate on the basis of common goals. Members are equal in status to one another. In order to accomplish their goals, associations then form stratified structures or bureaucracies. They become organizations.

Organizational and associational leadership together comprise what we mean by administrative leadership. Administrative leadership is informed by traditional management theory. The traditional tasks of managerial leadership include a cycle of planning (setting goals); organizing (recruiting); staffing (training); directing (supervising); and controlling (evaluating).[12]

Because the church is a unique form of organization, it must have more than organizational goals. Many believers become frustrated when denominational officials seem to demand institutional and quantitive success only. Another form of leadership necessary for the church to be the community of faith is spiritual leadership. Spiritual direction is provided in the congregation through preaching, teaching, prayer and meditation, administration of the sacraments, counseling, and the many other means of initiating persons into the faith.

Two strong needs exist in the church today. One is for trained pastoral leadership in administrative areas. The other is for strong spiritual leadership. Revitalization of the church requires a sensitive, proper balance between these. Assisting the church to reflect on its faith commitments, its sense of mission, and its outreach to the community, requires a special blend of leadership. Discovery of the unique nature and purpose of the church is the necessary starting point for developing the leadership it needs. In his classic study, *The Purpose of the Church and its Ministry,* H. Richard Niebuhr contended that an important element missing in theological education was a holistic, unified concept of the church and its mission. For Niebuhr, this is the very element needed to pull together the disparate elements of seminary education.

Reflecting on the Community of Faith

The first and most important administrative task, therefore, is to help believers critically reflect on what it means to be a community of faith. Such self-understanding has everything to do with what a congregation decides to do or not do together in its worship, witness, and work.

Alvin Lindgren emphasizes the community of faith as "a community

11. Ibid., p. 50.
12. Ibid., p. 83.

of persons to whom and through whom God's love is revealed."[13] "See what love [God] has given us, that we should be called children of God; and so we are" (1 Jn 3:1). The faith community is where grace, forgiveness, and unconditional love are radicalized. But even in the faith community we inevitably fail one another, and so we must depend on a power greater than ourselves. It is none other than the power of God's love that redeems our mutual failures. Through such love within the community of faith, our existence is altered *toward* redemption. We show up precisely in order to find out *how* to live redemptively in the world.

Though agape, love is radicalized in the faith community, the love and fellowship we experience together is not the most decisive thing about us. Rather, it is the startling redefinition of the status of the stranger.[14] We are called to love not only people like us but to embrace those who are so utterly alien to us. Within the Realm of God, we are called to see all persons as our fellow creatures and fellow sufferers. The stranger is redefined as the neighbor. Hospitality to the stranger, according to John Koenig, is the key to the entire biblical witness.[15]

To provide hospitality is to create an environment where the stranger is welcomed and received as gift, blessing, and fellow creature, rather than treated as threat, intruder, or enemy. Moreover, biblical hospitality means *actively* to seek out the poor, the homeless, the hungry, the needy (Mt 25:31-46). To be sure, we are invited to enjoy intimate fellowship with one another within the faith community. But if we mistake coziness and like-mindedness for genuine hospitality to the stranger we forfeit our call, as the faith community, to be midwife to the community of God's justice and peace.

Within this understanding, the church's ministry in general is rooted in teaching and learning how, more faithfully, more wholeheartedly, more deliberately, to participate in God's creative and redemptive work in the world. Administration is leadership or ministry exercised to help the people of God, corporately and individually, discover and carry out specific ways of participating in God's mission. Through administration, we seek ways to encourage, to empower, and to equip lay persons themselves to do religious education ministry where they daily live and work. We also

---

13. Alvin J. Lindgren, *Foundations for Purposeful Church Administration* (Nashville: Abingdon, 1965), p. 42.

14. Edward Farley, *Ecclesial Man* (Philadelphia: Fortress, 1976), see chapter six.

15. John Koenig, *New Testament Hospitality: Partnership with Strangers as Promise and Mission* (Philadelphia: Fortress, 1985).

help the congregation as a whole decide how it best can serve God's reality in its unique cultural context.

Areas of Administrative Skill

As Thomas Oden points out, there are three basic areas of administrative concern in the local congregation. 1) *General administration*. This includes an overall cycle of goal-setting, planning, organizing, and evaluating the mission of the congregation. 2) *Educational administration*. This includes helping to enlist, train, and support teachers in the congregation as well as engaging in teaching the laity oneself. 3) *Business and financial administration*. This involves helping to mobilize and effectively manage the resources necessary for the church to carry out its ministry.[16]

Of course these areas overlap and intertwine and cannot be neatly separated. One specific task of this chapter is to explore administrative dimensions of religious education, particularly in regard to budgetary and financial considerations. As we shall explore below, *stewardship* is a notion that interconnects these dimensions of administrative leadership, while recognizing their distinctive areas of practice in the congregation.

Whatever the area of administration, according to Robert Katz there are three types of skills needed by an effective administrator: human, technical, and conceptual.[17] Effective leadership in religious education ministry first and foremost requires interpersonal skills in working with people. Church administration from the outset is concerned with people, not programs. Human beings and their needs are the "raw material" of administration. This fact is all the more true in small membership churches. Because of their very nature, small congregations are relationally oriented rather than program oriented. They specialize in warm, intimate, and intense relationships.

This means that small membership churches evaluate their pastor in human, relational terms rather than in programatic or functional terms. The people want to know the pastor as a "real person" who shares the common lot of humanity.

In meetings, therefore, the fellowship or relational agenda is as important, at times more important, than the task-oriented agenda. Meetings of

---

16. Oden, *Pastoral Theology,* p. 158.

17. Robert Katz, "Skills of an Effective Administrator," *Harvard Business Review* (January-February 1955), pp. 35-36, as quoted in Kathryn V. Feyereisen, A. John Fiorino, and Arlene T. Nowak, *Supervision and Curriculum Renewal: A Systems Approach* (New York: Appleton-Century-Crofts, 1970), p. 38.

the administrative board (council, session, vestry) are gatherings of the "family clan." They are important as settings where nurture, fellowship, and care are demonstrated, and so members need to be given generous time to account for one another's presence.

This human side of administration has traditionally been treated by way of attention to group dynamics, communications theory, conflict management, human relations training, leadership styles, and so forth. Insights are drawn from psychology, sociology, and other human, behavioral sciences.

There are a host of administrative processes that require interpersonal skills. These include, for instance, planning, goal setting, organizing, making decisions, building morale or motivating, communicating, initiating change, delegating authority, negotiating, resolving conflict, supervising, evaluating. All of these, though they involve technical know-how as well, require sensitivity in dealing with the feelings, commitments, values, and biases of other persons. True, many of the human skills are painfully acquired, but effective leadership is not possible without them. The intensity of small membership churches magnifies this reality all the more.

The technical skills of administrative leadership have to do with practical "how to" knowledge. In the small membership congregation this can range from running a filmstrip projector (or nowadays VCR equipment!) to fixing a leaky faucet to technical knowledge about church finance, such as insurance, wills, tax laws, and the like. Technical skills and interpersonal skills overlap, of course, in helping any group accomplish its goals. An excellent summary of skills drawn from contemporary management theory is found in Charles Keating', *The Leadership Book*.[18] Writing especially for church leaders, Keating treats such topics as task and relationship functions of leadership, ways of handling conflict, learning to "read" a group, modes of decision making, planning procedures, delegating authority, and time management, among many others.

The conceptual skills related to administrative leadership have to do, in part, with seeing the church as an organization as well as a faith community. It involves "the ability to see the organization as a whole; it includes recognizing how . . . the various functions of the organization depend on one another, and how changes in any one part affects all the others. Recognizing these relationships and perceiving the significant elements in any situation, the administrator should then be able to act in a way which advances the overall welfare of the total organization."[19]

---

18. Keating, *Leadership Book*.
19. Katz, "Skills of an Effective Administrator."

The church as organization is unique, yet it also holds much in common with other types of organizations. Effective administrative leadership requires as much insight into organizational dynamics as into individual personality dynamics.

There are many formal organizational theories. Organizational theory has to do with such notions as how an organization should be structured and managed, how people can best relate and groups best function, and what constitutes appropriate leadership. Components of organizational theory, whether the theory is explicitly or implicitly held, include the overall concept of the organization, preferred decision-making processes, the leader's function and style, strategies for conflict management, ways of relating to the environment, a view of human persons, patterns of human communications, and overall goals.

Every leader operates with at least an implicit theory-in-action. Many leaders are not entirely conscious of their preferred notions of leadership and organizational design. Effective leadership requires that our preferred yet often unconscious notions be brought to light and examined for their implications and impact. An excellent overview of five popular organizational theories is provided by Alvin Lindgren and Norman Shawchuck in *Management for Your Church*.[20]

In *Foundations for Purposeful Church Administration*, Lindgren calls attention to two basic approaches to church administration. The first is to focus on particular programs (usually "canned") for every area of the life of the church (the traditional six or eight functions of ministry, such as education, evangelism, outreach, etc.). Most books are written from this point of view, giving detailed prescriptions for setting up such programs. The second approach, which Lindgren advocates, is to explore a basic set of administrative principles (conceptual skills) that can be adapted in a broad range of church settings. Though the idea of a fixed program or "canned" approach to administration is rejected, this does not rule out learning from the experience of other congregations. The tested experience of other churches can be an important resource but only if flexibly adapted in light of the uniqueness of each setting.

As we noted above, in addition to the human, technical, and conceptual skills suggested by Katz, church administration requires skills ingredient to spiritual guidance of the congregation. Religious leadership involves a faith vision. Such a faith vision will influence virtually every aspect of

---

20. Alvin J. Lindgren and Norman Shawchuck, *Management for your Church* (Nashville: Abingdon, 1977).

the administrative enterprise. For instance, what the human, behavioral sciences tell us does not exhaust our understanding of what it means to be a human being. Our basic assumptions about human nature and our deeply held views of other humans beings make a great deal of administrative difference. This fact was demonstrated by Douglas McGregor in his work, *The Human Side of Enterprise*.[21] To belong to the Judeo-Christian tradition is to strive to see every human being and every aspect of human life together as being redeemed through God's creative and redemptive work in the world. The faith journey is a lifelong pilgrimage to orient our lives to this vision.

The fundamental conviction of our faith centers in our mutuality and our interrelatedness and, therefore, our call to provide hospitality to all that exists—precisely because it all has been created and given by God. However, our relatedness is broken and corrupted (the condition called sin). Yet we know that human sin is not the deepest reality of human existence. The deepest reality of our lives is that we are beings created in the image and likeness of God. We are sustained by a God of forgiveness and grace. We are conscious of ourselves as called to participate in all that God is and does to mend up our brokenness and to bind us together in a community of justice, peace, and radical equality.

As we can see, resources for religious administrative leadership involve not only managerial and organizational theory. Important resources include knowledge of God as witnessed to in the scriptures, as mediated through the Judeo-Christian tradition, as reflected upon by critical inquiry and reason, as realized in personal and corporate experience, and as appropriated through prayer and meditation, partaking of the sacraments, and the practice of other spiritual disciplines. So important is this fourth area of skill that Arthur Adams claims faith as the most important qualification of the administrative leader in the faith community.[22]

By and large, administrative skills (as well as spiritual guidance skills, we must note!) are among the least adequately covered subjects during the years of semi-nary training. For the most part they must be acquired—

---

21. Douglas McGregor, *The Human Side of Enterprise* (New York: McGraw-Hill, 1960). McGregor explored two sharply contrasting sets of assumptions about human nature, naming them as Theory X and Theory Y respectively. The former is a rather static, negative picture of human nature, while the latter is much more dynamic and positive. As McGregor demonstrated, these basic sets involve sharply different implications for administrative and managerial leadership.

22. Adams, *Effective Leadership*, p. 1.

sometimes painfully—through on-the-job training in the congregation and through workshops, reading, and other forms of continuing education. Unfortunately, seminary education may contribute to a subtle contempt of administrative matters—until the inevitable day one notices the absolute necessity of such training! In a series of studies conducted in the late 1950s Samuel Blizzard discovered that pastors felt that after seminary education they were least prepared for their role as organizer and administrator and wished for more training.[23]

Administration and Religious Education

As construed in this chapter, administration is one form of leadership through which the faith community is helped critically to reflect on its mission and ministry. In this fashion, there is a religious education dimension to administration, just as there is an administrative side to religious education. This reflects Seward Hiltner's contention that any function of ministry can be seen through the eyes of any other function.[24]

Set within a practical theological approach, there are key areas where the concerns of religious education and those of administration converge. 1) They both are concerned with helping the community of faith discover and realize itself as such. 2) They both seek to help the church reflect on how each area of ministry and each dimension of the church's life contributes to the overall mission of the church. 3) They both attempt to involve all members of the faith community in leadership and witness. The whole congregation is to be involved in making God's presence and love known.[25]

PLANNING FOR MINISTRY

Redemptive interpersonal relationships supply the key to administrative leadership in the community of faith. As Lindgren puts it, church administration must be God-centered and person-oriented. Fortunately, small membership churches seem naturally more committed to people than to programs. People, not programs, win people to God's mission in the world. Intentional planning is still needed, however, if the small membership church is to fulfill its mission and ministry in the world. Prioritizing and

23. See S. W. Blizzard, "The Minister's Dilemma," *Christian Century* 73:17 (April 25, 1956), pp. 508-510.

24. Hiltner, *Preface to Pastoral Theology.* Hiltner called this a "perspectival" approach to pastoral theology.

25. These three areas are inspired by Lindgren, *Foundations for Purposeful Church Administration,* see pp. 60-61.

planning goals for ministry is essential for strengthening religious education in the small church.

Planning should not totally fixate on easily measurable objectives, such as building a new church sign. Though by and large objectives should follow the SAM rule (specific, attainable by a specified date, and measurable), religious education ministry also includes goals more difficult to "operationalize."

Whatever planning model is adopted, it should be situated in the attempt to discern God's mission for one's own specific community of faith. Planning for religious education ministry is a process of discerning God's claim on this congregation in this time and place. For an excellent resource in planning that potentially can revitalize the small membership church see James Cushman, *Beyond Survival: Revitalizing the Small Church.*[26] Also see his chapter ten within this text.

If administrative leadership is to help the small membership church discover and fulfill its mission in the world, then much can be gained from paying attention to those churches that seem to have discovered how to be dynamic missional congregations. The point is not, as we made earlier, to adopt canned programs. Rather, it is to see what general principles can be learned from the experience of other local faith communities.

Recent research indicates that strong, missional churches, whether large or small in membership, plan their ministry by claiming their present strengths and building on them. Strengths are affirmed as gifts from God for the work of ministry in that specific church's time and place. It is God's presence in the life and mission of the congregation that compels it to move forward and receive the future that God has in store for it.[27]

Strong missional churches, according to the research of Kennon Callahan, tend to manifest the following seven *relational* characteristics.[28]

1. They have two to three specific, concrete missional objectives that involve strong groups in the congregation who are in mission with specific hurts, hungers, and hopes in the community.[29] Missional objectives are not

---

26. James Cushman, *Beyond Survival: Revitalizing the Small Church* (Parsons, W.V.: McClain, 1981).

27. Kennon L. Callahan, *Twelve Keys to an Effective Church: Strategic Planning for Mission* (San Francisco: Harper & Row, 1983), p. xxii.

28. Ibid. Callahan also lists five *functional* characteristics that are not included here.

29. "Concrete" refers to the actual delivery of effective help and hope in a competent, compassionate, and courageous manner. "Missional" refers to the fact that the church focuses both on individual and institutional hurts, hungers, and hopes. See Callahan, *Twelve Keys,* pp. 1-2.

artificially constructed in planning retreats, long-range committees, and board meetings. They emerge because a small number of people personally long for these hurts and hungers to be addressed.

2. They have a strong program of pastoral and lay visitation, on a weekly basis, with the unchurched, with newcomers, and with present members.

3. They have dynamic worship services, corporately planned, that are holistic in style and jointly led by the pastor and the laity.

4. They have significant relational groups in the congregation, where people may discover roots, place, and belonging.

5. They have strong leaders who are trained to be relational and caring with individuals rather than simply to fill functional slots.

6. They have streamlined structures and solid, participatory decision-making processes, planning on the basis of strengths, hopes, and clear objectives rather than needs and problems.

7. They have several competent programs and activities, realizing that people attract people more than programs do.

Administratively, these characteristics provide useful diagnostic and educational questions as the pastor and people in the small membership congregation begin to move through the planning process.

BUDGETING FOR MINISTRY

The congregation's plans for mission and ministry begin to be translated into actuality through the process of budgeting. Planning must precede budgeting, though examining the present budget is a useful way to raise issues concerning the church's sense of mission. In fact, perhaps the *easiest* place to begin reflecting on religious education ministry is with the current budget.

Scores of small membership church pastors say that they have no budget. Their church simply puts all financial matters into the hands of an experienced treasurer. Every congregation, however, must at least mentally or informally anticipate a list of expenditures for the year. That list is its budget. Every church has a budget; it just may not be a printed one.

A church budget can be put to a much greater use than it sometimes is. The budget is one of the most important (also one of the most neglected) educational tools at the pastor's disposal.[30] The budget can be read as a basic statement of the church's sense of mission. Sometimes it records

---

30. Lyle E. Schaller, "What Is a Budget?" in *Parish Planning* (Nashville: Abingdon, 1971), pp. 38-46.

hope for little more than mere institutional survival. A haphazardly planned budget probably means the church has resigned itself to the gap between what it now is and what it potentially can be. An intentionally planned budget, however, can become a significant means for revitalizing and for planning the total religious education ministry of the small membership church.

If a budget is carefully planned, it can provide one source of periodic evaluation throughout the year. The focus should be on religious education ministry performed rather than money spent, and so careful attention needs to be given to how the church treasurer makes the monthly financial report. For instance, the tone of the report, especially if given at the beginning of a meeting, can create a climate of undue pessimism and caution. But is can also be used to create an atmosphere of optimism, hope, and celebration of congregational ministry.

BUDGETING GUIDELINES

An informal survey among twenty-two pastors from Texas, Oklahoma, New Mexico, and Louisiana reveals a budgeting process commonly used in small membership congregations. In a hurried review, the finance committee goes over last year's budget, adding about five to ten percent for inflation, and that's that. "We don't spend a lot of time planning our budget," said the pastor of a twenty-five member church.[31]

Several congregations in the survey use no formal, printed budget at all. "I have not been successful in adopting a budget; the church tends to take care of expenses on their own, so to speak, without a budget," said one pastor. When asked if her church holds a pledge drive or stewardship campaign, another pastor responded, "No, (it's) not necessary; the money is always there." Similarly, another pastor said, "If any additional money is needed, just make an announcement of how much is needed and when, and it shows up." A rural pastor pointed out that his members "are opposed to stewardship campaigns and object to them. 'We're out of debt and we're grown enough to handle finances without being pesky,' they say."

These comments reflect typical attitudes of many small membership churches toward financial planning and budgeting. Small membership churches tend to manage their finances in a less systematic and more informal way than do larger churches. Churches with fewer than 150 members,

---

31. Where membership figures are mentioned in this section, they are based on the "average worship attendance" in the given congregation.

for instance, are much less likely than larger congregations to 1) conduct an annual every-member canvass or pledge drive, 2) place a major emphasis on stewardship, 3) use stewardship literature, 4) ask members to make a written financial commitment to that church, 5) adopt a year-round, printed budget.[32]

Time is running out for many of these attitudes and practices, though they may have in fact worked in the past. The chances are likely that they cannot sustain the financial viability of the small membership church into the future.

One of the most crucial dilemmas the small membership congregation faces is in the area of financing. Many small congregations barely squeak by in paying their pastor's salary, keeping up with apportionments or "church askings," and maintaining buildings and property, with very little left over for religious education ministry programs.

Because so many small congregations manage their finances from the hip pocket or out of the cash box, one of the most important tasks of the pastor as religious educator and as administrator lies in inspiring a vision of the importance of deliberate, systematic planning of the church budget. This will require pastors who can gracefully (and firmly!) respond to the inevitable resistance raised by the congregation when the pastor claims the importance of new approaches to financing. If small membership churches are to remain financially viable in an increasingly complex and inflationary economy, then traditional attitudes toward finances as well as traditional spending habits will finally have to change.

For example, as Manfred Holck explains, it appears that it generally may be better to borrow when inflation rates are high than to save in order to buy later.[33] That is, in an inflationary economy, a church may gain more from borrowing than from saving, as he technically demonstrates.[34] The real point is that coping with inflation will require many congregations to change long and deeply held financial habits and attitudes. Past approaches to church finance simply may not hold up any longer, especially for the small membership congregation.

---

32. Lyle E. Schaller, *The Small Church Is Different* (Nashville: Abingdon, 1982), pp. 67-68. Schaller suggests that the best source of data on attitudes toward giving is by Douglas W. Johnson, *North American Interchurch Study* (New York: National Council of Churches of Christ in the U.S.A., 1971), pp. 111-126.

33. Manfred Holck Jr., *Church Finance in a Complex Economy* (Nashville: Abingdon, 1983), p. 22.

34. Ibid., p. 23

One of the most helpful resources offering creative pointers in response to inflation is *Church Finance in a Complex Economy*.[35] Manfred Holck is a trained accountant as well as a pastor. He summarizes sixteen creative ways that congregations have used to offset the impact of inflation on their church's income. He also expands the number of creative options that members can use to give to the church, exploring ideas such as insurance policies, deferred giving, property gifts, stocks, and other giving incentives from the IRS.

Holck shows, moreover, how a congregation may increase the take-home pay of their pastor without necessarily increasing the cost to the church budget at a commensurate rate. Central office leaders are particularly responsible, he claims, for helping small membership congregations learn how more responsibly to develop a clergy compensation plan that meets the inflationary impact of the current consumer price index (CPI), while also taking advantage of special IRS tax breaks.

Constructing the Budget

The most common method of constructing the budget is called *line item budgeting*. This conventional format lists each anticipated expense item and then matches each line with the projected dollar amount. Typically, in small membership churches each member of the finance committee is given a copy of last year's budget, and then the committee simply goes down the page, looking at each item one by one, asking whether the figure should be raised, lowered, or kept the same. As one pastor put it, "We begin with the necessities (utilities, insurance, salaries, apportionments) and see what we can handle past that."

This process, as typically practiced, is governed by precedent and tradition more than by attempts to discern God's plan for the congregation. Once a budget is adopted, it is exceedingly difficult to add a certain line item, and even more difficult to drop an existing item! Moreover, by beginning with the "necessities," the focus is kept entirely on institutional maintenance and survival.

In the survey mentioned above, two of the twenty-two congregations follow an entirely different budgeting method. In their approach, the congregation "wipes the slate clean." First they prioritize and plan their ministries for the year. Then they figure out how much they can allocate for each item. The previous budget is only one tool among others in creating the new budget. This method is a useful way to break the cycle of prece-

---

35. Ibid.

dent and tradition. It is basically the method called *zero budgeting*.

Instead of beginning with last year's figures for each line item, begin with a zero beside each item. Assume that the zero is appropriate *unless* some other dollar amount can be justified. Ask whether this or that proposed item is the best way possible to help the congregation realize its mission. It is not uncommon for some items to be dropped outright, for some to be raised, and for some new program items to get included. (When using the line item approach, zero budgeting would apply only to program items and not, of course, to fixed costs and building debts.)[36]

In contrast to the conventional line item budget, another method of preparing the annual budget is growing in popularity. It is known as *program budgeting*. A program budget shifts the emphasis from money spent to ministry performed. It does this by dividing all the activities of the congregation into three or four categories of ministry and then allocating the total budget expenditures among those categories. It is best to begin with a few broad categories and then perhaps refine those in subsequent years. In this way, a congregation can readily see how its money is spent in the various ministries and activities of the church.

The following are examples of possible categories to begin with.[37]

worship	nurture and membership care
education/nurture	evangelism
fellowship	outreach/mission
ministry to members	preparing for mission
ministry to this community	doing mission
ministry beyond this community	enabling others for mission

In the beginning, it takes a little effort and creativity to decide how best to distribute items from the line item budget among the categories chosen for the program budget. When the program budget is adopted, the line item budget should always be used in addition to it.

In an example drawn from above, *nurture and membership care* refer to ministry with the church's present membership. Most of the cost of maintaining the church facilities would be designated in this category, as well as costs for CCD or Sunday school supplies, worship materials, the women and men's fellowship organizations, youth work, pastoral care, and other similar ministry.

Evangelism includes all the efforts made by the pastor and the people to reach the unchurched in the community. This includes the costs of witnessing to the unchurched and assimilating new members into the church.

Outreach/mission includes concerns related to the church's witness in both the immediate community and the wider world. A major item is the denominational apportionments or "church askings," as well as contributions to the work of the larger church, such as seminaries, church-related colleges, mission schools, children's homes, and so forth. Included also is the church's involvement in its own community, such as the local council of churches, food or clothing banks, and the like.

In some instances, a single budget item will be apportioned among all the categories, particularly the pastor's salary. The figures may not be absolutely precise in the way they are allocated. Nevertheless, they still provide a useful picture of how a congregation uses its financial resources.

The budget worksheet on the following page illustrates the concept of reallocation that is key to program budgeting. Total *administrative* costs must be distributed across the program categories chosen and the same for *building and grounds* costs. There are various procedures for this. A "price tag" must be assigned to the percentage of the pastor's time spent in each of the categories, including administration. The administrative supplies used by each must be approximated. The building and grounds costs could be figured according to the percentage of floor space used by each program, or on any other basis that seems appropriate. The worksheet illustrates the difference between the line item budget and the program budget.

The program budget is a creative index to the priorities of a congregation and to its spiritual health. What might it mean, for instance, if a congregation were spending 90 percent of its resources on itself, and only the remaining 10 percent on evangelism and mission/outreach?

It is useful for every congregation to know how much it is spending on (building) maintenance versus how much on religious education ministry. Most Protestant congregations spend between 15 and 35 percent of their income on the operation and maintenance of their facilities.[38] For most small congregations, however, the minister's salary is the largest budget item. When a congregation allocates more than 40 percent of its total budget for ministerial compensation, according to Lyle Schaller, it probably means that other program costs, or missions, or building maintenance are underfinanced.[39]

A program budget can potentially evoke questions as to why the percentage for one category is so much lower (or higher) than another category. It can also provide a vehicle for dialogue about the church's ministry

---

38. Schaller, *Parish Planning,* p. 52.
39. Schaller, *The Small Church Is Different,* p. 85.

PROGRAM BUDGETING

EXPENSE ITEM	TOTAL	BUILDING AND GROUNDS	ADMINISTRATION	NURTURE AND MEMBERSHIP CARE	EVANGELISM	OUTREACH AND MISSION
PASTOR'S SALARY	15,000		2,000	10,000	1,500	1,500
PASTOR'S BENEFITS	3,000		400	2,000	300	300
MAINTENANCE SALARY	9,000	9,000				
MAINTENANCE BENEFITS	1,500	1,500				
CLERICAL SALARY	6,000		2,000	3,000	500	500
CLERICAL BENEFITS	1,000		250	600	75	75
TELEPHONE	900		200	400	250	50
TRAVEL	2,000	300	300	800	450	150
OFFICE SUPPIES	1,500		500	500	300	200
DUPLICATING	500		100	300	50	50
POSTAGE	500		100	275	100	25
LITERATURE	2,000			1,500	350	150
SPECIAL EVENTS	500			300	100	100
UTILITIES	5,000	5,000				
PROPERTY INSURANCE	1,500	1,500				
BUILDING MAINTENANCE	2,500	2,500				
GROUNDS MAINTENANCE	1,500	1,500				
APPORTIONMENTS	4,000					
SUBTOTAL	57,900	21,300	5,850	19,675	3,975	7,100
REALLOCATE BUILDING AND GROUNDS	-0-	-21,300	3,000	15,000	1,300	2,000
SUBTOTAL	57,900	-0-	8,850	34,675	5,275	9,100
REALLOCATE ADMIN	-0-	-0-	-8,850	2,950	2,950	2,950
TOTAL	57,900	-0-	-0-	37,625	8,225	12,050

LINE ITEM BUDGET   INDIRECT COSTS REALLOCATION   PROGRAM BUDGET

and mission, making it more feasible for a small membership church to conduct an effective every-member canvass. Rather than going to homes to ask for money, callers can discuss the church's sense of religious education ministry instead. A stewardship campaign can be an important opportunity for spiritual growth, if conducted in a way that fits the ethos and style of the small congregation.

Whatever budgeting method is used, the key is for the pastor and people to keep the process focused on dialogue about religious education ministry. A carefully and prayerfully planned budget is an excellent way for the pastor to invite the congregation beyond a survival mentality into a renewed sense of doing God's mission.

STEWARDSHIP EDUCATION IN THE SMALL MEMBERSHIP CHURCH

It is commonly observed that "canned" stewardship programs do not tend to work well in small membership congregations. For instance, whereas the Every Member Response (EMR) or Every Member Canvass (EMC) is a popular strategy to raise the budget in medium to larger congregations, many small membership churches shy away from it. Unfortunately, this often owes to the congregation having previously made a poor attempt at the EMR and ending up with disastrous results. It too easily comes off as the church going begging for money, or being "pesky." Yet better-planned programs can be a tangible way for the congregation to go about the indispensable task of stewardship education. Stewardship is a much larger notion than finances, pledge cards, offering envelopes, and the like. Stewardship should be seen as a central way of life for the individual believer as well as the entire faith community.

The church simply cannot shy away from talking about finances. Yet talk about finances, tithing, pledging, budgets, and the like, should always take place within the context of comprehensive, year-round stewardship education. Though the responsible use of money is an important dimension of it, stewardship implies much more than use of financial resources.

The New Testament Greek word that we translate as "stewardship" is *oikonomia. Oikonomia* is a combination of two words: *oikos,* meaning "house" and *nemein,* meaning "to divide or distribute."[40] The most direct reference of *oikonomia* is to the administration or management of a house-

---

40. Richard B. Cunningham, *Creative Stewardship* (Nashville: Abingdon, 1979).

SUSANNE JOHNSON

hold. The *oikonomos,* or "steward," was entrusted with managing the business affairs of a household.[41] As Richard Cunningham points out, *oikonomos* (steward) is used only twenty times in the New Testament, and *oikonomia* (stewardship) only seven times. Yet they both belong to a family of Greek words that, when taken together, provide insights into the nature of stewardship, especially construed as a whole way of life.

Letty Russell suggests that the larger biblical notion of *oikonomia* refers to God's householding of the whole earth or whole created order. The Greek words *oikos* and *oikia* (house, household) later became key metaphors for the church, imaging it as the household of faith.[42] Russell reminds us, however, that in the New Testament the household image refers, not only to the church, but also to the eschatological reality of the new creation. Only in certain later New Testament writings did the eschatological metaphor dissolve into an ecclesial metaphor, such as in 1 Peter. The church as the household of faith is called to witness to God's housekeeping in all of creation. The faith community is where believers are helped to discern and to participate in God's housekeeping plan, which is to "mend creation."[43]

Cunningham also points out how the New Testament uses stewardship to refer to God's creative and redemptive work in all creation.[44] Believers are appointed to participate with God in this work. We have a share in who God is and what God does! Because we are God's own creatures, we are called into mutuality with all that God creates and loves. In this sense, then, stewardship becomes a whole way of life, for it is the way we actually participate in God's householding.

The life of faith, therefore, implies stewardship as a whole way of life. Stewardship requires the responsible use of time; of personal gifts (such as intellectual, physical, or spiritual gifts); of personal relationships. It includes how we relate to various orders within society and within the whole created order, such as marriage and family, labor, government, the natural world. Finally, stewardship includes our relationship to the world of material things.[45] This is important because money and the possessions

41. Ibid.

42. Ibid., p. 37.

43. Ibid., p. 71. Russell says she first heard this eschatological hope expressed by Krister Stendahl. He once said that theology is worrying about what God worries about each morning: the mending of creation!

44. Cunningham, *Creative Stewardship,* p. 23.

45. These categories are suggestive, not exhaustive. See Cunningham, ibid., especially chapters four and five.

it buys are an extension of one's very self.

Unfortunately, stewardship education in the church largely has been reduced to a matter of giving money to the church. As we have seen, this is too restricted an understanding. One could give generously to the church yet in fact be a very poor steward. The use of money and how it is spent and how it is given must be seen as one dimension of a larger way of life. This does not rule out the fact that the use of money is a primary clue to one's sense of stewardship.

As we can see, stewardship is a notion that is key both to religious education and to church administration. For the faith community to fulfill its mission and ministry, it requires believers who are willing to be stewards of everything that they *are* personally and spiritually, and everything that they *have* materially and financially. Matters of finance and budget take on a different significance when seen in the larger setting of stewardship education. Talk about the disposition of one's money and material resources is not simply a way to raise the budget. It is one among other ways to help believers learn how to go about the business of becoming responsible stewards.

In this respect the pastor must at least become informed enough to be able to set up workshops or classes on technical matters related to financial giving, such as wills, life insurance policies, income trusts, appreciated property gifts, and the like.[46]

Though the EMR is probably a good idea for the small membership church to reconsider and to make use of, it cannot be reduced to a several-week financial blitz once a year and still be an effective means of stewardship education in its deepest sense. Specific programs for stewardship education in the small member church and for raising the budget should be locally designed, not "canned." Such programs need to build on the personal, relational character of the small membership church and to help members see specific, tangible needs (to which they are typically eager to respond).

SUMMARY AND CONCLUSIONS

Over one-half the Protestant churches on this continent are considered small membership churches. Given their ubiquity, it is ironic, as Carl Dud-

---

46. In this regard, helpful resources are Cunningham, *Creative Stewardship;* Holck, *Church Finance;* and Douglas W. Johnson, *Finance in Your Church* (Nashville: Abingdon, 1986).

ley has noted, that the small congregation ever needed to be rediscovered by the denominations. But that is exactly what is happening. A new perception of the small membership church is emerging. Pastors of small membership churches can feel encouraged about the beginning shift in denominational attitudes.

The time is ripe for small congregations to change their self-image. As a natural result of their size, unique opportunities are open to small membership churches. Modern people are searching not for programs but for people—people with whom to be significantly involved. According to Kennon Callahan, strong congregations share a strong theology of community. They provide opportunities for intense caring and sharing. Small membership churches are experts at this!

For too long the small membership church tried to copy the ministry of larger congregations. Instead of delighting in the values of intergenerational education, it clamored to have closely graded Sunday school classes and then felt second-rate when it could not. Instead of getting mileage out of its entire youth group fitting into one van (or car!) to go to a football game or youth rally, it sought to join with other groups so it could fill a whole bus. It dutifully sought to meet the required organizational structure of its denomination whether it made the best administrative sense or not.

The small congregation can and is reversing this trend. The small membership church can affirm that its sense of mission and ministry is not of secondary importance to that of its central offices. Congregations can view the general boards and agencies as important resources to their own ongoing witness and work, rather than vice versa.

Insofar as possible, small membership churches need to develop an organizational structure and administrative style that fits their self-identity as a warm, close-knit caring family. They can decide not to function as a "local branch office" of the general boards and agencies, but rather can decide, on the basis of local needs and concerns, what is a faithful witness. Within the general guidelines of their own denominational policy, small congregations are entitled to a structure appropriate to their unique size, setting, and sense of ministry. This is all the more important for ethnic minority churches.

Small membership churches can also refuse to be intimidated by annual statistical report forms issued by their denomination. Often such forms are so intricate and complex that they leave small membership church leaders confused and intimidated. Such report forms often create the impression that success means a highly complex organizational structure, a long list of programs, a steady increase in new members, a record of increased financial resources, and a roster of new Sunday school and CCD classes. As long as success is reduced to statistics on a page, small congregations will stay trapped in an aura of despair and defeat.

Both the pastor and the people in small membership churches need to become more proactive within their central office on behalf of their unique needs. Much initiative can be exercised by members of small congregations to rally attention and support to the small membership church. Persons concerned for small congregations can form coalitions in order to insure their participation and their power in central office policies and plans.

Small membership churches will be revitalized as they claim the freedom themselves to discern the direction of religious education ministry in which God is calling them. The small membership church has a unique opportunity to equip the saints for religious education ministry!

Chapter Seven

Lay Religious Education Leadership and the Planning Process: Volunteers

BOB I. JOHNSON

INTRODUCTION

One of the active members of a small membership church greeted the new pastor by saying, "We'll do anything you can get us to do."[1] Now, that is putting it plainly. That comment is judgment on current church life which sees the pastor as having to do or to get done what needs doing in the church's ministry. The small parish is especially vulnerable to the implications of the greeting the pastor received.

The parishioner's comment suggests something about how things work in any organization; the small congregation is no exception. The pastor as religious educator is viewed as the leader who is supposed to initiate and implement plans. In a more optimistic interpretation of, "Pastor, we'll do anything you can get us to do," laity confess a willingness to work with the pastor in meaningful ministry. Lay religious education leaders emerge when laity feel they are being led to the high road of

---

1. Many pastors have had similar experiences. This is based on the experience of Bill Alexander, one of my students at Midwestern Baptist Theological Seminary.

being the people of God in some meaningful way.

This chapter is divided into two sections: mobilizing lay religious education leaders and using the planning process. The chapter offers help for the pastor of a small membership church in leading the congregation to be the people of God.

The author's approach begins with simple, less threatening ways to develop lay religious education leaders in purposeful planning for ministry. The suggestions move from beginning steps to more involved ones. Never, in this author's view, will any of the suggestions be beyond the use of at least some, if not most, small membership churches.

Mobilizing lay religious education leaders includes five basic steps: finding, securing, developing, supporting, and releasing leaders. In the small membership church lay religious education leaders include teachers, the CCD director, and other persons who serve in leadership roles, such as chairpersons of education and governing boards. The critical question of each congregation is, "Who are the religious education leaders?" Donald Griggs and Judy McKay Walther suggest that the roles of educational leaders can be examined two ways. The first approach is through questions: Who designs the religious education program, who invites religious education leaders to serve, who takes care of the leaders, who takes care of the rooms, who keeps the records and pays the bills, who orders the curriculum and supplies, and who leads the opening exercises? The second approach in identifying who the religious education leaders are names the following: the church board, the religious education committee, the pastor/priest, the church school superintendent, the teachers, and other leaders, such as persons in music, recreation, or crafts.[2] For each parish the answer may vary. The assumption of this chapter is that the pastor serves in the role of primary religious educator and that the pastor has prime responsibility to mobilize lay religious education leaders in the overall mission of the parish. A pastor decides what is appropriate for use in a given situation. Warning: Do not underestimate an informed, committed laity who have confidence in the integrity and intent of a clergy who is a servant leader.

The church needs to develop lay religious education leaders. The stronger the role of lay religious leaders, the greater the health and strength of a parish.[3] Clergy must hear the profundity and challenge through the

2. Donald L. Griggs and Judy McKay Walther, *Christian Education in the Small Church* (Valley Forge, Pa.: Judson, 1988), pp. 39-47.

3. Joyce Sasse, "The Rural Church in Action: A Handbook for Members," *Action Information* 15:6 (Washington, D.C.: The Alban Institute, 1989).

simple, earthy words of the greeting to the new pastor. It casts a mantle
of leadership on one, ready or not.

Leadership needed for one congregation may not be appropriate for
another parish. Knowing how to define leadership appropriate to each context is critical. William Phillips suggests that congregations express themselves and their leadership needs in four categories: passive and uninter-
ested in much more than "attendance" at worship and infrequent meetings;
active and willing to explore new possibilities but unclear in how to proceed; enthusiastic and clear in their sense of mission and purpose; experienced and engaged in creative ministry and plan to continue their previous practice of activities.[4] Each of these four congregations needs the
leadership of the pastor/priest, and each church has lay religious education
leaders who are providing leadership. The question is, "What leadership
exists and what leadership is appropriate?" Phillips suggests that churches
have leaders who are equipped with the eight leadership gifts needed in
ministry: visionary, inspiring, engager, interpreter, enabler, teacher, sup-
porter, and monitor.[5]

Leadership according to Steve Burt includes three basic dimensions:
leadership is relational, inspirational, and transformational.[6] A critical factor in examining appropriate leadership is observing the effect of knowing
who should lead and when. Being aware of the timing of appropriate leadership can unleash and free others to lead. Leadership is not about controlling others but about releasing and empowering lay religious education
leaders.

Tom Peters identifies three leadership tools for establishing direction:
The leader develops and encourages initiative from others to elaborate and
perfect an inspiring vision, lives the vision via the calendar (what you do
and do not spend time on), and practices implementing the vision.[7] Leadership means being able to articulate a vision appropriate to the context.
Perhaps the most delicate dimension is the leader's ability to encourage
others to shape and to incorporate their ideas into the vision. The real test
of leadership is often the willingness to let go so that ownership of the
vision can occur. More than three hundred definitions of leadership exist.

4. William J. Phillips, "In Search of a Leader," *Action Information* 16:3 (Washington, D.C.: The Alban Institute, 1988), pp. 1-6.

5. Ibid.

6. Steve Burt, *Activating Leadership in the Small Church* (Valley Forge, Pa.:
Judson, 1988), pp. 35-42.

7. Tom Peters, *Thriving on Chaos* (New York: Knopf, 1988), pp. 388-389.

One definition of effective leadership in terms of the pastor is: *Religious education leadership is self-giving service which enables the church to be people of God who reach appropriate goals while also meeting the needs for individual growth and ministry development.* An obvious part of this definition is a priority to develop others for ministry. Religious education is an effort of mutual ministry where clergy/priest and laity share ministry of religious education. The basic intent of shared ministry is to stress in the small membership church that the work of ministry is not reserved for professional pastors or priests but rather ministry is the function of lay persons who are willing to be the religious education leaders for the congregation and for the community. Shared ministry often means letting go of the central leadership role for clergy and encouraging new leadership roles for laity.[8] How does a leader begin to share ministry? Griggs and Walther identify five specific elements in the process of leadership development: Clarify what is expected of religious education leaders, invite persons to serve, assess persons' needs, equip leaders with skills necessary to be effective, and provide spiritual direction.[9] This role of empowering existing religious education leaders and calling for new leaders is one of the most rewarding privileges for the pastor of a small membership church. The pastor/priest has the opportunity to impact a very high percentage of parishioners directly and personally.

Pastors work with volunteers. Developing and encouraging existing and new religious education volunteer leaders necessitates a leader who is patient and deliberate as well as persuasive and enabling. Such a leader:

1. Knows exactly what needs to be accomplished.
2. Puts self in the other person's shoes.
3. Is willing to take risks (knows that success is never certain and defeat is never final).
4. Makes objectives decent and open.
5. Knows the difference between leading and pushing.
6. Views every person as one for whom Christ died.
7. Is willing to share power.[10]

---

8. Richard E. Colby and Charity Waymouth ,"Shared Ministry: Lay Leadership Development," in *Small Churches Are Beautiful* (New York: Harper & Row, 1977), pp. 94-105.

9. Griggs, and Walther, *Christian Education in the Small Church*, pp. 49-50.

10. Based on an interview with pastor George Webb, Brown Road Baptist Church, Mesa, Arizona.

The pastor as religious educator is not the producer, director, or the scapegoat for what does not happen. Neither are lay religious education leaders assistants to the pastor to help do "his"/"her" work. God has gifted persons to do the total ministry of the church. The entire church membership participates in ministry through its service to God and humankind. Religious education ministry is not the privileged activity of a select elite but the serious responsibility of all. Each member of the church is specially gifted to function in ministry of religious education according to that endowment.

MOBILIZING LAY RELIGIOUS EDUCATION LEADERS

Finding Lay Leaders

At least on our better days we agree that ministry belongs to the whole people of God. But how do we get folk in the right places to be effective lay religious education leaders and partners in ministry. Between 30 and 65 percent of the members in a typical congregation are willing to serve as leaders and workers if they know they are needed, challenged, assigned meaningful tasks, and are appreciated. Actually, the smaller the congregation the larger the number of persons willing to serve.[11]

Perhaps it would be useful to clarify what volunteers are *not*. Volunteers are not: professional staff, full-time workers, cannot be taken for granted, are not paid, and are not bound to a job for long periods of time.[12]

So, where and how can a pastor find and mobilize lay religious education leaders? In a small membership church leaders are not "lost" in the masses. Everyone knows their names. They are seen often. Although it might help at times, one is not going to find many surprises by going over the membership roles looking for prospective leaders. The pastoral leader learns to "find" religious education leaders in other ways. That means looking beyond the obvious. The obvious may be lack of training, past failures, negative response to previous enlistment efforts, personality conflicts, or other factors. The pastor as religious educator develops the ability to see a David in a block of marble, or to put it more to the subject, a Sunday school or CCD teacher in a plain human wrapper.

There are some basic communication skills that may help a pastor find new religious education leaders. The pastor practices one to one contact,

11. Douglas W. Johnson, *The Care and Feeding of Volunteers* (Nashville: Abingdon, 1978), p. 8.
12. Ibid., pp. 22-23.

spends quality time with individuals, encourages persons to tell their stories of being a church member. The pastor listens for key words or statements used. Perhaps in the course of a conversation the priest may ask for further explanation or clarification by the person. Statements and questions such as: "It sounds as if . . ." "I hear you saying that . . ." "Am I right, did you say that . . ." "What did you mean by . . ." "Tell me more about your experience of . . ." may be useful.

Other guides for listening to prospective lay religious education leaders include:

1. Assume a physical posture which indicates you are listening.
2. Give your undivided attention to the person speaking.
3. Stop talking and do not think about what you are going to say when the person gets through speaking.
4. Allow for the person to express strong feelings.
5. Encourage silence, be patient.
6. Withhold judgment and avoid giving advice until an appropriate time (which may never come).

When the pastor listens she/he envisions ministries that such persons would fit. Clergy might close this first conversation by setting another time to talk about how the person would like to minister through the church.

Other factors exist in finding lay religious education leaders. Listing the available opportunities for leadership and keeping it current is a critical task. It is wise to offer two or three options for each potential leader. This notion of multiple option works off the assumption that persons are always changing.[13] The group responsible for nominating church leaders develops and maintains such a list. This list includes the details of what is involved: what is to be done, how much time it takes, when it needs to be done, and the length of tenure. Post this informative list where appropriate in the building or in a church publication.[14]

Compile a list of members who are not serving as lay leaders. Contact them to learn of their interest in serving. Do not assume that a person will or will not serve in an area requiring their weekday work expertise. Most people, however, want a change from what they do vocationally when they serve through the church.

---

13. Ibid., pp. 35-53.

14. Ibid., Johnson gives an example of task, time requirement, and contact person on page 47.

Look for people who have been involved in ministry training sessions but are not serving as leaders. Look for people at transition points in their lives. Does their experience make it more or less likely they can be enlisted as a lay religious education leader? Some churches use an intern experience to introduce the perspective leader to the particular responsibility.[15] Be aware that some change is taking place which might make a new participation possible. Gather all the names of prospective leaders and then move to the enlistment stage.

Securing Lay Leaders

In whatever way your church nominates, decide on the persons who will be approached for various religious education leadership positions. Remember that people want to be a part of ministry that counts, has life to it, has a clear purpose, gives respect to persons, and provides empowerment for the task. Work with the nominating committee to insure that the person who does the inviting is aware of these particular points and stresses them when extending the invitation. In some cases the pastor is the most appropriate person to make the contact. Spend sufficient time in deciding who is the best person to extend the invitation.

Approaching potential leaders is not a simple task. Each leader has specific gifts and needs. Some leaders want all the details, others want a challenge, some desire the straight facts, while others want to work collegially as part of a team ministry. Communicate with each person about the leadership role in a way appropriate to the individual's personality and preferences.[16] Some people need to see the relevance of the role. They want to know that what they are being asked to do will benefit people and meet a real rather than an imagined need. Such people want to help in a good cause. The inviting person shows how what they are being asked to do will allow this to happen. When the potential religious education leader's important questions are answered the inviting person talks about time requirements and the duration of the specific responsibility. Be certain to speak about the support the leader can expect from the church and from co-workers. For any task to be important to a potential leader, it must also be important to others.

Some potential religious education leaders are challenged by a task.

---

15. Lyle E. Schaller and Charles A. Tidwell, *Creative Church Administration* (Nashville: Abingdon, 1975), pp. 82-93.

16. Based on the concepts in Stuart Atkins, *The Name of Your Game* (Beverly Hills, Calif.: Ellis & Steward, 1987).

This leader is not interested in the details of the task. S/he wants to know the bottom line and the available resources. Be clear on the parameters of the leader's responsibility. Bottom-line leaders may appear to be abrupt in their leadership style and may not be as sensitive to people's feelings. You may want to team this person with a leader who provides a balance of sensitivity.

Other religious education leaders need all the facts before they can talk about the relevance, challenge, or enjoyment of the task. This leader needs a reason to feel secure about saying "yes" to the task. This may be the reason some people are comfortable doing what for others would be a fairly menial task for a long time with no desire to move. The pastor's leadership style may need to be a low-key, nonthreatening approach. Have all the necessary information available when this leader is interviewed.

Further, other religious education leaders want to know that they are going to be part of a team and to have an opportunity for fellowship. These leaders are more person-oriented and may view structure and facts as secondary.

Some leaders are cause, bottom line, facts, or team-oriented. With some understanding of the person to be invited refer to the following steps as suggested guides for the actual face-to-face contact:

1. Make an appointment which is convenient to the person. Allow for privacy and adequate time. Never "hijack" a person in the sanctuary or hallway of the church building or when time is too limited. Avoid using the telephone. Speak to the person face-to-face.

2. Make the invitation effort a matter of prayer. Pray for the person and for yourself. Be sensitive to the work of the Spirit in this matter.

3. Be clear. Present the religious education ministry you are asking the person to consider. Point out its meaningfulness, challenge, details, and opportunities for fulfillment in the order appropriate to the needs of the individual.

4. Prepare something in writing to leave with the person. You might include a job description, list of co-workers, and resources available. Be certain that the materials are sensitive to the needs of your congregation. Allow time to answer questions.

5. Present the leadership role realistically. Point out the potentially bad as well as the good.

6. Describe any leadership development opportunities available both before and after the task is assumed. Point out the possibility for personal spiritual growth.[17]

---

17. Stanley J. Menking, *Helping Laity Help Others* (Philadelphia: Westminster, 1984), pp. 79-81. This is an excellent resource in understanding lay ministry.

7. Allow the person time to think, pray, and study before giving a decision. Ask the prospective leader if a week (or perhaps two) would be time enough to make a decision. Suggest that you will call in a few days to see if any clarification is needed.

8. Follow up as promised. Call in three or four days to provide clarification and make an appointment to go back to receive the person's decision. If the answer is negative, thank the person for the time given and encourage openness to the directing of the Spirit in what s/he will do as a part of ministry in and through the church.

These eight steps are to assist the pastors or laity as they extend the invitation to new religious education leaders to share ministry.

Developing Lay Religious Education Leaders

Developing those who volunteer to be lay religious education leaders is a vital role of the effective pastor.[18] It has to do with the equipping, enabling role (Eph 4) of the pastor-teacher. Jesus provided examples as he worked with "volunteers." The story in Mark 3:13-14 emphasizes that Jesus called the twelve to follow. Jesus shared ministry through followers who were willing to learn and to serve others. In Luke 10:1-2, Jesus assembled seventy followers, developed them, and sent them out by twos to share the gospel. Jesus did not forsake these followers. He planned for them to come together and to share the hardships and joys of ministry (Mk 6:30-31).

A pastoral leader develops lay religious education leaders by staying with them, by equipping them, by sending them out to do their work, and by bringing them together to hear reports and to examine their battle scars. Staying with them means healing wounds as well as giving new vision and strength to return to their ministry place. Staying with them means walking by where they are ministering with an encouraging word. Staying with them means asking occasionally, "Is there some way I can help you do your task better?"

There are many ways to develop lay religious education leaders. Three specific development strategies include: in-service training, seminars, and evaluation. These are some strategies that are effective in the small membership church.

In-service training is extremely helpful in developing lay religious edu-

---

18. James Michael Lee, "CCD Renewal" in *Renewing the Sunday School and the CCD,* ed. D. Campbell Wyckoff (Birmingham, Ala.: Religious Education Press, 1986), pp. 235-244.

cation leaders. A person should not be expected to go from the pew to solo assignment. In-service training gives the lay religious education leader an opportunity to learn the responsibilities while receiving supervision. In-service training is the time to learn through observation, questions, and role-playing.[19] Fortunately, training on the job is an accepted practice in many areas of the business and professional world. In a recent study of vital congregations, on the job experience was the normal pattern of training. People came to expect it. Rare indeed would be a small membership church in which none of its members is in a vocation or job which does not require regular learning to keep pace with the demands. Most pastors are comfortable teaching Bible studies. Lay religious education leaders can benefit from short-term biblical studies on Bible leaders, leadership styles, or the mission of the early church. The pastor as religious educator is to teach and to train others

to teach the Bible. The four basic tenets to remember are: In most parishes, the pastor is the only person who has formal training in the Bible; if the pastor does not share the Bible training and knowledge, it will not be known in the parish; if there are other trained persons it provides an opportunity to share in the development of lay religious education leaders; there is always the option of continuing education for the pastor to receive additional training in the Bible and how to teach it.[20]

Bible studies and leadership seminars are other strategies pastors can use in developing lay religious education leaders. Pastors may teach a course on conflict management to assist leaders in handling the natural tensions in ministry. But the clergy cannot do everything which needs to be done. Often leaders respond to leadership development opportunities beyond the local parish. Most churches find a wealth of fairly accessible opportunities provided by their central office. Care should be taken to see that these events meet the needs of lay religious education leaders in the smaller membership church. Too often central office staff indicate that smaller congregations scale down the ideas suggested for larger church use. The pastor in the smaller parish may want to agitate (lobby is a bit nicer word) for conferences specifically designed for the small membership church.

If lay religious education leaders have never participated in such lead-

---

19. Menking, *Helping Laity Help Others,* pp. 81-84. Also see Douglas W. Johnson, *Vitality Means Church Growth* (Nashville: Abingdon, 1989), pp. 65-68.

20. Dick Murray, *Teaching the Bible to Adults and Youth* (Nashville: Abingdon, 1987), p. 155.

ership development experiences, it may be hard to get started. If one leader attends and has a good experience, the pastor will not have to do the encouraging the next time such an event is promoted.

Evaluation is an essential strategy for the development of lay religious educators. This is a tricky matter fraught with some dangers, both real and imagined. A first response may be that these persons are volunteering their time and efforts and should not be subject to evaluation. Our fears may be fueled by past and mostly inadequate concepts of evaluation. Most people can recall the feeling when an incorrect answer was given to a question proposed by the teacher in school. The ease with which another student answered that same question may have been even more devastating. It is shortsighted, however, to dismiss the need for evaluation as a part of leadership development on these grounds.

Evaluation properly done may be one of the greatest favors a smaller membership church can do for its volunteer leaders. At best it is unthoughtful to ask a person to take a place of responsibility without stating what the church expects from that person, providing resources to do the task, and using some means of evaluation. Each lay religious education leader will want to know, How am I doing?

One of the fundamental principles of working with adults states that adults need feedback on their progress. Feedback for one pastor was a fifteen minute "check-in-time" when laity could tell how they were feeling about their work. It was a time to encourage questions, to offer assistance and to assure laity that the pastor cares for them.[21]

Self-evaluation probably is the most effective means of determining strengths, weaknesses, and then planning for improvement. Perhaps the lay religious education leader will agree to a leaders covenant or some such document to use in regular evaluations. A church could observe an annual covenant on Sunday or at an appropriate time when leaders can celebrate and renew the covenant.

Lay leaders can be given a list of questions for use in self-evaluation. The list might include:

1. Do I have concern for those I minister to and lead?
2. Do I delegate responsibility?
3. Do I ask for and respect the opinion of others?
4. Do I promote loyalty to the entire ministry of the church?
5. Do I give deserved and specific praise?
6. Do I keep my fellow workers informed appropriately?

---

21. Douglas A. Walrath, *Planning for Your Church* (Philadelphia: Westminster, 1984), pp. 14-19.

7. Do I include all who need to be involved in planning?
8. Do I deal with problems rather than personalities?
9. Do I have a way of assuring that assignments are completed succe fully?
10. Do I consult those who will be affected by action to be taken?
11. Do I see that those I lead receive proper orientation?
12. Do I seek to measure up to the standards fitting to my leadership role?[22]

Most evaluation in the small membership church will be informal. The pastor's role is to take whatever evaluation is done with lay religious education leaders and to translate it into appropriate praise for effectiveness and further leadership development opportunities.

Developing lay religious education leaders is a never-ending ministry opportunity and requires thoughtful ways of communicating a theological understanding of ministry (without always saying what one is doing) in preaching, teaching, and in personal conversation. It demands going back over what may be familiar territory to the pastor but often brand new or relatively unknown territory to the lay religious education leader.

Supporting Lay Leaders

Supporting as well as developing lay religious education leaders is an ongoing process. Support for lay religious education leaders refers to what is done after persons are involved in their leadership roles and have moved beyond the initial stages of orientation and training. To support lay religious education leaders is to equip persons to accomplish their ministry tasks. There are many strategies which can be used to equip and support leaders. An experienced friend or other leader a briefing session led by the pastor or an experienced leader, workshops, books, and periodicals are a few such strategies.[23] In supporting volunteers the pastor will continue many of the suggestions included in the material on developing leaders.

Willingness to listen is one of the most supportive acts of caring clergy can do. Not all needs are met nor all problems solved, but it is better to listen and lament with the lay religious education person than it is to decide it is not worth the time.

Asking the simple question, "How's it going?" and then genuine listening to the person reveals feelings, problems, solutions, and hopes related to the lay religious education leader's ministry. In using intentional support

---

22. Bob I. Johnson, "How to Plan and Evaluate," in *Christian Education Handbook*, Bruce P. Powers, ed. and comp. (Nashville: Broadman, 1981), p. 69.
23. Griggs and Walther, *Christian Education in the Small Church*, pp. 61-73.

strategies one can build a support base aimed at keeping lay religious education leaders walking on solid ground.

Developing empathy with the lay religious education leader is part of building a support system. The pastor seeks to get inside persons and look through another's eyes to know what the leader is thinking or feeling. One way to aid empathy is to take a sheet of paper, place the lay religious education leader's name at the top, and write everything you can think of which describes what is would be like to be that leader. Build this information into your support system for the leader. It will help as you seek to create an atmosphere in which the lay religious education leader is most likely to be equipped, supported, and motivated.

Lay religious education leaders need:

1. A sense of belonging to the overall purpose of the church's ministry.
2. A sense of shared planning of the objectives for the specific religious education ministry in which s/he is involved.
3. A feeling that the ministry objectives are able to be accomplished and that they make sense.
4. A feeling that the ministry contributes in some lasting way to the welfare of humankind and to the glory of God.
5. A clear and detailed understanding of what is expected of that leader and how much input in decisions s/he will be permitted.
6. A sense that progress is being made toward the ministry goals.
7. A consistent flow of needed information. (Most may be oral in the small membership church.)

Another dimension of the support system for the lay religious education leader is the pastor's support of the leader when approved ministry actions seem to fail and draw criticism from others. Ideally, planning occurs with the pastor and those involved in the ministry, a consensus reached about the approach that should be taken, and an agreement of support for each other regardless of the outcome. The pastor might say to a critic of a lay religious education leader in this case, "Everything had been agreed to, everyone thought it was the best approach but it just didn't turn out as we expected. This experience of conflict does not invalidate our ministry as religious education leaders, it contributes to our maturation."[24] For this kind of support to take place, clear communication must occur throughout the process.

Support for lay religious education leaders includes appropriate recognition and praise. While some might say that persons who minister through

---

24. Menking, *Helping Laity Help Others,* pp. 90-92.

the church should not expect to be recognized or praised, note that that is not the issue. While most people who serve as lay religious education leaders do not serve for the attention they get, the issue of recognition and praise is deeper. What do people need to maintain a sense of purpose and fulfillment in doing volunteer ministry? Leaders need to know and feel that what they are doing is counting for something worthwhile and long-lasting. They need to hear this from someone else. This expression of appreciation is surely a Christian grace to be cultivated.

What are some ways to show recognition and praise in the small membership church? It is best to be specific. Handwritten notes are effective. Praise the leader in front of others when possible. Recognition during a worship service or other church meeting is appropriate if certain precautions are taken. Be sure you are consistent, specific, and truthful in your practice of public praise.

Support for the lay religious education leader may include accepting that the leader does not feel it possible to continue in his/her ministry role. Offer to spend some time with the person. Make suggestions of resources which may serve to refresh the person. By all means continue to see the person as one of ultimate worth and not as one to be discarded because s/he is no longer "working in the church."

Releasing the Lay Leader

Releasing is the intentional act of declaring the lay religious education leader as an equal partner in ministry, fully capable under God of determining what one's ministry should be. Releasing also includes commissioning that person to follow the Spirit's leadership. Up to this point the discussion has at least implied a church-centered ministry for lay religious education leaders; that is, a ministry mostly practiced through the activities of the church. To be certain, such ministry is necessary, but it ought not to be the total story. Business folk remind us that there are no results inside their own walls. The result of a business is a satisfied customer. The result of a hospital is a healed patient. The result of a school is a student who has learned something and lives and works by that in the years to come. The result of a church is a changed life released into a desperately needy world where that life makes a difference. The church may be compared to a base camp for mountain climbers. The conventional wisdom of climbers has it that the success of your climb depends on the strength of your base camp. The church base must be strong, but it must also produce mountain climbers if it is truly to be the church.

In view of this concept some of our lay religious education leaders must be released from ministry within the walls of the church building to minister beyond. A pastor works at helping the church to see that both kinds of ministries are viable. One way to affirm ministry beyond the base camp is through a commissioning service. Persons who take on special tasks vital to the church's mission can be included. Would it also be appropriate to commission a person who may feel that coaching a Little League baseball team is a ministry calling? The intimacy possible in a small membership church adds to the meaningfulness of commissioning the church's own to be out "priesting in the world."

Another way of releasing the lay religious education leader is through a shared ministry, one in which secrets of the trade and power are freely given to all the ministering people of God. Secrets of the trade means the knotty biblical and theological problems the pastor wrestles with, how to preach and teach, how to visit, and kindred matters. Lay religious education leaders are capable of handling such matters. The small membership church is an ideal setting for attending to these issues, through developing conversations about the preaching, encouraging lay religious educators to visit and to participate in new ecumenical ministries.

Giving power away is something Jesus did as if there were no shortage at all. "You feed them. You heal them. You can even walk on water if your faith is strong enough. You will be doing greater things than I have done." In the kingdom it is this way, the more power of authority you give away, the more there is to share. In practical application when a person is given a responsibility to minister, make certain that authority is given as well.

PLANNING WITH LAY LEADERS

Planning which covers both long and short-range time periods is rare in most small membership churches. The usually predictable exception is the new or fairly new congregation. Newer congregations may be more aware of the need for planning because of the times in which we live, the necessity for growth to survive, and the natural desire to include others in something new and exciting.

The age of the congregation bears heavy weight in the consideration of planning. A church's self-image and attitudes help to shape the planning process. Does the church believe it has any reason to feel good about who it is? Is there anything the church is or has which is worth giving away to others through the ministry of its people? Answers to questions such as these must be assessed before proceeding with a plan for the lay religious education leaders in the parish.

To propose a formal planning process in many small membership churches might produce less than the "spiritual" experience we dream it could be. Some lay persons might react with statements indicating that this has never been done before; the church knows what it ought to be doing; there aren't any opportunities for growth; planning would interfere with the work of the Holy Spirit. Unfortunately, some pastors reflect some of these attitudes. One of the characteristics of a vital small or large congregation is a basic positive attitude. In fact, lay religious education leaders in vital congregations are positive, conscientious, and spiritually motivated to become leaders.[25] Clergy need to begin in the most basic and low-key way.

If the pastor has reservations about planning then these must be resolved first. Then, a plan for planning must be developed by the pastor, at least a plan for how to proceed. Here one needs the suggested wisdom of a serpent and the harmlessness of a dove.

A Most Basic Approach

In a new parish, arrange a meeting with some appropriate group in the church (or the entire congregation) to talk about how to get off to a good start as pastoral leader. State that you are interested in knowing what the congregation needs to do to be the church it ought to be. Take suggestions, write them on newsprint or chalkboard. Brainstorm, evaluate, create an atmosphere where no suggestion is more important than any other. Ask people to suspend judgment on any idea. The process may be slow, and may require patience. If someone's contribution is "fix the roof on the building," follow their suggestion with questions such as: How do we go about fixing the roof? Is someone in charge of such needs? How do we pay for it? Do the members of the church usually do this kind of work as a group project? When should this be done? If the pastor can lead the group through answering such questions, then the group has entered into a meaningful planning process.

The pastor might continue to ask for other responses. If several other suggestions are made, it may become necessary to prioritize the items and plan the human and financial resources needed to accomplish them. The church is planning without ever calling it that. Also, if the group stays with this process long enough, the pastor may lead the group to think of needs related more to ministry beyond the church walls. It may be that someone will mention the needs of families in the mobile home park down the road,

---

25. Johnson, *Vitality Means Church Growth,* pp. 46-52.

or the high-rise apartment across the street, which the church up to now has ignored. Though issues such as this may be more controversial than mending the roof, ask some of the same questions in discussing these ministry possibilities. Another perspective on encouraging new ministries or to use when examining existing ministries includes three criteria for evaluating the idea: Will it involve our members in reaching out, will it impact our community and does it offer the possibility of a continuing ministry for our parish.[26]

It is appropriate to introduce the concept of dreaming in this context.[27] Point out that any church begins with a dream about what it should be and do. Encourage lay leaders to think about the original dream of the church founders and to re-dream and/or re-create that dream today.

With this simple and, yet, *subtle* approach to beginning planning clergy may be able to take lay religious education leaders a step at a time toward longer-range planning. Early in the effort, the pastor must give attention to the self-image issue. Self-image is absolutely crucial in a church's development toward truly being the people of God. The small membership church is well aware of what it cannot do. It knows its finances and people resources are limited. It knows there are many ministry needs it is not meeting. Such understanding often leads to tentative, apologetic efforts or no effort at all. A pastor complicates matters by directing sermons only at the weak areas, urging greater commitment, more efforts at evangelism, and more generous monetary giving.

It is far better to hold consistently before the congregation its strengths. One way to build on strengths is to invite members to talk about what they like about the church, or what the church has done for them which gives them strength. Ask the people to name the good things about the church that are out there on the community grapevine. Display these before the group and save them for later reference when the church begins planning for how to capitalize on their strengths to be more effectively the people of God on mission in their community.

Asking a small membership church to do a "strengths versus weaknesses" assessment does not seem to be as useful when church leaders probably know too well the church's weaknesses.

The basic principle is that when a congregation expands it strengths, the church becomes more effective in mission. The corollary is that when a congregation becomes preoccupied with weaknesses the church begins

---

26. Lyle E. Schaller, *Getting Things Done* (Nashville: Abingdon, 1986), p. 114.
27. Robert Dale, *To Dream Again* (Nashville: Broadman, 1981), p. 5.

to lose its strengths.[28] The church begins the planning process by identifying strengths.

When the church has decided on what its top two or three strengths are, the pastor can lead them to make these the central thrust of the church's religious education ministry. These strengths might be the worship services, the Bible study program, or the caring nature of the fellowship. Whatever they are, begin with strengths to develop greater strength. As an example, say that the Bible study program is a strength but upon examining that strength the discovery is made that there are several younger couples for whom there is no study group which exactly fits their needs. Without really disrupting any other group a new group could be formed if a nucleus of participants can be found. The pastor may lead the group during its formative stages and may involve a lay religious education leader who is connected to the power base of the church. By so doing, communication is assured with those who traditionally are the decision makers.

Developing a strength provides the church an area of ministry in which to excel. It provides a specific and positive way for the church to present itself to the community. One of the questions which can be asked in this process is: What would we like for the community to know about our church? Accenting the strengths of a parish provides an identity around which the church can find anchor and from which lay religious education leaders can develop ministry.

Taking Planning to the Next Level

Planning enables the church to act in positive ways in being the servant people of God in the world. Planning helps the church to determine the nature of God's presence in the world and joins God in the ministry of creation and redemption.[29] Planning challenges the church beyond its human resources to remain open to the presence of the Spirit. The pastor is enabled through planning to emphasize that as the church is moved by the Spirit it is lifted above a mundane, self-serving agenda and becomes the people of God in the world. This belief about the critical role of the Spirit lies behind all that is said about planning in the small membership church.

The spiritual growth and development of lay religious education leaders is a critical part of planning. To be intentional about the spiritual devel-

---

28. Kennon L. Callahan, *Twelve Keys to an Effective Church* (San Francisco: Harper & Row, 1983), pp. xi-xix.

29. Paul Hanson, "The Identity and Purpose of the Church," *Theology Today* 42:3.

opment of leaders is to plan to invite persons to reflect and to share from their own faith life journeys. Lay religious education leaders seek spiritual direction.[30] Pastors can offer the possibilities for spiritual growth to occur through planning. Some possibilities include planning for: times in prayer, Bible study, and/or sharing groups; structure, a plan for ways to use the time of spiritual development; and commitment, to be committed to spiritual growth as a high priority.[31]

Four specific ways planning can strengthen religious education in the small membership church:

1. Planning helps to develop the decision-making process and individual lay religious education leaders who are decision makers. One crucial question for the smaller parish is, How do we make decisions? To be an effective decision maker, one practices making decisions with a view to improve decision-making skills each time through the process. The final results of planning are important, but the process of planning is also important.

2. Planning aims at the best use of human and non-human resources. Each ministry of religious education has a certain amount of money, time, building space, and people. Planning helps to determine the best use of these resources.

3. Planning helps religious education leaders to view how the entire church is related through its parts: the whole, of course, always being greater than the sum of its parts. Planning helps leaders to enlarge their perspective, to see why and how to strengthen the church's ministry.

4. Planning is based on and helps to refine further the church's reason for being. The church has overall goals, and the congregation also has individual members who have directions set for themselves. Effective planning respects individual maturity while reaching for overall church goals. It does not allow either to nudge the other out of the picture.

To speak specifically of the religious education ministry, planning is the intentional effort of engaging lay religious education leaders in understanding the purpose of the church and in formulating goals and action plans to fulfill that purpose.

The call *to be* is the first task of the small membership church. No church small or large should be involved in activities simply for the sake

---

30. Johnson, *Vitality Means Church Growth*, pp. 51-52.

31. William R. Nelson, *Ministry Formation for Effective Leadership* (Nashville: Abingdon, 1988), pp. 141-146. Griggs and Walther, *Christian Education in the Small Church,* pp. 68-73.

of being active. A vast difference exists between "offering the cup of cold water" for the sake of the offering of the water and "offering the cup of cold water" in Jesus' name.

If a church already has a purpose statement adopted and written, then planning for the various religious education ministries can proceed. Assess the purpose statement to determine if it is adequate or if it needs to be rewritten. Guide the planning by asking: Does what is planned help to fulfill the larger purpose of the church?

Beware of resistances to planning. Worthwhile plans produce new patterns of thought and action. The truth is—people resist planned change. Furthermore, people are immersed in the routine of the church's religious education ministry and may see no need for planning or may feel inadequate as planners. Some leaders resist because planning demands new commitments to the future. Another resistance to planning is influence protection. Some leaders may feel that a personal favorite project would be passed over. Be aware that approval of an idea or plan is not necessarily support.[32] Confront resistance by maintaining a positive pressure in a persuasive way. Point out reasons for planning and highlight small past successes which grew out of intentional planning.

Involve as many persons as possible. A planning group seeks to include all who could be a part of such an effort. It may be awkward in some small membership churches to become accustomed to a representative group planning for the whole group. The rule of thumb in selecting a long-range planning committee and a long-range steering committee is 20 percent of your average worship attendance. For example, if the average worship attendance if fifty, the long-range planning committee needs fifteen persons and a steering committee of five persons. If the service worship attendance is a hundred the planning committee is twenty and the steering committee is five.[33] Make sure that clear communication takes place. Broader involvement through a planning group decreases inappropriate resistance and increases commitment. Remember that lay leaders in the church tend to support what they help to create.

In keeping with emphasizing strengths in the small membership church, look for potential religious education ministry opportunities rather than problems. A church may have sought to maintain a youth ministry with fewer and fewer prospective participants, while it has given little or no

32. Schaller, *Getting Things Done*, pp. 118-119.

33. Kennon L. Callahan, *Twelve Keys to an Effective Church: The Leader's Guide* (San Francisco: Harper & Row, 1987), pp. 57-61.

attention to a potential religious education ministry with older persons. Problems can be depressing; discovering potential can give new life and self-esteem to a planning group.

Using Priority Lists

Design a simple form to be used to get people to express the potentials they see for the religious education ministry of the church. Place at the top something like, "Possible Dreams," or "Dreaming About Priorities." Beneath the title place these instructions: Write the potential ministry opportunities you feel our religious education ministry has. Do not limit your dreaming by a lack of such resources as people, money, or space. Then number a half-dozen or so blank spaces for the persons to use. At the bottom of the sheet ask the person to indicate which of the suggestions should get Number One priority and in which one would s/he be willing to participate actively.[34]

Another possibility lies in the use of a prepared list of possible priorities in the religious education ministry. The list could be used to stimulate ideas for planning. Such a list might include:

1. More training for Bible teachers
2. More physical facilities, including lighting and seating
3. Additional visual aids
4. A better system for greeting and encouraging visitors to return
5. More organization-sponsored fellowship
6. More money for religious education
7. An intentional outreach ministry
8. Stronger mission education
9. More emphasis on family education
10. Enlistment of inactive members
11. More emphasis on specific ministries by the members
12. Classes for the mentally retarded
13. Provisions for the physically handicapped
14. More emphasis on prayer
15. Regular planning by the lay religious education leaders
16. Greater punctuality on the part of leaders
17. More participation from members and leaders in curriculum planning
18. More programs on political and social issues

---

34. See Kenneth D. Blazier, *Workbook for Planning Christian Education,* (Valley Forge, Pa.: Judson, 1983) for a useful planning process.

19. An improved member training program

20. Better use of recreation

21. Weekday learning opportunities for older adults

Begin with the suggestions of the lay religious education leaders or the congregation as a whole to identify the probable priorities of the religious education ministry. The religious education committee, church cabinet (or council), planning team, or whatever group has the assignment for planning can then tabulate the results and incorporate the ideas into the planning process. Care should be taken not to move too rapidly in adopting new priorities. It is wiser to begin with one or two ideas which have broad support and a high probability of being implemented. A new project should meet these criteria:

1. Is consistent with the overall purpose of the church

2. Does meet a valid need

3. Has at least one person who can provide leadership

4. Includes resources available for support

To restate a point already made in this chapter, most small membership churches do not plan and do not write down those plans in any formal way. For those churches which have moved to such a practice, or wish to do so, a project planning sheet may be useful:

PROJECT PLANNING SHEET

Project Title: _____

How Does This Project Help to Fulfill the Overall Purpose of the Church?

_____

_____

_____

Specific Project Goal(s): _____

_____

_____

Needs This Project Can Meet: _____

_____

_____

Resources Needed: _____

_____

_____

Actions to Take: _____

_____   _____

_____   _____

_____   _____

Person(s) in charge: _____

Date to Begin: _____ Date to Complete: _____

Perceived Impact on the Overall Religious Education Ministry of the Congregation:

_____

_____

Moving to the Ultimate

For the small congregation ready for regular, specific, comprehensive, and goal-oriented planning of its religious education ministry, further steps can be taken. For the church wishing to begin, theoretically at least, with a blank sheet of paper there are some other possibilities. The church writes a stated purpose of missional objective(s). The purpose or missional objective statement tells why a church exists. Spinning off the church's purpose or missional objective is an objective for the religious education ministry of the church. The objective of religious education tells the intent, the hope, the clear reason for teaching and learning in a particular congregation. The statement below produced by representatives of sixteen Protestant denominations may be helpful in formulating the church's statement (note the need for some inclusive language):

> The objective of Christian education is that all persons be aware of God through his self-disclosure, especially his redeeming love—to the end that they may know who they are and what their human situation means, grow as sons of God rooted in the Christian community, live in the spirit of God in every relationship, fulfill their common discipleship in the world, and abide in the Christian hope.[35]

35. Cooperative Curriculum Project, *The Church's Educational Ministry: A Curriculum Plan* (St. Louis: Bethany, 1965), p. 8.

The next step is for leaders to form specific ways that the church's religious education ministry can fulfill the objective. The religious education objective is fulfilled through specific, attainable, measurable goals. Goals as used here have several characteristics which set them apart from the broader term, objective. They are:

1. Specific	5. Written
2. Attainable	6. Participative
3. Worthwhile	7. Deadlined
4. Consistent	8. Flexible

An example of such a goal might be: Our goal is to increase the average attendance of the Sunday school by five persons (or by 10 percent) to fifty-five by June 1, 19___ . Another example might be: Our goal is for 80 percent of the leaders in the religious education ministry to complete a church-sponsored training course by January 1, 19___ .

The small membership church develops its goals out of possibly three or four areas which it knows to be important to its life and work. Based on the objective above, the church might designate those areas as nurture, evangelism, and fellowship. The planning process answers the question: How can we fulfill the needs of these areas of religious education? Remember that all goals are written and implemented to fulfill the broader vision of the objective.

Planning can be done in a retreat setting at a time preceding the beginning of a new church year. An overnight retreat may not be as appropriate as an evening or an all-day event. Small membership church religious education leaders may be more comfortable meeting at the church building or in someone's home. Work for 100 percent participation and commitment in the planning process by the lay religious education leaders involved. An agenda for the planning session might be:

1. A time of personal reflection. Use a question like, What has been most meaningful in your religious education experience this past year?

2. Examine the church goals. Identify the specific goals which relate to the ministry of religious education.

3. Reflect on the past. Ask: What are the good events, experiences, opportunities which have happened in our religious education ministry?

4. Generate the high potential ideas for the coming year. Ask: What are the challenging possibilities for involvement of religious education in the church's goals?

5. Examine the space and equipment needs. Are they adequate? What can be done to improve them?

6. Identify the training needs. What training should be provided for our religious education leaders?

7. Encourage ongoing planning. Ask: Are we planning throughout the year in order to be most effective in our task?

8. Examine policies and procedures. Do these need to be updated or changed?

9. Inquire about curriculum plans. What is the curriculum plan for the coming year in each (age) group or class?

10. Plan for personal growth. Ask each religious education leader to plan for specific ways they will grow spiritually. Encourage leaders involved in the planning retreat, beforehand, to be thinking of such plans.

Regular, Ongoing Planning

Groups or individuals can meet weekly or monthly for planning. Most of this kind of planning is related to the teaching-learning experience in the upcoming session. Included in this planning can be:

1. A purchased or self-devised plan sheet
2. Consideration of the main purpose or goal of the lesson
3. Determination of what truth in the scripture passage is being communicated to the learner
4. Goals or objectives for one's teaching
5. Choosing educational methods appropriate to the goals
6. Listing resources needed
7. Thorough study of the biblical/lesson materials
8. Choosing ways of helping the learner to apply the study experience to life
9. Prayer

Planning supports the church religious education leadership in evaluating the effectiveness of the religious education ministry. Planning sets standards by which to make this evaluation. Standards are formulated by the church, adapted from others, or used exactly as produced by a religious education specialist or by one's central office.

How much planning is too much in a small membership church? It is too much when the process begins to erode the unique and vital strengths of a small congregation. What is enough planning? When the process enhances the strengths of the church and moves the church to be the people of God on mission in their setting of today's world.

The pastor referred to at the beginning of the chapter decided to take the comment of the church member as a challenge. He began by preaching biblical messages on the meaning and purpose of the church. Vision and dream were highlighted. Special Bible studies emphasized what a church was to be and do. The pastor gave several weeks to such an effort. During a Sunday evening worship service, the pastor set up three chalkboards in front of the congregation. On one he wrote one year, three years on another, and five years on the third board. He asked the congregation to suggest what they would like to accomplish in those three time periods. Their first, and somewhat uneasy, response was: Get more people. The pastor patiently led them to think in more specific ways about religious education ministry possibilities.

The people had trouble, however, thinking in the three and five-year time periods. The pastor settled for a one year projection. The suggestions were recorded. Afterward, the pastor entered them into the computer. For the next meeting he prepared a handout based on the computer printout of suggestions. The people were asked to prioritize four religious education ministry opportunities from the list. A value was placed on each vote: 10 points for a first-place vote; 7 for a second-place vote; 5 for a third-place vote; and 3 for a fourth-place vote. The values were tabulated and the four items receiving the highest number of points were adopted as priorities for the coming year. In subsequent meetings the religious education leaders decided on specific goals and action plans to be implemented throughout the year. The man who told the new pastor, "We'll do anything you can get us to do," found himself, as well as others, viewing religious education ministry as belonging to all the people of God. Ministry was no longer something the pastor "got" someone to do.

LEAVING A LEGACY

Working with lay religious education leaders in the planning process of the church's ministry is surely kingdom work at its best. If the pastor is given to leading the church to be and do what God wants it to be and do, then one of the discovered joys in the process will be the blossoming through the empowering of lay religious education leaders. The task of mobilizing lay religious education leaders and using a planning process is twofold: empowering existing leaders and calling forth new religious education leaders. Clergy are not able to do ministry alone. The ministry of religious education is a mutual effort with clergy and laity. The great legacy one can leave in a small membership church is a people who are more Christian and more intentional in joining God in fulfilling God's purposes of creation and redemption in today's world.

Chapter Eight

Curriculum in the Small Membership Church

D. CAMPBELL WYCKOFF

INTRODUCTION

Curriculum workers have the task of putting together a comprehensive and practical plan that takes into account everything that they know about religious education—the teaching and mission of the church, the character of the Christian life, the learning process, and the challenges and opportunities in the situation of the learners. The persons closest to the process, planners and teachers in the local church, have the key responsibility, since they are the ones who know the particular needs and opportunities in the situation of the learners, and they are the ones who will make it happen, if it happens. They have available to them consultants and resources. The consultants are usually persons designated by their communions to work on curriculum matters with curriculum workers in the local church. The resources are usually curriculum series prepared by national curriculum workers.

As a rule the curriculum, the church's plan for its educational work, consists of a set of rather simple ingredients that are structurally consistent with curriculum as it is worked out both in secular and religious education. Ralph Tyler uses a set of four questions to identify these ingredients:

1. What educational purposes should the school seek to attain?
2. What educational experiences can be provided that are likely to attain these purposes?
3. How can these educational experiences be effectively organized?
4. How can we determine whether these purposes are being attained?[1]

Substitute "church" for "school" in the first question and these questions become immediately applicable to the planning of the curriculum of religious education.

The so-called "Tyler rationale" has been seriously criticized on several scores. Most of the criticism stems from its wooden use as a too-rationalized scheme, opening the ways for "behavioral objectives" to limit the scope of religious education to behaviors that may be empirically measured. There are those also who in their use of it assume the status quo as the norm for determining objectives. Further, it can be used in such a way as to discourage free exploration of the field of experience. All of these are important danger signals for religious education curriculum planners.[2]

The area most likely to be overlooked in planning the curriculum is, strangely, that of aesthetic experience. One would think that, since the aesthetic experience is one of intense emotion (variously expressed in music, drama, the graphic arts, and literature), it would be at the heart of the curriculum plan. Cognitive experience and rational values have, however, been given greater emphasis. Notable attempts are being made to correct this imbalance.[3]

---

1. Ralph W. Tyler, *Basic Principles of Curriculum and Instruction* (Chicago: University of Chicago Press, 1949), p. 1 and *passim*.

2. See James B. MacDonald and David E. Purpel, "Curriculum Planning: Visions and Metaphors," in *Curriculum: An Introduction to the Field*, 2nd. ed., ed. James R. Gress (Berkeley, Calif.: McCutchan, 1988), pp. 305-321. See also William Pinar, ed., *Curriculum Theorizing, The Reconceptualists* (Berkeley, Calif.: McCutchan, 1975).

3. In the secular field, a case in point is Elliot W. Eisner, *The Educational Imagination*, 2nd. ed. (New York: Macmillan, 1985). In religious education, see Maria Harris, *Teaching and Religious Imagination* (San Francisco: Harper & Row, 1987).

Further, in much of religious education curriculum the component of appropriate action is seriously underplayed. There have been attempts to build curriculums on an "action-reflection" model, in which engagement in action integral to various aspects of the Christian life leads to analytical reflection on that action, making use of biblical, theological, and ethical resources, thus enabling growth in understanding and the formulation of a basis for more effective modes of action. Such attempts have not been notably successful, due largely to the unusual demands that they place on teachers and leaders. Yet here, as in the case of aesthetic experience, it is strange that action-reflection has not been more strongly supported, since it is central to mature Christian experience.

Such *caveats* with respect to the Tyler rationale point up the importance of the determination of objectives that are fully in character with the Christian faith and life. Such objectives are sometimes stated very briefly, as in the now classic *Objective of Christian Education for Senior High Young People:*

> The objective of Christian education is to help persons to be aware of God's self-disclosure and seeking love in Jesus Christ, and to respond in faith and love, to the end that they may know who they are and what their human situation means, grow as children of God in the Christian community, live in the Spirit of God in every relationship, fulfill their common discipleship in the world, and abide in the Christian hope.[4]

The pervasive influence of such a statement of the objective of religious education is attested to by surveys of subsequent Protestant curricula.[5]

At the other extreme is the Cooperative Curriculum Project of the National Council of Churches, which, after a focus on a later version of the above objective, spins out objectives and learning activities in 788 pages of detail.[6]

---

4. *The Objective of Christian Education for Senior High Young People* (New York: National Council of Churches, 1958). One word of the original has been changed to put it in inclusive language.

5. See, for instance, Howard P. Colson and Raymond M. Rigdon, *Understanding Your Church Curriculum,* rev. ed. (Nashville: Broadman, 1981). Note especially chapter 2, "Revolution in Christian Education," and Appendices A and B.

6. *The Church's Educational Ministry: A Curriculum Plan* (St. Louis: Bethany, 1965). An even more sophisticated analysis of objectives, illustrative of the highest degree of mastery of the field, is Benjamin Bloom et al., *Taxonomy of Educational*

Whether expressed in pithy form or in extended analysis, the objectives of religious education must reflect the whole nature of the Christian teaching-learning act, perhaps best indicated by such texts as Deuteronomy 6:4-9 (teach the Word of God diligently to your children at all times and through every act); Psalm 78 ("tell to the coming generation the glorious deeds of the Lord"); Malachi 2:1-9 (teachers must be utterly faithful); Matthew 7:29 (the convincing and converting authority of parabolic teaching, coupled with a life of complete integrity).

In deciding on appropriate learning experiences and organizing them into a curriculum, curriculum workers seek methods that will specifically implement the objectives that have been chosen and models that will help teachers to lead learners through step-by-step processes like exploration, discovery, appropriation, and response in action.[7] One such model, suggested by Donald Griggs, uses this sequence of steps: Enter, Engage, Explore, Express, Embody, and Empower.

Curriculum evaluation is a matter of systematically comparing results with intentions. This may be done at the most fundamental level of religious education: How do the ideas, aspirations, motivations, action patterns, and behaviors of the learners compare with the intentions of the curriculum in these matters? It may be done at the level of the teaching act: How faithfully have teachers and learners carried out the intentions of the curriculum? It may be done at the level of curriculum materials: How fully and accurately do the materials reflect the intentions of those who planned them?

In some matters, evaluation may be quite precise. This is the case, for instance, with things like biblical knowledge, the historical development of the faith, the ideas of particular religious leaders, and the positions of

---

Objectives, Cognitive and Affective Domains (New York: McKay, 1956 and 1964). The analysis of the affective domain uses a structure analogous to that of developing religious experience. It is mirrored to a degree in a subsequent volume produced by the Cooperative Curriculum Project, *Tools of Curriculum Development for the Church's Educational Ministry* (Anderson, Ind.: Warner, 1967).

7. The importance of selecting methods appropriate to the Christian faith and life is explored in Robert R. Boehlke, *Theories of Learning in Christian Education* (Philadelphia: Westminster, 1962). An attempt to nudge religious education into innovative methods is Evelyn M. Huber's, *Doing Christian Education in New Ways* (Valley Forge, Pa.: Judson, 1978). The matter of models is fully explored (in secular settings, but applicable to religious education) in Bruce Joyce and Marsha Weil, *Models of Teaching,* 3rd. ed. (Englewood Cliffs, N.J.: Prentice-Hall, 1986).

the church on personal and social ethics. In other cases, such precision is out of the question. For instance, uniformity is undesirable in the personal expression of faith and in creative response of the religious affections. Here a range of outcomes is to be expected and encouraged. The evaluative questions are how and to what degree the outcomes enrich and enhance our grasp of the curriculum's purposes.

THE SMALL MEMBERSHIP CHURCH

Literature on the small membership church is very helpful in defining such churches, insisting on the variety of forms that they take, and enlarging our vision of their program and mission. It is not so helpful on specific matters relating to religious education.

Nevertheless, it is worthwhile to pick up from the literature some of the characteristics of small membership churches that may have bearing on the educational plans that they devise and adopt. First, there seems to be some agreement that a small membership church is one that has about 250 members or less. Second, small membership churches are found in every kind of setting—urban downtown, inner-city, suburban, town and village, and open country. Third, some small membership churches are growing and have relatively high morale and hope. Some are stable and either comfortable with the situation or concerned about slipping into decline. Some are in decline and are either characterized by low morale or by a creative search for new types of service to new constituencies. Some are intentionally small, and as they grow continue to segment. Fourth, significant among small membership churches are those with special purposes— mission, fellowship, mutual caring, and social action.[8] If the situation of a church conditions its plan for religious education, as I am maintaining, these differences among small
membership churches make for somewhat different curriculum needs.

The ethos of the small membership church is also a factor in determining curriculum needs and possibilities. Carl Dudley paints the positive side of the picture: "In a big world, the small church has remained intimate. In a fast world, the small church has been steady. In an expensive world, the small church has remained plain. In a complex world, the small church has remained simple. In a rational world, the small church has kept feelings.

---

8. Based on a review of Carl S. Dudley, *Making the Small Church Effective* (Nashville: Abingdon, 1978) and Jackson W. Carroll, ed., *Small Churches Are Beautiful* (San Francisco: Harper & Row, 1977).

In a mobile world, the small church has been an anchor. In an anonymous world, the small church calls us by name—by nickname! As a result, small churches have survived where others have failed."[9] Although he does not make the point, it may well be that his analysis of the ethos of the small membership church contains clues for the characteristics of the curriculum that is appropriate for it.

Alone among current authors on the small membership church, Donald Griggs and Judy McKay Walther discuss in depth the questions surrounding curriculum.[10] Fundamentally, they find that sound curriculum planning requires "a sense of direction, the affirmation of some basic goals for Christian education, and a recognition that curriculum involves more than ordering materials for teachers."[11] It is important to note that these conditions are to be met *in the local church itself*. They present a seven-step process by which these conditions may be met and provide practical guidance on the effective choice and utilization of curriculum materials.

Lest at this point we slip into the assumption that the CCD/Sunday school and religious education are to be equated in the small membership church, we need to be reminded that the research done by Warren Hartman has identified at least five different "audiences" for religious education in the local church--those seeking fellowship, those seeking the traditional Sunday school, those seeking study in depth, those seeking training for dealing with social concerns, and some who combine two or more of these interests.[12] The CCD or Sunday school cannot satisfy all these groups. Other agencies are needed, each with distinctive curriculum needs.

Jack Seymour hammers the point home by insisting that the Sunday school has an exploratory, introductory, and foundational function "on which more systematic and cumulative settings for study may be built."[13] There is no reason to believe that this is not true of the small membership parish. The clear implication is that in the small membership church the

---

9. Dudley, *Making the Small Church Effective*, p. 176.

10. Donald L. Griggs and Judy McKay Walther, *Christian Education in the Small Church* (Valley Forge, Pa.: Judson, 1988). See chapter 6, "Selecting, Adapting, and Using Curriculum."

11. Ibid., p. 78.

12. Warren J. Hartman, *Five Audiences, Identifying Groups in Your Church* (Nashville: Abingdon, 1987).

13. Jack L. Seymour, "A Reforming Movement: The Story of Protestant Sunday School," in *Renewing the Sunday School and the CCD,* ed. D. Campbell Wyckoff (Birmingham, Ala.: Religious Education Press, 1986), p. 24.

urriculum of the CCD or Sunday school will help persons to know *of* the faith, while other groups, with appropriate curricula will take on the task of deepening and enriching what the CCD or Sunday school has started.

THE GRASS ROOTS SITUATION

Believing that a realistic assessment of the status of curriculum in the small membership church necessitates some first-hand investigation, I decided to look into what is actually happening in a variety of churches. Four denominations were selected, representing different types of churches—the Roman Catholic Church, the Southern Baptist Church (conservative, aggressive, growing), the Presbyterian Church, U.S.A. (Protestant mainstream), and the Assemblies of God (Pentecostal). For the sake of convenience, the jurisdiction of each of them within which I live was used.

After securing some statistical and descriptive data on the small membership churches involved, I asked the following questions:[14]

Who in the church does the actual educational planning?
To what effect? (Programs, persons served, leadership.)
What special educational resources do these churches have?
    In the parish? (Personnel, equipment, etc.)
    From outside the parish? (Consultants, training opportunities, etc.)
What curriculum materials are being used?
What curriculum materials are recommended for them? Why?

The Roman Catholic Church

The Archdiocese of Santa Fe covers 61,142 square miles in the central and northeastern sections of New Mexico. It includes the two largest cities in the state, Albuquerque (with a population of some 350,000) and Santa Fe, the state capital (about 50,000). Its arid, sparsely settled character is indicated by the fact that the third largest town within its bounds is Las Vegas (New Mexico, not Nevada), with a population of less than 15,000.

Paul Horgan has called the culture of the area a "heroic triad,"[15] for it consists of a rich mixture of Native American (Pueblo and Mescalero Apache), Hispanic (dating back to the early sixteenth century), and Anglo-American

---

14. I gratefully acknowledge the help of Catherine Abeyta, George Warren, Jaime Quinones, and David Vistine in gathering these data.

15. Paul Horgan, *The Heroic Triad* (New York: Holt, Rinehart and Winston, 1970).

(an influx since the Civil War, primarily in commerce and ranching).

The archdiocese consists of ninety-four parishes and 216 missions, missions being clustered around parishes, to provide added strength in leadership and in program. Parishes are for the most part quite large; missions tend to be small in membership and located in villages and open country, although there are small member missions in urban areas as well. About 60 percent of the Catholic population is Hispanic, the rest being divided between the Native Americans (mainly the nineteen Pueblos) and the Anglos. Liaison is maintained with the Tekakwitha Conference, which serves Native American groups across diocesan lines.

In theology, liturgy, and instruction 70 percent of the parishes and missions would reflect post-Vatican II views and practices.

While some missions have their own parish councils, most of them have members who serve on the council of the parish to which they are attached. In 90 percent of the cases, educational planning is done by the pastor, together with the parish council. Leadership of the educational program consists of certified directors of religious education, noncertified parish religious education coordinators, and catechist-teachers. Directors of religious education and parish religious education coordinators ordinarily serve on the parish council.

In the small member situations, resources for full parish religious education are most often not available. Religious education then focuses on sacramental preparation (with parents, for infant baptism, and with appropriate ages for Eucharist, Confirmation, and Reconciliation). Thus, sacramental preparation predominates, with sequential religious education (K-8), the Rite for Christian Initiation of Adults, and adult education (scripture instruction, and things like parenting and seasonal programs—Advent and Lent, in particular), following in order.

Most of the buildings consist of a sanctuary and a hall. There may be one to three rooms in addition. All of the space has to serve many functions. None is reserved exclusively for religious education purposes. A non-school model prevails, with many classes meeting in homes. Even the office of the director of religious education is often used for daily chapel.

The archdiocese maintains a staff and two audio-visual centers, which are available to all groups. The audio-visual center in Albuquerque is well stocked with books, videotapes, and the like, but has not built up an adequate supply of equipment (VCRs, for instance). The one in the northern office at the San Juan Pueblo, serving the northern deaneries and parishes, is in the beginning stages.

Archdiocesan training events include an annual adult education conference, and a catechetical conference for workers with children and youth. In addition, about two major training events per year are held in each of the eight deaneries. The archdiocesan director of religious education and her associate meet with the coordinators once a month and also provide on-site services as requested. Nationally known leaders are often called in for conferences and special services. Events outside the archdiocese are announced, but not heavily promoted. Clustering and networking for training and for youth programs are stressed.

The major publishers whose curriculum materials are both recommended and used are Silver Burdett-Ginn, Our Sunday Visitor, Winston, Sadlier, W.C. Brown. Special sacramental preparation books are those most used, with grade-level books where the program justifies them. If teachers are lacking, audio-visual materials are used instead.

For the Hispanic groups, components in Spanish are available. For Native American groups, the impact of the Tekakwitha Conference is just beginning to be felt. The Santa Fe Institute for Spirituality also provides one week a year on Native American spirituality.

The New Mexico Baptist Convention

The New Mexico Baptist Convention covers the entire state, comprising the churches in the state that are connected with the Southern Baptist Convention, an aggressive, growing, conservative church. Small membership churches number 274 out of a total of 367. It has to be noted, however, that in certain cases Sunday school membership is larger than church membership. There are 67,058 resident members in the churches, and 60,413 members in the Sunday schools. Participation in the Church Training Union (a more intensive educational program than the Sunday school, has decreased somewhat, and stands at 16,559. Lay institutes, with regular curriculum leading to a diploma, and six-week modules, tend to take its place. The Women's Missionary Union educational program for all ages has 6,657 members, and tends to be used more in small membership churches. The Brotherhood has a corresponding program for men and boys.

Open country churches are fewer (10.9 percent) than the national figure for the Southern Baptist Convention (37.9 percent). Twenty-four of the fifty-seven churches in Albuquerque are small membership churches. About one-third of the small membership churches are in centers of 10,000-50,000 population. The rest are in towns and villages.

Of the 274 small membership churches, about 200 are predominantly Anglo, forty to fifty are predominantly Hispanic, and eleven or twelve are predominantly Native American.

Differences among the churches are not primarily theological. They are more likely to differ in the kind of music they use, the degree of formality in worship, in practices like the ordination of women as deacons, and (while insisting on immersion) on the emphasis placed on rebaptism.

Religious education planning is done by the pastor and the Sunday school council. (The council may consist of teachers, or of directors of departments.) It is recommended that the Sunday school council report to the church council on planning matters. Heavy emphasis is put on annual planning. Since the church year runs from October 1 through September 30, the heavy load of planning has to be over by August.

The associations within the state convention offer training events. Recent emphases have been on the ABCs of church planning and on the pastor who is also the church's principal religious educator. One of the two major conference centers of the Southern Baptist Convention is located at Glorieta, New Mexico, a few miles from Santa Fe, but its use by New Mexico people is not great. They do not seem to be geared to week-long events.

Typical religious education programs include the Sunday school, the Church Training Union, missionary education for all ages (separate groups for men and women), a graded church music program, and ministry with families, singles, senior adults, and students. Churches subscribe to the Baptist Television Network services. Forty-four churches in the state, many of them small membership churches, now subscribe.

Professional personnel involved in the religious education program are the pastor and often a part-time director of religious education. More and more churches are employing persons for combinations of music, education, and youth work.

Building and equipment are most often quite adequate, with a separate space for each educational unit.

Resources outside the parish include religious education consultants at the convention level and (at the association level) persons who combine religious education and mission responsibilities. There is one Baptist Book Store in the state, but churches do not use it as much as they do the A.T.&T. 800 number (and in some cases in-church computer services) by which they may order directly from the Sunday School Board in Nashville. There are also periodic training opportunities.

While the generally recommended curriculum material for small membership churches is the Convention Uniform Series, there is a significant number of churches that use other materials or (for adult classes) no materials to supplement the Bible itself. Some churches order selectively by age groups. Ease of preparation, attractiveness, and acceptance by workers are major criteria in the selection of materials.

The Presbyterian Church (U.S.A.)

The Presbytery of Santa Fe covers over half of New Mexico, and has forty-two churches, of which thirty-two are small membership churches (250 members or less). Of the thirty-two, about half are urban. Except for two in the open country, the rest are located in villages.[16] Eleven are predominantly Hispanic, and one (with three chapels) is Native American.

These small membership churches are moderate to conservative theologically, with two exceptions. One of the exceptions is a church that stresses close fellowship and experimental worship; the other has a membership that consists to a significant degree of university people. The ethnic churches are without exception conservative.

Religious education planning is generally done, under the leadership of the pastor, by the religious education committee of the parish, reporting to the church's session (the board of elders). With two exceptions, all have Sunday schools. Three have organized youth groups. In addition to adult Sunday school classes, most have mid-week Bible study groups. A significant number have family night programs, with a variety of appropriate activities serving children, families, youth, and adults.

Most pastors are also teachers, while certain lay people who teach also serve occasionally as preachers. A number of the lay persons have special training, being professional teachers or educational administrators. The average church teacher has some educational work beyond high school. One member in an open country church is a rancher who holds a Ph.D. A number of teachers are business people, and those in the Santa Fe area are employed by the Los Alamos National Laboratories.

The presbytery employs an associate executive, among whose duties is that of consulting with the churches on religious education program, including curriculum. There is also a Christian education committee that is responsible for the training of teachers and leaders, as well as assisting the churches in the selection and use of curriculum materials. Ghost Ranch, the denominational study center, is in the presbytery and is used by many teachers and leaders.

Sixteen of the churches use the recommended denominational curricu-

---

16. At one time, one of the open country churches, with five members, had the distinction of being the smallest in the denomination. It has recently grown, and has twice as many members and five times the attendance it once had.

lum material. A few of the others use material from other similar denominations. Two use a published curriculum in which the individual learner proceeds at his or her own pace.[17] A number use the materials produced by the David C. Cook Publishing Company, one of the largest independent curriculum publishers.

In advising the churches on their choice of curriculum materials, the associate executive and the educational unit counsel that they select those materials that reflect their needs as a congregation. They point out, however, that there are certain materials that will not be of help. If materials are chosen from other denominations, churches are encouraged to supplement them with courses, pamphlets, filmstrips, and other materials that promote denominational identity.

Teachers of small membership churches themselves report that they want curriculum materials that are "friendly," that are not too difficult to comprehend, and that do not require an inordinate amount of preparation time.

The Assemblies of God

The New Mexico District of the Assemblies of God includes all the churches in the state, with the exception of those Hispanic churches that are a part of the Central Latin American District. While related to the national denomination, the Central Latin American District is independent of the New Mexico District. This accounts for the relatively low number of Hispanic churches in the New Mexico District. There are six geographical sections in the District.

Because of the nature of membership in the Assemblies of God, churches of 150 members or less are small membership churches. Of the 100 churches in the district, seventy-eight are in this category. Of these, twenty-one are in urban areas, five in the open country, and the remaining fifty-two in villages or small towns.

The churches are very likely to include persons of various ethnic backgrounds —Native American, Hispanic, and Anglo. However, sixteen are predominantly Native American; three Hispanic (see the proviso above); and fifty-nine, Anglo.

The churches are theologically conservative, most being very fundamental. Some of their religious education differences, however, are in worship styles and types of music used. All are Pentecostal, but none of the

---

17. The St. John Curriculum, developed by Kenneth Clark, Canon Educator at St. John's Cathedral, Albuquerque, and published by Youth Club, Inc.

small membership churches uses ecstatic worship. They are of the wing of the church that holds to the need for radical conversion, and not of the "faith leads to prosperity" wing.

The denomination, through its "Directions for the Decade of Harvest" emphasis, stresses careful, systematic educational planning at the congregational level. The key agency for this planning is a committee, chaired by the superintendent of the Sunday school, with the pastor as a member *ex officio,* and usually acting as the main resource person. The plan is for voluntary use, but its use is strengthened by visits of national and district officers to the sections and churches, and by elected sectional Sunday school representatives, who are pastors or associate pastors serving in this capacity as part of their beyond-the-parish duties. At the local level, in practice, the pastor usually takes the lead in religious education planning, working with the Sunday school superintendent.

The result is a local program that is a blend of Sunday school, missions education, and evangelism. The key is a strong Bible-centered Sunday school where the Word of God can be taught. Missions education characteristically takes place through the BGMC (Boys and Girls Missionary Crusade), whose materials are mainly used about once a month in the children's church. In addition, there are monthly youth rallies in each section, a summer camping program for pre-teens and youth, and AIM trips (Ambassadors in Mission), often to other countries, for youth.

When the denominational plan is followed, there is provision for the Sunday school main session, extension classes (at other times than the Sunday school hour), branch schools (intended to develop into autonomous congregations), additional children's ministries, family ministries, single adult ministries, groups for persons with special needs, and missions education. Most commonly, the elements that are found in the small membership churches, besides the Sunday school, are children's ministries, marriage enrichment, extension classes, and missions education. Senior ministries are in beginning stages, and there are a few instances of groups for persons with special needs.

Leadership education in the parish is done by the pastor and the Sunday school superintendent. The pastor has special responsibility for training the Sunday school superintendent. Most small membership churches consist of a sanctuary, fellowship hall, and several classrooms. Audio-visual equipment is available and used.

Resources available to the churches from outside center in the sectional Sunday school representatives. They meet annually with the Youth and Christian Education Director of the district, using training materials from the national office. These sectional representatives do needs analyses of the parishes and conduct training missions at least once a year. When the district director visits the section, usually once a year, a Sunday school training event is planned, and the sectional representative conducts a workshop during the function. National officers and seminary personnel are also used in the sections and parishes from time to time. Leadership material (a "Book-of-the-Year," evaluation forms, job descriptions, and the like) is available from the national publishing house. In addition, the publishing house has regional representatives who counsel on curriculum and leadership matters.

The denominational curriculum, "Radiant Life," with appropriate materials for all ages, is recommended and generally used, especially in small membership churches. Its emphases are on scripture, doctrine (stressing the Pentecostal faith), and personal needs. Missions education is woven in, with supplementary material for the BGMC. Periodically, the publishing house conducts a survey of needs, to keep the curriculum relevant. There is little deviation from the curriculum at the children's level. At the youth level, there are a few cases of teachers doing "what they are led to teach." There is likely to be more flexible use of the adult material, with shorter modules provided for optional use. A Spanish translation of the curriculum, "Vida Radiante," is available.

SPECIAL PROJECTS

There are a number of special curriculum projects with which I have been personally involved that bear on the matter of curriculum in the small membership church. They have so shaped my thinking on curriculum in general, as well as on curriculum in the small membership church, that I feel justified in discussing them here.

My professional work started in two mission schools in the Southern Mountains of Appalachia. Interest in the area had been sparked by experiences in college in which we were required to live and work for a period in the mountains of Western North Carolina. The culture, church life, and educational ways of the Appalachian people were further opened up in these early teaching experiences, which involved close contact with the churches and their Sunday schools and vacation schools. One of my assignments was to help to develop a rural life center that was to assist with the religious, educational, and economic development of one of the presbyteries in the Cumberland Mountains. One of the emphases was on curriculum development, in which we worked out experimental units for the children's level, including attempts at music, storytelling, and creative dramatics of an indigenous character. This was followed by the design and conduct of workshops for training in the effective use and evaluation of the material.

The ultimate fruition of this experience came much later when I was invited to join the staff of the Appalachian Curriculum Project of Joint Educational Development. The product of that project was published as the book, *Beautiful upon the Mountains, A Handbook for Church Education in Appalachia*.[18] The project was begun at the instigation of the Cumberland Presbyterian Church, which was seeking the development of indigenous materials that the church would accept and use. It developed that one of the regular series of *Christian Education: Shared Approaches* provided what they needed, so the project changed direction and worked on curriculum ideas that would supplement and enrich the work of the Sunday school as the basic institution. Three approaches eventuated. The first was built on a family/congregation model, since in Appalachia the culture is fundamentally transmitted by the family, and the congregation tends to operate on the dynamics of an extended family. The second was a music/youth model, since the culture is permeated by music of an indigenous character, to which youth, in particular, is drawn. The third used as experience/story/vision model, based upon Thomas Groome's shared praxis teaching model. This was deemed to be appropriate because of the long experience of a number of Appalachian congregations with study and action groups concentrating on local educational and economic problems and projects.

An interim period on the staff of the Greater New York Federation of Churches was useful in discovering how important interchurch experiences were for youth in small member urban congregations. Working with the Youth Council of the Federation in designing and conducting a city-wide study conference for youth on "The Challenge of International Christianity" provided an unusual experience in curriculum building for an interchurch group.

When I joined the national staff of the denomination in rural church and Indian work, I found them in the midst of a project on writing curriculum materials for Native American churches. Here the emphasis was on three

---

18. D. Campbell Wyckoff et al., *Beautiful upon the Mountains, A Handbook for Church Education in Appalachia* (Memphis: Board of Christian Education of the Cumberland Presbyterian Church, 1984). Harold Davis chaired the project and John Spangler provided staff services.

kinds of stories from the experience of the people themselves—stories in the folk tradition that dealt with religious themes, stories in the folk tradition that paralleled biblical stories, and stories from the experience of the people with the church and its leaders.

Later we worked on vacation church school units designed for the rural and ethnic churches with which we worked. After the publication and distribution of a vacation school unit based on the experience of Hispanic churches, the project was taken over by the curriculum people on the denomination's Board of Christian Education, and continued for several years.

At the same time, several workshops were held in the Southwest, in which workers with Hispanic and Native American churches and schools were trained in the development of their own approaches to and materials for weekday religious education classes. Many of the approaches used in these workshops were based upon the experience of the Children's Committee of the New York State Council of Churches in building materials for rural religious education and for weekday religious education in rural released time schools.

Further experience with Native American curriculum came much later, in a brief stint as a consultant to the project in this area conducted by the National Council of the Episcopal Church. With much the same motivation as that of the Tekakwitha Conference of the Roman Catholic Church, the Episcopal Church gathered a group of Native Americans to devise materials that could be used both in Native American congregations to deepen their religious experience by exploring their particular cultural and religious heritage, and by other congregations in raising their consciousness of Native Americans and their contributions to the church. An interesting format was worked out. The curriculum was designed to be printed on posters, with stories and activities on one side of the posters, and paintings by Indian artists and photographs on the other side, picking up the themes of the stories.

Two units of the National Council of Churches, one dealing with international affairs, and the other with Christian education, were asked to form a joint committee on international affairs education in the churches. I chaired the joint committee. It was in this connection that we saw and used the possibilities of an action-reflection model in religious education. Although not specifically touching on small membership churches, the practical possibilities in the model became apparent, and I now believe that its use in small membership churches is a real possibility, perhaps more practical and effective under certain conditions than an instructional model.

Editorial work on the curriculum of the Caribbean Conference of Churches proved particularly instructive in its attention to the needs of small membership churches, its training of volunteers as editors, writers, and key persons in interpretation and leadership development, and in its superb work in incorporating indigenous qualities in its stories, activities, art work, and music. Its sets of "teaching pictures" are among the best ever produced, and its enlistment of recognized musicians and lyricists in writing special songs and hymns is unparalleled.

Design work on an Arabic curriculum, for use mainly among small membership churches in Lebanon, Jordan, Egypt, and among the Palestinians led to new understanding and appreciation of the force of culture and enculturation on the ways in which religion may be taught. People in different cultures learn in different ways, and the activities and approaches that are used must mirror those ways of learning. Furthermore, when for years a people has been under the influence of an outside culture (as in the case of French influence on Lebanese education), a new culture with mixed values and ways, and with mixed assumptions about education, comes into being. Three of the significant discoveries in this connection were that four different versions of the curriculum had to be worked out because of cultural differences among the Arabic Christians, that leadership development had to be done differently in each context, and that curriculum writers and editors can do their jobs best when they have role-played as learners.

Finally, although there is a general assumption among national curriculum developers that the materials they produce are quite suitable for small membership churches, it has been instructive to observe attempts to deal with more specific needs of small membership churches through the adaptation of existing materials by counseling on how to use them with broadly graded groups, and by developing intergenerational programs.

Guidelines

What do these data imply for curriculum in the small membership church? How may the small membership church put together a comprehensive and practical plan that takes into account everything that it knows about religious education—the teaching and mission of the church, the character of the Christian life, the learning process, and the challenges and opportunities in the situation of the learners?

This is a task in which the whole church has a stake, but it is not one on which a large group can do the spadework. A group is called for, made up of the most experienced hands and informed minds on the Christian faith and religious education. It is important that the pastor as primary religious educator be involved in the work of the group at every step. The group's task is to formulate an educational plan for the local church that suits its character and function. Throughout its work the group will consult widely with persons inside and outside the parish, read the basic literature on the task of religious education, become familiar with available curriculum plans and resources, and test its ideas from time to time with those whose job it will be to approve and implement the plan. When it is ready to do its final reporting, it will provide interpretation in turn to the church's religious education committee, its governing board, and the congregation.

Purposes

The group's attention turns first to clarification of what religious education is to accomplish in the local church. This may be simple or complex, depending on how clear the church is about its particular mission. Most churches today have mission statements that guide their life and work. If the particular church does not have such a statement, its formulation constitutes a priority task. With a working mission statement, the group deals with the question: What must the religious education work of the church accomplish, in order that the church's mission may be fully and effectively fulfilled? In other words, what do our people (at various ages and stages of life and experience) need to know and become in order to come to maturity in Christ and understand and undertake the church's mission?

It will occur to the group, as it works on the purposes of religious education for the church, that there is more than curriculum materials and resources involved. They have to deal with questions of leadership and leadership development; program and the kind of organization that will carry the program adequately; suitable housing, equipment, and teaching and learning supplies; scheduling various aspects of the program; and finance. Without adequate attention to these matters, the purposes cannot be accomplished. On the other hand, in the small membership church they must be handled economically or the plan will be too grandiose to carry out.

Learning Activities

With purposes clear, the group's attention turns to appropriate learning activities. The first requirement is a good idea of what the content of the curriculum is to be, in terms of subject matter and experience. The subject matter covers the necessary knowledge of the Bible, the faith, and the personal and social demands of discipleship. The experience component deals with those factors and actions that make for personal growth and change and with the skills with which the Christian regularly comes to and implements decisions.

Fundamentally, the choice of learning activities is guided by the principle that persons learn the Christian faith and life by rich and reflective involvement in the worship, witness, and work of the church in its various ministries. Thus, the learning activities that are chosen for the education plan will be those that stress worship, study, fellowship, creativity, stewardship, and witness, service, and social action.

The choice of learning activities will also be guided by the character of the small membership church. The small membership church may work more like a family than the larger church, implying that appropriate learning activities will be more like informal learning in the family than like formal learning in a school. There will be an atmosphere of closeness, warmth, intimacy, and informality, difficult to achieve except in the small membership church.

Further, the choice of learning activities will be to a significant degree determined by the makeup of the membership. Many small membership churches have a particular ethnic heritage. Many are located in places where the people engage in similar occupations or share particular patterns of life. In some churches, the members are brought together because they share particular visions of Christian faith and discipleship. These all need to be fully reflected in the kinds of learning activities that are chosen.

Organization of the Curriculum

With purposes and appropriate learning activities worked out, the group deals with the question of how the program is to be organized. Since curricula always have sequences of learning activities, is the sequence of the program to be primarily logical (determined by sequential growth of ideas) or psychological (determined by sequential growth of experience)? Can a more fluid sequence be used that is determined by the developing experience of the church, rather than the individual?

The organization of the program also involves decisions about grouping. In this particular situation, is the emphasis to be more on a graded program or on an intergenerational program? If graded, how is the grading to be worked out so that there is balance in the number of participants in each segment of the program?

Materials and Resources

With the skeletal ideas of the purposes, learning activities, and organization that it wants, the group is in a position to turn to examine materials and resources and make an informed decision on what to recommend. Ordinarily, it is wise to consider the materials and resources that are recommended by the denomination. If, however, they prove not to fit, other options are examined. The group may in the long run decide that it needs to do a job of "mix and match" in order to get what it wants, or to develop its own materials and resources, in whole or in part. Developing your own materials, however is a long and difficult process, and should not be undertaken lightly or without professional help.

Elements in Implementation

Considerations of leadership and leadership development; program organization; housing, equipment, and supplies; scheduling; and finance, having been on the group's mind all along, must now be given full attention. The decisions that are made on these matters have to be a realistic balance of practical needs and possibilities, on the one hand, and realistic implementation of the curricular decisions, on the other hand. Curricular decisions may have to be modified at this point, to some degree. *Do* recommend a plan that has real promise of being implemented in the local situation. *Do not* recommend a curriculum that cannot be adequately carried through. Perhaps the balance is to be found in a plan that presents challenge but that does not spell defeat from the very beginning.

Final Action

The report that the group prepares and submits to the religious education committee, the church's governing group, and the congregation highlights its recommendations on materials and resources and includes enough of its thinking on purposes, learning activities, the organization of the curriculum, and practical matters of implementation to make its reasons for making the recommendations clear. It also includes its recommendations on steps to be taken to put the plan into effect.

Chapter Nine

Conflict, Feuds, and Border Wars

DONALD E. BOSSART

INTRODUCTION

Conflict is a dynamic present in every local church. The critical question is whether the conflict is constructive or destructive. Understanding the dynamics of conflict is a necessary part of making them constructive. These dynamics can differ in the small membership church from that of the large membership church. This chapter will attempt to describe that difference and how it affects religious education and the creative resolve of conflict.

My beginning teaching new pastors-educators at seminary was with a class of graduating seniors called a senior seminar. The goal of this seminar was to deal with matters of importance and concern before going out to serve in full-time work. The most frequent and serious topic raised was how to deal with conflict. These students had just enough experience in part-time ministry while attending seminary to know how difficult it was to manage the conflict in their parishes. Most of their experience was in the small membership church. They did not know what to do to creatively manage what they saw there. The conflict seemed so pervasive, so entrenched, so debilitating when it affected the small membership church. They came to realize that the effectiveness of their ministry may well rest on how well they learn to deal with this conflict.

Ministry tends to be taught from the perspective of the large membership church. The model is certainly over the 200 membership figure. Most pastor-educators who teach at the seminary have come from the large membership church, both in their own background as well as in their parish experience. By contrast, most seminary graduates leave school and enter the small membership church for the early years of their ministry.

It has also been established that over half of active Protestants worship in and experience religious education in congregations with attendance of seventy-five or less every Sunday.[1] Many Catholics also worship in small parishes. Yet church leaders and denominations see the large membership church as normative. The perspective of the seminary and the denomination sets the tone for the expectations of the seminary graduate. However, the immediate experience and the pattern for years to come for the new pastor-educator is to be with the small membership church.

Population shifts have been toward the rural areas, from the city to the less populated areas. These shifts have brought people who have been members of the large membership church and placed them in the midst of established, small membership churches. Experience and expectation differ, creating the groundwork for new conflict.

IMPORTANT DIFFERENCES

If seminary training tends to focus on the large membership church, then some of the important differences between the small membership and the large membership churches need to be enumerated. These differences will be relevant to one concerned about religious education and the creative utilization of conflict.

A major difference is the unique organizational style of each church. The large membership churches are typically organized around a functional design and a representational system. The governing bodies tend to be made up of persons who represent large groups in various divisions of the church's operations and programing. Smooth functioning and performance

1. Lyle E. Schaller, *The Small Church Is Different* (Nashville: Abingdon, 1982), p. 10.

are priorities. Leadership focuses on administration to oversee this process. The ties that hold people together in the large membership church are organizational-functional ties. Personal ties are related to smaller segments of the church organization or programing. The central tie or loyalty for all is the minister or staff. Few, it any, persons are involved in all aspects of the church. Commitment is quite selective, and goals have a wide range of diversity. Planning is quite complex and is done so in long-range perspective. Power is in the hands of officers who have been elected because they have earned their positions by leadership within the church as well as from outside the church. They have demonstrated their competency by their work and their commitment. They are truly representative. Their power is the power of office and of abilities.[2] Conflict management dynamics based on this context will follow.

The small membership church reflects a different organizational structure. It is not just a scaled-down version of the large membership church. This difference is critical for the understanding of conflict dynamics. Carl Dudley, church researcher/writer, has described the unique characteristic of the small membership church as a single cell: a primary group to which everyone identifies and associates. All belong, know about, and care for each member. This single cell carries a long common history which is measured by significant events, preserving a culture that vitally affects the present and future operations of the church.[3] This points to a critical dimension of religious education in the small membership church. This cell reflects a relational characteristic that contrasts to the large membership church's functional characteristic. It is the individual who counts and for whom care is extended by all. Almost every member knows the name and the history of each of the others. When members are absent from meetings or worship, it is a person who is absent, not a name, or number, or count. It is also the individual who does the work of the church, not a committee. These persons who do the work as laity in leadership do so not necessarily because they have proven themselves in and outside the church but because they are a part of a historic church family of generations of religious education leadership and who now ought to be growing into the leadership of the present and future. In fact, most of the decision making in the small membership church is done by a consensus of the body as a whole. It is more of a participatory democracy than a representative orga-

2. Ibid., pp. 18-40.
3. Carl S. Dudley, *Unique Dynamics of the Small Church* (Washington, D.C.: The Alban Institute, 1977).

nization. Most meetings are of an open nature, containing plenty of social fellowship time for all present, rather than the heavy, task-oriented agendas of the large membership churches. Goals and loyalties are more focused as a whole body, having strong rootage in the past. Commitment of members is based upon heritage and tradition, which has strong kinship ties. Power in the small membership church is usually kept close to kinship ties. A very few persons tend to set direction and wield power in the congregation, often holding critical offices or responsibilities for many years. Even when these power leaders leave their church offices, they continue to exercise control over important decisions. Power in the small membership church tends to be in the hands of the laity in contrast to the greater personal power in the clergy-staff of the large membership church.[4]

In sum, Lyle Schaller, expert on the small membership church, has described the basic ties of this organization. The people are tied to: 1) each other, 2) a meeting place, 3) kinfolk, 4) a family-like organization, 5) a women's organization and its goals, 6) local traditions and customs, 7) Sunday school, and 8) a church cemetery.[5]

These basic characteristics, as they relate to religious education and conflict dynamics in the small membership church, will be developed later. There is a factor that remains formative when relating to conflict dynamics. It is the rather obvious characteristic of limited resources. Amazing support is often given to the small membership church from the few members that it has. Crises emerge with their financial problems, yet the church members seem to be able to rise to the challenge and pride themselves in their ability to do so when the crunch is on.

The resources are limited and they must make choices for the application of their budget. The members would often like to be able to do things which they simply cannot. For example, they may wish to retain full-time pastoral services or religious education leadership, such as in youth work or music leadership. These expenditures are very often beyond their capacities. They are aware of large membership churches and the ability they have to hire such leadership. The pastor-educator has visions for this small congregation, but the resources just are not there to reach that vision. The frustration of a consistent shortage of funds and unmet goals often brings a low self-image or low morale to the congregation and its professional leadership. The church can get a feeling of being abused or ignored in the larger church structure and project a bleak future for themselves. With such

---

4. Schaller, *The Small Church Is Different*, pp. 18-51.
5. Ibid., p. 52.

a low self-image, commitment from the worshipers can begin to drop and divisiveness emerge. Leadership can become only dutiful and appear uncaring. Hope for solvency and strength seems distant, and blame is projected both within and without. The professional leadership can become a scapegoat for all ills unless she/he is continually showing care and concern through calling and involvement with the crisis events of the members. This potential for low self-image or worth, often stemming from the reality of limited resources of funds or persons, is the point that begins my theoretical assumptions.

THEORETICAL ASSUMPTIONS

1. All conflict begins intrapersonally. The degree of self-worth or self-esteem felt by the individual is the core to constructive conflict resolution. To the degree that one feels a lack of self-worth, one will have difficulty dealing with conflict constructively or creatively.

A premise in conflict theory is that the conflicting parties are responsible for their own actions and therefore for the direction of relationships that follow. People create the interactions of conflict out of their own inner needs, which can entrap them into endless rounds of destructive conflict. A change in a person's individual behavior can change the whole interaction system.[6]

A lack of self-worth raises the defensiveness of the person, making conflict more difficult to process creatively. It may well come down to the psycho-theological point of whether one gets self-worth from others or from within the self and one's God. Establishing self-worth from others is a very tenuous process. To feel that it has already been given to us from our God frees us from dependency on others, as long as we maintain faith in our belief system. The understanding of self-worth is a basic factor in beginning to deal with religious education and conflict dynamics. The factor of low self-image can be a characteristic of the small membership church and therefore a contributor to the tension and a deterrent to dealing creatively with conflict therein. The source of the self-esteem problem can be within either the pastor-educator or the laity, or both. Thus, the issue of self-worth is of basic concern in coming to terms with conflict.[7]

---

6. J.L. Hocker and W.W. Wilmot, *Interpersonal Conflict,* 2nd. ed. (Dubuque, Iowa: William C. Brown, 1978, 1985), pp. 158-159.

7. Donald E. Bossart, *Creative Conflict in Religious Education and Church Administration* (Birmingham, Ala.: Religious Education Press, 1980), pp. 66-70.

2. The second assumption is that all conflict begins intrapersonally and becomes interpersonal when it is projected outward onto others. Projection is a well-established psychological theory which states that projection feeds on our inner, ongoing battle. That battle is between our shoulds and our wants. The conflict within is one in which we as individuals strive to find some equilibrium. It is not a struggle which can come to an end with a decision that holds once and for all. The degree to which we find an acceptable equilibrium between our shoulds and our wants is the degree to which we find self-worth and project less conflict out onto others. This equilibrium comes from the full acceptance of ourselves, warts and all, and is helped by the conviction that our God has made us and lovingly accepts us as well. This acquired self-worth helps in dealing more creatively and less defensively with the conflict projected out onto us from others. Psychiatrist Sigmund Freud helps to delineate this inner conflict with his description of the battle between our superego (shoulds) and our id (wants). In a sense, then, each of us is the source of all conflict. To the degree that we have not found satisfactory equilibrium with our own inner conflict, we project that conflict out onto others. This is not a popular maxim, since we all tend to believe that others are the source of our conflict and wish to blame them for our conflicting situations.[8]

3. The third assumption is that the problem is not the problem but rather the state of the individual and the resulting relationship with others. This maxim comes from Blaine Hartford who was with the Niagara Institute of Behavioral Science. It builds on the earlier premise that all conflict begins within. Therefore, if we tend to focus on the apparent problem that emerges in interpersonal conflict, we may forget to look to the inner person to find the source motivation for the interpersonal conflict. Preoccupation with the apparent problem can divert energy and time, leading to nonresolution and frustration. Self-awareness is vital to the understanding of religious education and conflict dynamics and the movement toward successful resolution.

4. The final assumption is that conflict can be creative. In fact, conflict is the source of all growth. This is not to say that all conflict is creative. But it is to say that there is no growth without the successful dealing with conflict within. Each person tends to both want to change and grow and not want to change and grow. Preference is for the comfortable status quo or equilibrium we have already established rather than to reach out for the growth and change that is possible. Other times we are compelled by the

---

8. Ibid., pp. 64-66.

growth possibility and move toward change and goals we have set or accepted for ourselves. Conflict must first come to our already established perceptions and beliefs before we are moved to bring about any changes or growth.

This theory is based on the developmental concepts of Erik Erikson and Jean Piaget. It has been put into a theory of moral development in stages by Lawrence Kohlberg, utilizing the dynamics of conflict in change to move from one stage to the next in growth.[9]

DYNAMIC SOURCES

Three further dynamic sources for conflict have a helpful bearing on understanding religious education and conflict.

1. Perceptual differences are a major element in the creation of conflict. This is reflected in the definition of conflict by Hocker and Wilmot as "an expressed struggle between at least two interdependent parties who *perceive* incompatible goals, scarce rewards, and interference from the other party in achieving their goals."[10] It is a natural assumption that what we see is in fact reality. However, both superficial as well as scientific testing shows us that what we "see" is not necessarily reality. We tend to filter out what we do not want to see, or else we are overwhelmed with data and cannot handle it all at one time. Our very beginnings as a child start a screening process which begins selective reception of the data around us, creating a phenomena of "our world" in contrast to the "real" world. Data that does not conform to "our world" is filtered in order not to create inner conflict. We therefore do not "see" everything, or rather "let in" all data. This unconscious process sets us up for future conflict, as we assume what we let in is the whole or real world. Our perception of a problem may not therefore be the perception of a problem which another sees, and yet we assume that it is.

Understanding another person's thinking is not just a helpful measure to solve problems. The other's thinking *is the problem*. Differences in conflict are defined by the difference between your thinking and theirs.[11]

Take the example of the first meeting of another person. At the first

9. Lawrence Kohlberg, "Education, Moral Development, and Faith," *Journal of Moral Education* 4 (1974), pp. 5-16.

10. Hocker and Wilmot, *Interpersonal Conflict,* p. 23.

11. Roger Fisher and William Ury, *Getting to Yes* (Boston: Houghton Mifflin, 1981), p. 22.

instance of meeting a stranger, it is said that over two thousand pieces of data are made available to us. This experience is overwhelming. We cannot handle it all at once. So we do the next most natural thing. We selectively take on some of the data from the person and start our relationship with that. This is not particularly a problem, as long as we are aware of what we are doing. Unfortunately, we do not operate with only partial data of a person but tend to fill in the gaps with our own data to meet our needs. We therefore create that person that we meet in order to meet our needs. We can quickly stereotype the person to fit the likeness of someone we have met before in order to know how to relate to them. This stereotyping is not too problematic as long as we recognize what we are doing and gradually allow the person to continue to reveal themselves to us as we are able to receive them. Then, of course, we need to be aware of our constant filtering process.

What really makes this perceptual problem so immense is the fact that most of the data that we confront from the world around us is not processed through our consciousness. This we know from contemporary research in cognitive psychology. Daniel Goleman of Harvard University puts the best research together on this subject in his book, *Vital Lies, Simple Truths*. Research indicates that we filter out and store in the unconscious the data we take in through perception, leaving very little to be processed through the preconscious and out into the conscious mind for our conscious action and decision making. We do make some decisions from our unconscious data as well. However, we think that we are making our decisions from the well-considered conscious data.[12] You can see how perception affects conflict and conflict resolution.

2. A second major source of conflict comes from our assumption that what we intend to say to another person is what they hear. This is not necessarily true.

The Communication Gap theory tells us that the process of thinking an idea, translating it into words and action for another to hear, results in a possible miscomprehension of the idea. When a person thinks of an idea, he/she must translate that idea into words and/or actions (encode) which characterizes the idea and its meaning and conveys the message intended. These words and actions are then decoded by the receiver into the meanings that they have with them, which are not necessarily the same as that of the sender. This creates the possibility of a gap between the message

---

12. Daniel Goleman, *Vital Lies, Simple Truths* (New York: Simon and Schuster, 1985), pp. 84-90.

sent by the sender and the one received by the receiver. Misunderstandings occur. sometimes without the persons being aware of the gap in communication. The opportunity to clarify and verify the information is not always present. Our assumption is that what we say is what is heard. From this position, conflict can surface easily and with surprise.

3. The third major source of conflict is the dynamic of power. In itself, power is a neutral term. It can be defined as a force necessary to achieve an end or a goal. It has neither a good nor a bad connotation until it is made clear that it is one person's end or goal over another's. We tend to view power as a force over against us or of our force acting upon another. It is the acting out of the win/lose approach, which says there is only a limited resource over which we must fight. There must be a winner and a loser.

Power can be achieved by way of election to an office. An office conveys authority. Power can also be given to a person by virtue of their physical presence or strength of personality. The latter power can be either latent and unused, or it can be expressed and utilized for some purpose or goal.

Power basically comes from within, surging from our inner sense of worth. It comes from the capacity to accept the whole of oneself, the bad with the good, forging it into a unity of personhood. This releases power toward accomplishment that would otherwise be wasted in the struggle within to gain self-worth and esteem. This power of self-worth and self-confidence breaks the need for defensive behavior, making handling of conflict more constructive and growth producing.

Essentially, there is no such thing as pure equality of power in relations. But that is not actually important. What is important is whether or not there is a *felt* equilibrium of power in relationships. Equilibrium is achieved when a person feels that she/he is heard and taken seriously by another or others. In a conflict, this may be all that a person wants, i.e., to be taken seriously in the proceedings, whether or not their ideas are finally adopted. A sense of equilibrium of power is a necessary dynamic in working toward conflict resolution or conflict utilization toward growth.[13]

The importance of power balancing is confirmed by the research/writing of Hocker and Wilmot. Power imbalance can harm relationships, particularly due to the many different assessments of power. Power balancing can increase the possibilities for productive conflict utilization by limiting the power of a high-power party, empowering a low-power party, or restructuring the conflict from win/lose to win/win dynamics.[14]

---

13. Bossart, *Creative Conflict,* pp. 98-105.
14. Hocker and Wilmot, *Interpersonal Conflict,* p. 90.

CONFLICT DYNAMICS

I. Individualistic Approach

How do the dynamics of conflict get started? Conflict usually begins with the feeling of chaos. There is the sense that something is wrong, but we do not know what it is. Sometimes we do not really want to know what is wrong, for then we would have to deal with it, or at least find ways to deny it. But chaos is not a pleasant stance in which to be. We usually press to find out what is wrong. If we do not, there is likely someone who is willing to tell us because they think we ought to know.

Once we become aware that there is an issue or disagreement, the reality of the competition hits us. This is where we can become ego involved and get hurt or hurt another. It is the dangerous stage of conflict dynamics. We can become so involved (and threatened) that we may say something we did not really want to say or find ourselves polarized from others and find our association with them endangered.

In order to protect ourselves from this dangerous situation, we may tend to avoid conflict, or at least the competitive stage just described, and try to bypass that stage and move toward collaboration or reconciliation. If this dynamic is operating in a group, the group will come to the first possible solution to the apparent conflict in order to avoid the continuation of competition and the possible threat to relationships. This is called groupthink, a phrase coined by sociologist Irving Janis. This dynamic does not resolve the conflict but merely pushes it into the background or underground. As the issue is not actually settled, it will surface again later. The threat to the relationship is too much to risk, so the goal or task must be sacrificed. This jump from chaos, past competition, into collaboration or reconciliation may be expressed in theological terms as "cheap grace." The attainment of a desired state without passing through the suffering or work of competition bypasses the creative possibilities of the conflict. The creativity is in the healthy debate and sharing of various ideas around the problem in order to have perceptions checked and possibilities aired that would never come to one person alone. The pluralism of ideas that defines the conflict also releases new possibilities that come from the uniqueness of each individual through the gift of their creation.

There is also a barrier to moving from the competitive stage and the collaborative stage which must be broken in order for the conflict dynamic to flow from the win/lose of competition to the win/win creativity of competition. One name given to such strategy is that of brainstorming around a problem. It involves the sharing of ideas for potential resolution of an agreed-upon problem without the immediate evaluation of those ideas. The offering of ideas frees persons from the fear of evaluation, allowing a free flow of expression that has the greatest creativity within it. The important point here is separating the act of creating options from the act of deciding. Roger Fisher and William Ury, of the Harvard Negotiation Project, maintain that the discussion of options is a vital difference from taking positions. With positions, one side will automatically conflict with another. With options, other options are invited in a more creative sharing process. The process tends to be more open than closed.[15] Evaluation must eventually follow along the guidelines of agreed-upon criteria for a consensual resolution.

The barrier of the competitive stage is in the inability to listen to one another in order to creatively come to a mutually satisfying solution. The capacity to accomplish this move depends on the freedom from defensive response, resting back on the sense of self-worth and esteem. Can the move be made from a cultural stance of win/lose to a creative stance of win/win? This could allow for the willingness to risk the dangers of competitive conflict for the creative possibilities in it and the growth that could come from it for all parties. It is like embodying the Chinese character for the word conflict, which includes both risk and opportunity.

II. A Systems Approach

The preceding material has been presented from an individualistic perspective. There is another perspective that needs to be contributed before looking at the implications for religious education in the small membership church. This view on conflict dynamics reflects a systems theory. A systems approach says that all persons involved are united into a total system that dictates their individual action. These systems can be either rigid and unchanging, establishing what are called rituals, or they can be flexible or adaptive avoiding being stuck in certain behavior patterns. Essentially, a system is a structured interrelationship of persons, in which the behavior of one dictates the relational pattern of others. The cohesiveness of the relationship of persons will usually determine how adaptable the system is to conflict dynamics within it.

Assessing conflict dynamics through systems theory helps to see repetitive patterns by which parties function and the way in which they process information. Systems operate in a circular pattern from cause to effect, with individuals behaving in a programed fashion, each facilitating the

---

15. Fisher and Ury, *Getting to Yes,* p. 67.

other to carry out his/her role. Religious education in the small membership church is a natural context for the playing out of this dynamic. Conflict in such an arrangement can serve a function in the church by substituting for intimacy, problem solving, or for sharing feelings of dissatisfaction. Understanding the structure and rules of these systems can help to move the church to a more creative use of the conflict that is experienced.[16]

Speed Leas, who has worked in conflict resolution with many churches and other public organizations, thinks that when conflict is submerged it works at cross purposes within the organization. A leader's skill and wisdom are critical in order to surface issues for healthy debate and resolution. If the leader is uncomfortable with getting others to express their differences, the organization is going to have even greater difficulty. Problems continue and become repetitive, even when scapegoated leaders are removed. People have the feeling that if conflict issues surface and others are asked what dissatifactions they have new conflict will arise that did not already exist. Confronting issues or bringing them to the surface is likened to bringing people to attack each other, especially as it might upset a preexistent system at work. Actually, raising submerged conflict is necessary for the creative existence of any organization.[17]

IMPLICATIONS FOR RELIGIOUS EDUCATION IN THE SMALL MEMBERSHIP CHURCH

A unique characteristic of the small membership church was described by Carl Dudley earlier as that of a single cell. This refers to the unitary nature of a primary group, to which each belongs and for whom each cares. In such closely knit groups there is a high frequency of interaction and high personality involvement which tend to suppress conflict. At the same time, hostility engendered over time tends to accumulate and intensify. When conflict finally does break out, it usually does so with explosive character. The conflict dynamic that emerges does not just include the immediate issue but also contains the past accumulation that has been denied expression. The closer the group, the more intense the conflict seems to be. In large membership churches, individuals do not have such high frequency of interaction with the whole group or with total personality involvement. This distance lessens

---

16. Hocker and Wilmot, *Interpersonal Conflict,* pp. 53-60, 131-132.

17. Speed B. Leas, *Creative Leadership Series: Leadership and Conflict* (Nashville: Abingdon, 1982, 1986), pp. 63-65.

the personally disruptive nature of the conflict felt internally in the group.

When a closely knit group faces conflict externally, the group tends to be strengthened and come closer together to face the danger. Group identity is strengthened and the groups boundaries are made more clear. External conflict can help clarify the objectives of the group and enhance the power for achievement. Such external threats as closure by the central office or financial crises can often strengthen the group for a longer term of existence.

The single cell, closely knit group will tend to be more concerned about each other and less interested in new persons or membership growth. This exclusionary character can be problematic for new pastor-educators who bring with them plans for an expanded religious education program and a growing congregation. In fact, these new ideas have come more than once to the small membership church. The pastor-educator who brings them again can find him/herself caught either between divisive factions long established, such as family feuds, or between the staff offices and local tradition instead of either side of a real issue. Lyle Schaller has suggested that the pastor-educator of a small membership church functions more as a chaplain than a leader. The real leadership resides in the continuing lay leadership within the congregation.[18]

Carl Dudley also raises an important point for the new pastor-educator to be aware. Many small membership churches use conflict for their own catharsis. When they allow themselves to fight, they do so in an extended family setting as a kind of affirmation of the larger bond that holds them together. They feel free, therefore, to release their emotions, affection as well as anger. They raise a stylized response to issues, such as: the Blues are always the pro side, the Reds are always against, and the Greens won't play the game.[19] This is similar to the role and status description given to the various members of a small membership church, like the legitimizer, the communicator, the "aginer," and the peacemaker. Rules are established, even though unsaid, which tend to protect the important relationships, just like in a family system.[20]

Conflict is harder to manage in the small membership church because

---

18. Schaller, *The Small Church Is Different,* pp. 54-55.

19. Carl Dudley, "The Art of Pastoring a Small Congregation," in *New Possibilities for Small Churches,* ed. Douglas Alan Walrath (New York: Pilgrim, 1983), p. 52.

20. Mike Massa, "Administration and Leadership," in *Ministry Resources* (Minneapolis: Augsburg, 1986), p. 11.

of the mini-culture in which people live. This relational community does not necessarily live by rational decisions based on logical investigation and orderly conflict management procedures. Votes and decision making are weighted by leadership within, not coherent argument. Family ties and history hold people together, not considered commitments or the outcome of any particular decision.[21]

Relationships must be protected in the decision-making process. It is important to understand that the entire congregation is involved in decision making, either formally at all church meetings or informally at various places and various times throughout the community. It can be a long process but one which will eventuate by consensus. Consensus methodology is important here as it helps to protect the all-important relationships within the body of the single cell. As in the norm of consensus, the outcome is not necessarily what anyone originally wanted, but it is what everyone is willing to live with having met certain basic needs. This preserves the community as much as possible. The leadership for this process is focused on a few people who have this power conveyed upon them by the members of the congregation. The persons may or may not be officeholders, but power is given to them to do the task. Often such leaders may inherit their power through family bloodlines.[22]

CONSENSUS AND SUPPORTIVE LEADERSHIP

Consensus methodology in decision making in the small membership church requires some critical understandings if it is to allow for creative conflict management. Even if the process is less formal in this size organization, some structural concerns are still to be noted. Consensus making requires a focus on integrative goals, or goals which bring people together around basic needs. Fisher and Ury describe a block to creative problem solving which consists in the acceptance of the notion that there is a fixed pie of resources. The more for you, the less for me. However, shared interests produce agreements good for all parties. Latent shared interests lie in every conflict. The unearthing of them will create the excitement of joint gain and mutually advantageous relationships.[23]

It is too often assumed that the congregation has or is aware of integrated goals. Good religious education leaders must keep these goals before

---

21. Dudley, *Unique Dynamics of the Small Church*, p. 20.
22. Massa, *Administration and Leadership*, pp. 5-10.
23. Fisher and Ury, *Getting to Yes*, pp. 73-77.

the people or else help them develop new ones if they are in fact changing. Religious educators must work especially hard in the more social and less orderly atmosphere of the smallmembership church. Status and relationships must be maintained at the same time as orderly movement from stage to stage in consensus. If full consensus would endanger relationships, partial consensus or practical consensus is possibly attainable. In the midst of the problem-solving process, religious educators must be able to work at deemphasizing status and depersonalizing the process as much as possible as ideas are shared and solutions projected. This keeps the issue of threat to status and relationships as minimal as possible. Religious educators must be as supportive to all as possible, affirming the contributions of all. Each member must feel that his/her experience has been a supported one, which in turn builds and maintains a sense of personal worth and belonging. This affirmation of the win/win style of problem solving is necessary for the continuing smooth functioning of religious education within the mini-culture of the small membership church. Awareness of tradition and roles will help the religious educator not to be caught in the assumption that the problem that has come to the surface is really the problem. The problem is usually not the problem, but rather the state of the individuals and their resulting relationship with one another. Supportive and relationally aware leadership can make all the difference in trying to move such groups toward consensus and creative, stable relationships. These are the keys to personal growth in the life of religious education in the small membership church.

Leadership awareness should also include sensitivity to the three major sources of conflict described earlier. The first is to be aware of the differing perspectives possible around a community problem and to be more tolerant of the differing approaches to solution. Helping people come to a common perspective initially will help immensely in the problem-solving stage. Such a common perspective stage should also include delving into "the problem is not the problem" issue.

Second, religious educators must constantly work at clarifying the meaning of the communication between parties. In the small membership church, natural leadership should know each party and be able to derive meaning from such knowledge. This can be invaluable in working toward consensus.

The third source of conflict noted for leadership awareness was the dynamics of power. The critical dynamic here is the power equilibrium felt by all. There is no actual equality of power in the organization or community, but there is a necessary equilibrium which assures that each is important, is heard, and recognized as an integral part of the congregation. The supportive style of religious educators must be able to sustain this felt equilibrium.

If these sources of conflict are remembered by the supportive style of the natural leadership of the congregation, relations and status will be kept functionally intact and consensus, win/win type decision making will be facilitated. This type of leadership provides valuable religious education for the parish as well. Religious education in the parish, especially the small membership parish, occurs throughout the whole of the activities of the organization, not just in the CCD, Sunday school, or classroom sessions of study activities. Demonstration of the supportive leadership described shows respect for the uniqueness and value of the individual. Caring and love are present, giving each a feeling of the worth and esteem that is his/hers by creation. The integral place of each member in the congregation affirms both the right and the responsibility each must have for fully functioning behavior. This is necessary in order that all may grow as individuals and as a church. Theological education, shared as a theology of reconciliation, is affirmed over a judgmental theology. Win/lose experience perpetuates a theology of judgment. There must always be a right and a wrong in such theology. But the win/win approach to conflict resolution affirms the worth, value, and integrity of the individual, showing the reconciling nature of the Christian community.

Supportive religious education leadership is not a pacifying style that keeps the community together by avoidance and being nice persons. The religious educator confronts issues and not people, acting as if all persons have something to contribute through their uniqueness. This leadership style affirms the power and the presence of the Holy Spirit, letting it work through relationships, preserving the relationships. Religious education leadership of the small membership church would do well to be trained in both small-group dynamics as well as theology. If the leadership is lay, then training programs need to be available in their areas. If the leadership is clergy, then seminary education needs to take this concern seriously enough to make it both available and integral to degree work.

SHARED LEADERSHIP

A frequently occurring situation for conflict in the small membership church is the lack of sufficient resources to maintain full-time pastoral-educational leadership and the resultant need to have shared leadership with other congregations. Shared time and loyalty creates situations where one or more congregations may feel slighted in either time or the love and care desired of pastoral-educational leadership. The leadership role in the small membership church has been described as a "lover" more than an organizer and leader. Loving care is foremost in need by congregations.[24] The conflict comes when two congregations try to share their "lover." National church practice has increased in the use of yoked or larger parishes, which puts either one person with multiple churches, or two or more persons with five or seven churches. In any case, the conflict arises as to which church will gain favored status for the time of the pastor as religious educator. A sense of self-worth and esteem can come from the perceived favored status. Self-image is already low with the need to be in such an arrangement. The resulting morale can affect the work of the parish and the conflict experienced by the leadership. Part-time religious education leadership is sometimes utilized with seminary students, retired clergy, or part-time lay leadership, all of which require the congregation to share such persons with another sector. It has been suggested that if the "lover" can be shared within the community, such as part-time pastoral-educational work and part-time secular work within the same community, this can result in less conflict than the sharing of leadership between different communities and different churches.[25]

It is most difficult for a pastor-educator to serve churches which differ in need and character. The churches can differ in theological stance, program need, cultural heritage, community differences, and style of congregational life. Such differences can present tension between churches and communities as well as with the pastor-educator's own tendencies and commitments. The scheduling required to serve these different needs leads to conflict, and ultimately relates to the self-image of the churches and their sense worth and esteem. The ripple effect reaches into the life and functioning of each. The professional religious educator can easily become a scapegoat for problems that arise from these conflicts. Internal problems are projected onto the available, visible, and responsible person. The tendency for short-term appointments or calls to small membership churches increases this sense of unworthiness and feeling of neglect by the national bodies.[26]

Mergers are another source of conflict for the small membership church. Governing bodies will often try to merge two or more small membership

---

24. Walrath, *New Possibilities,* p. 57.
25. Schaller, *The Small Church Is Different,* pp. 90-91.
26. Ibid., pp. 146-151.

churches in order to put together a more economically efficient organization. This efficient reorganization goal has not often come to pass. The process is often devastating to the members of one or both churches. Both churches bring a self-esteem problem for having to merge in the first place. They couldn't make it on their own. History and tradition suffers from both original churches as a new entity is born. Relationships, status and roles, power equilibrium, and religious education leadership are all threatened in the process. A single cell balanced in relationships and tradition does not necessarily grow into a more healthy unit by forced union with another single cell. Many characteristics would have to match in order to grow into a healthy new functioning organism. National church leaders, pastor-educators, as well as congregational leaders risk scapegoating as low esteem and resulting hostility enter the merging process. Shared perspective, communication, and equilibrium of power all get scrambled and submerged in merger dynamics.

CONFLICT RESOLUTION AND UTILIZATION

Finding resolution and utilization of the conflict dynamics for growth in the small membership church organization requires not only self-awareness by the leadership but also some skills. It will take more than just will to get past the tendency to blame others for one's own undesirable situation and to get beyond the imaging of bigness as the standard for one's well-being. It is the growth of persons that is the goal of religious education, not the size of the organization or the size of the budget. Small can be beautiful. This needs to be heard and internalized by both congregation and pastor-educator before the self-image of each attains worth and esteem.

A positive climate and a cooperative process, utilizing win/win dynamics will go far toward achieving desired ends and goals for all concerned. This should not be impossible given a reconciliation theology in the church instead of a judgmental one. The following suggestions can be helpful to supportive religious education leadership outlined earlier.

1. Develop a cooperative attitude by focusing on the collective, integrative goal of the congregation.
2. Incorporate the participation of as many as possible in the clarification of goal and ensuing process.
3. Develop a basic community support for the contributions of each, affirming their value and uniqueness.
4. Encourage reflective consideration before the presentation and defense of viewpoints.

5. Develop a positive attitude toward disagreement as a useful means for gaining perspective.
6. Keep issues and personalities separate.
7. Work toward consensus through compromise and win/win process, searching always for ways to resolve differences creatively.
8. Keep the climate of communication and interaction open and non-threatening.[27]

If full consensus is impossible to attain in the situation, work toward partial or practical consensus. These guidelines can be useful in the movement toward consensus in religious education.

Reference has been made throughout this chapter regarding a process called win/win versus the win/lose process. It might be helpful to spell out win/win more specifically in the resolution and utilization section. Power has been defined earlier as a force necessary to achieve an end or a goal. It can make all the difference if that goal is a collective one or only an individual one over against others. In the win/lose scenario, there are those who have power and those who are without it. In the win/win state, power is in a relative state of equilibrium that allows for the beneficial experience of all. The balance moves from individual power to group empowerment. This power in the group derives from the individuals affirming the goals of the group while at the same time maintaining their sense of personal worth and importance. Individuals within the group feel the capacity to influence others when they feel they are valued by the group. The corresponding feeling of self-worth extended by the group allows for individual self-acceptance and reconciliation, which frees the person to participate fully and openly and with a sense of satisfaction. When the group power grows in this fashion, it does not benefit one party at the expense of another. This process increases the problem-solving potential of the group, strengthening both task and maintenance factors.[28]

Religious education leadership training should include skills at utilizing the win/win process. Training programs should include small group dynamic skills that help religious educators develop their personal power base so that they avoid insecure behavior. Activities which encourage

---

27. Gerald M. Phillips, Douglas J. Pedersen, and Julian T. Wood, *Group Discussion: A Practical Guide to Participation and Leadership* (Boston: Houghton Mifflin, 1979), p. 67.

28. Rensis Likert and Jane Likert, *New Ways of Managing Conflict* (New York: McGraw-Hill, 1976), pp. 269-282.

acceptance and trust can be learned. Depth listening and responding should be taught. To take seriously the points made concerning the filtering process of our individual perceptions, the inclusion of skills in filtering out assumptions and doing reality testing is needed. The identification of integrative goals and the keeping of such in the forefront of discussion is a skill needed in religious education leadership training. Finally, the discovery of creative alternatives, the agreement process for criteria of selection, and the contracting for chosen alternatives would round out religious education leadership training.

Training of this nature and with such priorities takes seriously the nature of religious education in the small membership church and community and aids in the management and utilization of conflict found therein. Even the "aginer" can be brought into the win/win process with individual respect.

An eleven-step process, advocated by Blaine Hartford of the Niagara Institute of Behavioral Science, brings these various dynamics into one procedure for consensus building. It takes most seriously the relational base of religious education in the small membership congregation. It will help to deal with substantive conflict, though not so well with the nonsubstantive or intransigence that can occur in the small community. The following is the proposal:

1 Begin by attempting to clarify differences that have arisen. Work at cleaning up communication so that what is left is real difference.
2. Review similarities and overlap of views. Try to find a consensus or norm for the group upon which to build.
3. Stimulate the honest expression of feelings or reasons for oppositions. This is important in attempting to remove personal blocks to relationships.
4 Define the shared interdependence in the congregation around integrative goals, needs, and resources.
5. Check out the feeling tone for the development of trust since the beginning of this process. If there is no improved trust, return to step one and start over. If trust is present, proceed.
6. Finally, define the problem as now perceived.
7. Look creatively for alternative ways to getting at the problem. A good procedure here is to use brainstorming, which has the advantage of non-evaluative offering of ideas.
8. Isolate some alternatives and test for feasibility.
9. Select an alternative that shows possibility for all using consensus methodology.
10. Get all involved in the implementation of the choice.

11. Evaluate the choice by all after some distance from the problem. If not positive, return to another choice.[29]

The consensus process in #9 is helped by the awareness of #11 in that there is anticipation of an evaluation time which keeps the choice of an alternative from being cast in concrete. Step #9 is often made most difficult because of the fear that there will never be a second chance to review the choice.

The context of religious education in the small membership church provides a worthy challenge to its leadership to bring creative utilization to the conflict dynamics they experience. The unique character of this closely knit group provides possibilities for growth as well as for destructiveness. May this material make a contribution to those growth possibilities.

---

29. Bossart, *Creative Conflict*, pp. 236-237.

Chapter Ten

The Future of Religious Education in the Small Membership Church

JAMES E. CUSHMAN

INTRODUCTION

The small membership church is here to stay. That is the initial affirmation to make when one ponders the future of smaller churches. The tenacity of small congregations to continue to exist, to hang on in spite of overwhelming odds, attests to the fact that the small membership church will be with us as long as the church continues as an institution.

But what does the future hold for smaller congregations? I believe that the answer to that question lies in the attitudes of central office leaders and local small church leaders of the various denominations.[1]

There are signs that the time has been fulfilled for smaller churches to

---

1. Carl S. Dudley, *Making the Small Church Effective* (Nashville: Abingdon, 1978), pp. 13-27, pp. 157-178. For further discussion see Douglas A. Walrath, *Finding Options for Ministry in Small Churches* (Valley Forge, Pa.: Judson, 1988).

begin to thrive rather than simply persist to exist. Numerous societal trends indicate that many people are looking for what the small membership church has to offer.[2] But in order for small churches to emerge as significant places for ministry and mission, major attitudinal changes need to take place among middle-level central office church leaders.

The major problem with the small membership church today is that is has been perceived as a problem. Although there may be complex issues related to enhancing the ministry of small congregations in the present cultural context, the problem does not rest primarily with the small membership church but with the dominant value systems of the major denominations.

It is the uncritical acceptance of institutional values of growth, wealth, and program production that has created an atmosphere in which the small membership church is perceived as a problem. Instead of being a problem, the small congregation by its very nature may well offer some answers for the contemporary American church.

At the same time it must be recognized that the vitality of many small membership churches has been weakened by experiencing the alienation of existing on the fringe of the larger church. In most instances that experience of corporate alienation can be traced to the unique cultural environment of the particular small congregation. Small membership churches are found in rural, small town, suburban, and urban settings. Many racial ethnic churches are small, and other small congregations reside in regional contexts which leave unique cultural imprints upon the particular small membership church. This has resulted in the adoption of community folkways and patterns of corporate behavior which seem unusual to participants of larger churches.[3]

Therefore some view small membership churches as being out of step, less productive, and potentially not viable as congregations. The subsequent tendency has been for middle-level central office personnel to develop strategies to help small membership churches grow, develop, and

---

2. For readings on revitalization and redevelopment see: James E. Cushman, *Evangelization in the Small Church* (Decatur, Ga.: CTS Press, 1988); Carl S. Dudley and Douglas, A. Walrath, *Developing Your Small Church Potential* (Valley Forge, Pa.: Judson, 1988); and Arlen Rothauge, *Reshaping a Congregation for a New Future* (New York: Episcopal Church Center, 1985); James Cushman, *Beyond Survival: Revitalizing the Small Church* (Parsons, W. V.: McClain, 1981).

3. Anthony G. Pappas, *Entering the World of the Small Church* (Washington D.C.: The Alban Institute, 1988), pp. 8-15.

become more like large churches or, when that fails, to encourage mergers or closures.

The frequent result has been a loss of self-esteem on the part of pastors and leaders of small membership churches. Therefore some churches have lost the ability effectively to reach out to new persons in the name of Jesus Christ or the will to become engaged in religious education ministry to the larger community.

Affirming Small Church Life

At the same time, some of the unique patterns of congregational behavior of small membership churches result in qualities of corporate living that are needed within our denominations and society as a whole. When one considers the future of religious education in the small membership church it is important to reiterate some of these qualities of congregational life, for the health of the small congregation begins with affirming and building upon these very qualities.

The first quality of religious education in parish life in the small membership church that can be affirmed is an alternative way of doing things. At the middle-level central office most denominations are highly organized and bureaucratized, with goals, committees, departments, divisions, units, and task forces for planning and doing everything. At central office gatherings, Roberts Rules of Order are often followed with motions, amendments, and amendments to amendments. It all gets very complex and confusing at times.

Small membership churches demonstrate through practice that life can be much simpler than that. They remind us that there are alternative ways of planning and making decisions that work just as well as contemporary approaches to organizational development. Some issues are decided better by consensus, by talking about them until agreement is reached. Sometimes a committee is not required to solve a problem. There are times when a need exists and people can make a spontaneous response . . . no committees, no meetings . . . the need is perceived and people respond.

What small membership churches can teach the larger churches is that the bottom line for all the deciding and planning and doing is people. People must remain the priority in all the things that are planned and done. And sometimes that is forgotten.

A second quality of religious education and parish life that the small membership church offers the larger church is a value system that is an alternative to the dominant cultural norms of twentieth-century American society. In a society that says that bigger is better, small membership churches demonstrate that size isn't everything.[4]

In denominations in which mission is often equated with producing programs, smaller congregations offer the reminder that mission is people. People are the recipients of mission. People are the performers of mission. In an era in which newness and change for the sake of change are highly valued, small membership churches offer the caution that change is not always positive for all people.

Changes sometimes mean that people lose identity, experience dislocation, pain, and trauma. Sometimes there is something to be said for stability. Yes, small membership churches offer a counter-balance to the dominant cultural norms of growth, production, and change that so shape the major denominations today.

The third quality of religious education and congregational life that small membership churches offer is a very practical form of inclusiveness. Most mainline Protestant denominations, and more recently the Catholic church, place a priority on inclusiveness. There is the desire to include racial minorities, women, and persons of different social classes more fully in the church. And yet, in spite of all the rhetoric, the church hierarchies of mainline denominations are still dominated primarily by middle-aged, white males.

One of the most severe critiques of small membership churches is that the people of those churches demonstrate very exclusive attitudes. There may be some truth in that perception.

On the other hand, most of the racial ethnic mainline churches are small membership churches. Most blue-collar mainline churches are small. For all the overt sexism in small congregations, most of the women clergy end up serving as pastors of small membership churches. Many small congregations are located in places where societal problems are the most acute such as the inner-city, small towns, Appalachia, Native American villages, and other economically depressed regions.

Small membership churches possibly offer about the only first-hand religious education contact mainline denominations have with the places and people that are most ignored and oppressed by the dominant society. The small membership church may be the only place where relevant inclusiveness regularly occurs.

---

4. The work of Carl S. Dudley in *Unique Dynamics of the Small Church* (Washington D.C.: The Alban Institute, 1977) focuses on the "single cell" nature of the small congregation, why it may remain small, and why the qualities of smallness are maintained.

The fourth characteristic of religious education and congregational life to be affirmed is that the laity of small membership churches generally have a higher level of commitment to the local church. It is a fact that in small congregations a much higher percentage of members participate. There are few, if any, fringe members. Lay persons generally give a higher percentage of their income to the ministry of the church. In fact the level of personal commitment to the local institution is difficult to fathom.

Members of small congregations can tolerate bad preaching, conflicted relationships, marginal finances, and poor programs. Still the people attend and remain involved in the church. The main reason that many smaller congregations have not been closed is not that the middle-level central office administration often has not tried. It is because the laity absolutely refuse to allow the church to be closed. After all, they are the ones who have the keys to the church door, and it remains open in one form or another as long as the building stands. That is a level of personal commitment to a local institution that most in our day and time find strange.

The fifth quality of small church congregational life to be affirmed is the centrality of worship and religious education.[5] There is no doubt that worship and religious education are absolutely central to the life of the small membership church. The methods and approaches may not be the most trendy, but these two emphases are not questioned. When asked, laity in small membership churches will always list meaningful worship and a good Sunday school or CCD as the two most important aspects of congregational life.

The sixth quality of religious education and congregational life to be affirmed and admired is the assumption by most of the laity that the Christian faith really should make a difference in how one lives. We have all heard someone say during a time of difficulty or trouble, "Have faith and everything will be okay." The fact is that many of our small membership churches have been living by that basic premise for generations. Every time a pastor leaves, or the budget is prepared, or a dependable lay person dies or moves away, the faith to hold on and depend upon God's grace becomes a living reality in our small membership churches.

The seventh quality of religious education and parish life to be affirmed within the small membership church and the one which undergirds all the rest is the richness of intimacy and caring that can be encountered there. The small congregation exists to undergird human relationships. It is a

---

5. Donald L. Griggs, and Judy McKay Walther, *Christian Education in the Small Church* (Valley Forge, Pa.: Judson, 1988), pp. 99-109.

place in which all the people know each other and want to know each other. And in a dispersed, depersonalized society that is a quality much to be admired. In fact the small membership church may well be the one place left where the true meaning of human community can still be experienced.

These are but a few of the unique qualities of religious education and congregational life that the small membership church offers. And it is essential that central office personnel learn to appreciate and publicly affirm these qualities instead of evaluating small membership churches by large membership church criteria. That is an important first step toward revitalizing small membership church ministry. But what additional changes need to occur in order for the small congregation to become more vital in the future?

Three Hopes for the Future

There are at least three essential foci that are needed in the future to ensure that small membership churches will be able to continue vital religious education ministry. I would term them hopes for the future health of small membership churches. First, there is the need for better training and support for clergy leadership of small membership churches. Second, there needs to be an increased emphasis upon the laity of the small membership church discovering the unique calling of the particular congregation in its community context. Finally, there needs to be an increased emphasis upon alternative models for doing ministry, not as last resort approaches, but as better ways of engaging in ministry.

1. *The Hope of Better Clergy Training and Support.* Carl Dudley has correctly observed that small membership churches are more apt to thrive when the pastor is a "lover of people." At the same time central office leaders often look for clergy leaders who are competent enablers, who can help a congregation develop effective programs of ministry and mission. Seminaries are usually oriented toward educating future clergy leaders to be scholarly theologians in residence who posseses biblical exegetical skills. These three views of ministry may not be completely contradictory, but they certainly embody differing visions of the priorities of ministry for clergy leaders.

In addition, at the present time the recognition and reward system of most mainline denominations values and honors those clergy leaders who move up to the largest churches or into positions of institutional leadership at the central office level. It is little wonder that many small membership church pastors feel undervalued with lingering feelings of failure.

Successful religious education ministry with small membership churches can seldom be measured by membership growth figures, budget increases, or brick and mortar memorials. Effective ministry is measured more in terms of the quality and depth of the pastor's relationships with the laity and whether the congregation begins to envision itself as a context for vital ministry.[6] Traditionally, seminaries have not trained, and middle-level central office leaders have not affirmed and supported clergy for this type of ministry

There are signs that more relevant training for pastors of small congregations is emerging. There is a growing number of programs in various denominations aimed specifically at training clergy for more effective ministry with small membership churches.

The United Methodist Centers for Town and Rural Ministry, the Missouri School of Religion of the Disciples of Christ, the Institute of Land and Theology of the University of Dubuque and Wartburg Seminaries, the Small Church Leadership Program of Bangor Seminary, and the Appalachian Ministries Educational Resource Center, sponsored by CORA and a number of denominations, are some of the training programs for small membership church clergy that are presently emerging.

However, much more needs to be done. There is a tremendous need for training tenured seminary faculty members and middle-level central office officials in understanding the character and dynamics of small membership churches and the type of clergy leadership needed to enhance religious education ministry. And with the large percentage of seminary graduates who serve small congregations, one wonders why more seminaries do not require an introductory course on small membership church ministry.

In addition, new nurture and support systems for small membership church pastors are needed at the middle-level central office. Programs are needed to build self-worth, lend emotional support, ensure adequate financial compensation, provide relevant continuing education, and give recognition to clergy of small membership churches. The future vitality of the small membership church depends upon committed clergy leaders who have a love for small membership church ministry.

2. *Discovering the Unique Calling of the Congregation.* A basic biblical affirmation is that God calls persons in the fullness of time to minister for

---

6. Steve Burt, *Activating Leadership in the Small Church* (Valley Forge, Pa.: Judson, 1988), pp. 27-42. For further readings on pastoral adjustment see: John C. Fletcher, *Religious Authenticity in the Clergy* (Washington D.C.: The Alban Institute, 1983).

special purposes, in specific social contexts. One of the debilitating factors of religious education in many small membership churches is the absence of any dynamic sense of corporate calling. It follows that in order to strengthen the vitality of small membership church ministry in the future, clergy and lay leaders of small congregations need to focus time and energy on enabling the members to discover the unique calling of the particular church. This entails helping each church understand its unique identity in relationship to its specific cultural and community context.

Middle-level central office officials often attempt to coerce small membership churches to come to terms with mission by superimposing a business-oriented goal-setting process on the congregation. Invariably such processes are aimed at encouraging the congregation to reorganize and restructure to do more effective programing so that the institutional goals can be met. The approach seldom works with small membership congregations.

The beginning point for a smaller congregation to understand and become excited about religious education ministry is to come to terms with its own unique identity. The identity of a congregation is no simple matter. It is a complex, interwoven story, written over generations. It includes the stories of the persons and families who constitute the church and the images and ghosts of those who have gone before.

James Hopewell, in his book *Congregation: Stories and Structures* stated, "A group of people cannot regularly gather for what they feel to be religious purposes without developing a complex network of signals and symbols and conventions—in short, a subculture—that gains its own logic and then functions in a way peculiar to that group."[7] It was Hopewell's contention that no new person is fully part of a congregation until that person understands and is adopted into that subculture.

There are at least six components of identity that need to be understood for a congregation to fully come to grips with its unique calling and ministry. It begins with the congregation's name. If one thinks that name is unrelated to identity, try suggesting to some members of a church that the name should be changed and observe the reaction.

But name here means more than the mere words, FIRST UNITED METHODIST CHURCH. Name symbolizes the purpose, direction, and character of the church from its beginning times. The name embodies the origins of the congregation, why it originally came into being, and how

---

7. James F. Hopewell, *Congregation: Stories and Structures* (Philadelphia: Fortress, 1987), p. 5.

its original purpose and ministry was perceived.

The second component of congregational identity is history and tradition. Written histories of churches record the names of pastors, members, officers, and events that have occurred. And those are all important. But the real history of the church is oral, that is, the stories of the families who have made up the church. One does not understand religious education in a church until one knows its stories.[8]

The third ingredient of identity is the denominational affiliation. This can be a subject of pride or apology depending upon the situation. And always there is another layer of stories related to this slice of identity. "I remember when those folks from the bishop's office came and told us we had to do such and such or we'd be closed." That's part of the church's identity.

Symbols are a major part of a church's identity. The most powerful symbol is the church building itself. It houses the corporate memory. An older member walks through the sanctuary and immediately recalls persons and events, some of which carry great meaning. And the building holds other symbols such as plaques, pictures, windows, furniture, and artifacts, all of which carry memories and stories.

The fifth part of congregational identity is ritual. There is of course the worship ritual. For some congregations, changing the worship ritual or introducing the unfamiliar such as a new hymn into that ritual, is quite disrupting.

There are other rituals in addition to the worship rituals that also embody the church's identity. There are all the informal rituals such as the couple that arrives late every week, the three men who stand outside the vestibule and talk until just before the service starts, or the way that two persons who do not really like each other turn to avoid talking with one another each week. Ritual is a large part of a church's identity.

Sixth, and perhaps most significant, is the corporate worldview. Every congregation embodies a dominant worldview.[9] The worldview is not the spoken theology of persons in the congregation as much as the attitude of life that is reflected in how the people live, understand religious education, and minister together. Hopewell draws upon Greek drama to discuss four basic worldviews that may be lived out by various congregations. They include the gnostic, canonic, charismatic, and empiric.[10]

---

8. Ibid., pp. 140-149.
9. Ibid., pp. 87-100.
10. Ibid., p. 69.

The gnostic or comic affirms that life is basically good. Nature works together in harmony. To live well, one needs to stay in tune with the natural rhythms of life.

The canonic or tragic worldview asserts that life is difficult and tragic. Only by recognizing God's plan and rigorously living according to that plan can one ever find a moment of happiness.

The charismatic or romantic view sees life as an adventure, heroic in nature. Evil is present, but through God's Holy Spirit one can be empowered to overcome anything.

The empiric or ironic worldview encourages one to become partners with God and take charge of life. Life is both good and evil, and humans need to learn to control the evil and work for the good. People must work together and help one another to bring about change and become co-creators with God.

The point is that every congregation has a dominant corporate worldview which the congregation lives out. That worldview determines how the people of that church respond to the world around them, and especially to other people.

All of these factors, name, history, ritual, symbols, denomination affiliation, and worldview constitute a church's corporate identity. And this identity to a great extent determines a congregation's willingness and ability to become engaged in religious education ministry. Part of what this means is that if small membership congregations are to develop more vital and effective religious education in the future, the clergy and laity of smaller congregations will need to begin to come to terms with congregational identity in order to discover who God is calling them to be and what God is calling them to do in the world today.

But in order to discover that unique corporate calling, small membership churches not only need to come to terms with their own identity but also grow to understand the cultural community context in which they exist.[11]

The religious education of any congregation takes place within the context of a larger community and is greatly influenced by that community. An initial point of reference for attempting to understand the community context of ministry is to come to some basic understanding of the meaning of community. Pastors and laity of small membership churches need to learn to define what they mean by community. Everything from a tribal clan, to New York City, to the entire human race on

---

11. Dudley, *Making the Small Church Effective,* pp. 138-156.

the globe has been described by someone as community.

In more traditional terms, community is considered to have three basic elements. First it is a group of persons who know each other and have regular face-to-face contact. Second, a community implies that there is some cooperative action to meet personal and group needs. Third, a community has a center, a basic system of beliefs, folkways, and memory that hold it together.

In the classical sense, every small membership church is a community. And most of them exist within an area, town, or neighborhood that could also be termed a community. That community is the congregation's context for religious education ministry.

The most helpful definition of community for a congregation, however, probably comes from the people of that particular church. Every church needs to define its own community context. The community context is quite simply the persons in the defined area to which a particular congregation is attempting to minister. Only the people of a particular church can make that definition.

But defining community is not enough. There must be a basic understanding of the dynamics of that community context before a congregation can minister effectively. And again, there are at least five basic aspects of community context that need to be understood if a church is to minister effectively.

The first is community history. What have been the key elements of the community's history that have affected the life and ministry of the congregation over the years? What have been the major life-shaping events? Who have been the leading persons and institutions in the community? These are all questions of community history that need to be understood in order for a church to begin to understand the context for its corporate call to ministry.

The second aspect of community that needs to be understood is who lives there? What is being referred to is community demographics. How can the population of this community be described in terms of race, age, sex, education, occupation, income level, and family status? How does the community demographic profile compare with the church's demographic profile? How can this kind of church minister with effective religious education in this kind of community?

Persons in small membership churches seldom view community demographics as being very important. They usually assume that they know who is in their community. Sometimes they do. More often they do not.[12]

---

12. Ibid., pp. 78-91.

And the fact is a church cannot carry out relevant religious education ministry within a community unless there is a firm understanding of who lives in that community and what the major needs of those persons happen to be.

The third essential aspect of community that needs to be understood by persons in a congregation is the structure of the community and how if functions. How are decisions made? Who are the decision makers? Who gets things done? If a church is to minister effectively within a given community context there must be a basic understanding of community structure.

The fourth important understanding of community context concerns ecumenical climate? What other churches are present in the community? What is the size, orientation of religious education ministry, and influence of each? How well do the churches cooperate with each other?

To discover the unique corporate calling that God might have for a congregation, it is helpful to begin to understand the unique role and function of each of the other churches in the community. And if a small membership congregation is to minister effectively in religious education within community it is true that many ministries can be carried out better in concert with other churches.

Finally, a church must come to an understanding of the primary human needs in the community. Effective religious education ministry in the church is need based. We reach people when we are aware of their needs and adjust ministry to meet those needs.

Within a local community the people of a particular church should have a basic awareness of major community issues, what changes are taking place, how the lives of various people are being affected by changes, how community institutions are responding to present problems, and how the church can best respond to community needs.

Small membership congregations have all the necessary resources to care for people. The problem is that there is often a tendency to define too narrowly who should be part of the church's care and concern.

It is clear that if the religious education ministry of small membership churches is to be strengthened, in the future much greater emphasis must be placed upon understanding God's unique calling for the particular congregation. For that to happen, small membership church clergy and laity must come to terms with church identity in the context of community. The question ultimately to be answered is how does God want this kind of church to minister in this kind of community? Answering that question is to discover corporate calling.

3. *Alternative Forms of Ministry*. Finally, the future health of the small membership church is dependent upon the increased use of alternative forms of ministry as better ways of doing ministry. By alternative forms of ministry I am speaking of alternative approaches for clergy leadership (tentmaking) and structural arrangements (cooperative parishes), to cite two examples.

In the past, alternative forms have been promoted among small membership churches by middle-level central office officials. But more often than not they have been encouraged as last resort attempts at maintaining some form of viable ministry, rather than better ways of engaging in religious education ministry.

The underlying justification has often been, "Try this for a while and as soon as your small church grows, becomes stronger and more viable, you can abandon it." The underlying goal for the small membership church is still perceived as growing until it can be a "normal" congregation with a full-time pastor and a fully funded program. It is this "last resort" approach which has doomed many such projects to failure.

For example, the use of tentmaking or bi-vocational clergy, has been experimented with for a number of years in small membership congregations.[13] Churches are encouraged to consider a tentmaking arrangement primarily because of financial factors. The fact is that tentmaking arrangements are often much better ways of engaging in ministry, even if a congregation had plenty of financial resources. The tentmaking pastor is in a position to extend ministry into the secular work situation which greatly enhances the strength of the church's religious education ministry. That is the real justification for tentmaking, not financial viability.

Cooperative parish development is also frequently encouraged from a financial perspective. By cooperating in ministry the participating churches can pool resources, share clergy, and save money. And of course that is a consideration. But the most attractive justification is that cooperative parish arrangements provide the opportunity for churches to plan religious education ministry jointly for an area, and that greatly strengthens the ministry and outreach of the churches. Usually it is a better way to approach

---

13. Some of the resources available on options for ministry include: John Elliott, *Our Pastor Has an Outside Job* (Valley Forge, Pa.: Judson, 1980); Lowery L. James Jr., ed., *Case Histories on Tentmakers* (Wilton, Conn.: Morehouse-Barlow, 1976); Douglas A. Walrath, *New Possibilities for Small Churches* (New York: Pilgrim , 1983); and Luther M. Dorr, *The Bivocational Pastor* (Nashville: Broadman, 1988).

religious education ministry whether the churches involved are large or small.

The future health of religious education in small membership churches is dependent upon the increased use of such alternative models of ministry. But to be successful they cannot be approached as last-resort attempts for keeping the doors opened. Alternative models should be developed as means of enabling the small membership church to carry out more relevant and vital religious education ministry.

At this particular juncture, the future of religious education in the small membership church is hopeful. Smaller congregations offer mainline denominations the opportunity to minister to people in places and ways that are impossible for larger congregations. They are often located in areas where need is most critical. The people who comprise small membership congregations are by and large deeply committed to the church.

The primary need is for denominational middle-level central office leaders to affirm the small membership church as a vital context for religious education ministry and develop ways to strengthen small membership church ministry, rather than planning how to mold small congregations into miniature versions of large congregations. If that practical reorientation can begin to occur many small membership churches can begin to thrive, rather than just survive.

About the Contributors

DONALD E. BOSSART is Associate Professor of Interpersonal Ministries and Coordinator of Justice and Peace Study Program at Iliff School of Theology, Denver, Colorado. He is the author of *Creative Conflict in Religious Education and Church Administration*. Service to the church and community includes: preaching in local churches and mediation for local community and church organizations.

RONALD H. CRAM is Associate Professor of Christian Education at Presbyterian School of Christian Education, Richmond, Virginia. He authored *Understanding Trends in Protestant Religious Education in 20th Century America* as well as numerous other articles, books, and curriculum resources. Service to the church and community includes: Sunday school teacher, member of a local church worship committee and editorial consultant for *EX AUDITU: An Annual of the Frederick Neumann Symposium on Theological Interpretation of Scripture*.

JAMES E. CUSHMAN is Associate for Small Church Development, Presbyterian Church (U.S.A.), Louisville, Kentucky. He authored *Beyond Survival: Revitalizing the Small Church* and *Evangelism in the Small Church*. He is a pastor and has directed projects such as the West Virginia Mountain Project.

GARY EUGENE FARLEY is Associate Director of the Home Mission Board's Rural-Urban Missions Department. He authored books and numerous articles which appear in *Faculty Studies, Church Training, and*

Associational Bulletin. He is listed in Outstanding Young Men, American Men of Science, and Personalities of the South.

NANCY T. FOLTZ is Leadership Development Director for Western Pennsylvania Conference, the United Methodist Church. She is adjunct faculty in Christian Education at Pittsburgh Theological Seminary. She was a contributing editor for *Handbook of Adult Religious Education* and has authored articles, curriculum, and a video tape series *Journey of Faith: Stories of Marriage and Divorce.*

BOB I. JOHNSON is Associate Professor of Church Administration and Religious Education, Midwestern Baptist Theological Seminary, Kansas City, Missouri. His chapters appear in *Christian Education Handbook for Church Leaders* and *Christian Administration Handbook.* Other articles appear in publications such as *Adult Leadership Magazine.*

SUSANNE JOHNSON is Associate Dean for Community Life, Perkins School of Theology, Dallas, Texas. She teaches courses in Christian education. Her publications include: a chapter in "The Person in Spirituality," *Theological Issues in Christian Religious Education* and a book, *Christian Spiritual Formation in the Congregation and Classroom.* Her experience includes preaching in rural churches in Oklahoma, Director of Christian Education and adjunct faculty for Phillips University, Oklahoma, and Princeton Theological Seminary, New Jersey. She is listed in Outstanding Young Women of America.

PAMELA MITCHELL is Assistant Professor of Christian Education and Communication at United Theological Seminary, Dayton, Ohio. Her teaching includes courses in Foundations of Religious Education, Beginning a Teaching Ministry, and Curriculum and Resources for Teaching. She has published curriculum on homelessness, *Let Us Rise Up and Build,* and articles such as "What Is Curriculum? Alternatives in Western Historical Perspective."

WILLIAM H. WILLIMON is Dean of the University and Professor of Christian Ministry at Duke University, Durham, North Carolina. He is the author of thirty books, including *Worship and Preaching in the Small Church* and *Worship As Pastoral Care.* He has lectured and taught in Canada, Europe, and Asia. In 1988, he served on the theological faculty of the University of Bonn, West Germany.

D. CAMPBELL WYCKOFF is Thomas W. Synnott Professor of Christian Education, Emeritus, Princeton Theological Seminary. He lives in Albuquerque, New Mexico, and serves as an elder in the First Presbyterian Church there. He is also General Editor of the Kerygma Program.

Index of Names

Index of Subjects

Acoustics in church, 108-109
Action-reflection teaching procedure, 166
Administration, 98-100, 113-137
  budgeting, 126-133
    construction of, 129-133
      line item, 129
      program, 130
      zero, 129-130
    examples of, 130-131
      building and grounds, 131
      evangelism, 130
      nurture and care, 130
      outreach/mission, 131
    guidelines for, 127-129
    ministry, relation to, 126-127
  bureaucracy, obstructionism of, 98-100
  community of faith, relation to, 118-120
    empowering laity, 119-120
    grace and, 119
    hospitality and, 119
    love and, 119
  definition of, 117-118
  diakonia, as, 114
  leadership, relation to, 117-118
    types of, 117-118

  ministry, relation to, 113
  planning for, 124-126
    dynamic congregations, following lead of, 125
    relational characteristics and, 125-126
  practical theology, as branch of, 114-117
    enabling religious education of laity, 116-118
    holism and, 115
    ministry of church, proper focus, as, 116
    pastoral theology, relation to, 115
  service, as, 114
  skill, areas of, 120-124
    conceptual skills and, 121-122
      organizational theory and, 122
    evaluation and, 120-121
    how-to knowledge, 121
    management theory and, 121
    principles vs. programs, 122-123
    seminary education, inadequate preparation for, 123-124
    social sciences, place of, 121
    spiritual guidance skills, 122-123
  stewardship education, 133-135
    concept of, 133